Delivering Welfare

Public Policy and Management

Series Editor: Professor R.A.W. Rhodes, Department of Politics, University of York.

The effectiveness of public policies is a matter of public concern and the efficiency with which policies are put into practice is a continuing problem for governments of all political persuasions. This series contributes to these debates by publishing informed, in-depth and contemporary analyses of public administration, public policy and public management.

The intention is to go beyond the usual textbook approach to the analysis of public policy and management and to encourage authors to move debate about their issue forward. In this sense, each book both describes current thinking and research, and explores future policy directions. Accessibility is a key feature and, as a result, the series will appeal to academics and their students as well as to the informed practitioner.

Current Titles Include:

Delivering Welfare

The Governance of the Social Services
in the 1990s

Tony Butcher

Open University Press
Buckingham · Philadelphia

Open University Press
Celtic Court
22 Ballmoor
Buckingham
MK18 1XW

and

1900 Frost Road, Suite 101
Bristol, PA 19007, USA

First Published 1995

A catalogue record of this book is available from the British Library

ISBN   0 335 15710 6 (pbk)   0 335 15711 4 (hbk)

Library of Congress Cataloging-in-Publication Data
Butcher, Tony.
    Delivering welfare : the governance of the social services in the
1990s / Tony Butcher.
        p.   cm. — (Public policy and management)
    Includes bibliographical references and index.
    ISBN 0-335-15711-4 (hbk) — ISBN 0-335-15710-6 (pbk)
    1. Public welfare administration—Great Britain. I. Title.
II. Series.
HV248.B89   1995
354.410084—dc20   94-43713
                                                         CIP

Typeset by Dorwyn Ltd, Rowlands Castle, Hants
Printed in Great Britain by St Edmundsbury Press Ltd, Bury St Edmunds, Suffolk

Contents

Preface

This book provides an introduction to the delivery of welfare for students of British social policy and public administration. It describes and discusses the organization of the 'public face' of welfare delivery at the central and local levels – concentrating on the five core social services of social security, health care, education, housing and the personal social services – and the arrangements for coordination, accountability and public involvement. It also focuses on a number of key issues that have attracted attention in recent years – particularly since the election of the Conservative Government in 1979 – and the new directions that welfare delivery has taken.

The public sector organizations responsible for the delivery of welfare – central government's social service departments, elected local authorities and the institutions of the National Health Service – have been subjected to radical changes since 1979. Developments since the election of the first Thatcher Government have challenged the public administration model of welfare delivery associated with the developments of the immediate post-war period, with the result that what have been described as the 'really decisive' debates of the 1980s and the 1990s have been about the organization and delivery of the social services, rather than about social policy (Glennerster 1992b: 15). Major developments since the late 1970s include the changing role of local government in welfare delivery, especially the transformation of elected local authorities from front-line delivery agencies of the welfare state into enabling authorities; the growing privatization and marketization of welfare delivery; the increased emphasis on efficiency and value for money in the operations of welfare delivery agencies; and the growing attention being given to consumerism and customer sensitivity in the delivery of the social services, as reflected in the Citizen's Charter and other developments. As the book will discuss, long-standing assumptions about the organization and delivery of welfare have been increasingly questioned and important changes have taken place.

The idea for this book originated in the realization that the literature of social policy and administration contained no comprehensive and up-to-date overview of the organization of welfare delivery and recent developments. Textbooks on social policy and administration tend to concentrate on approaches to the study of social policy, the historical development of state welfare provision, accounts of the main social services and discussions of current policy issues, with a relative neglect of issues involving the organization and delivery of welfare. Whilst surveys of some recent developments – such as the changing role of local government – can be found in the literature of public administration, little attempt has been made to draw together the implications of all these developments for the organization of welfare delivery.

There are, of course, a number of studies of specific developments in welfare delivery, including the decentralization of local services (Hoggett and Hambleton (eds) 1988), the growing attention given to consumerism (Deakin and Wright (eds) 1990), and the increasing use of performance indicators in the social services (Carter *et al.* 1992), whilst another book in the Open University Press's Public Policy and Management series, *Markets and Managers*, edited by Peter Taylor-Gooby and Robyn Lawson (1993), examines the emergence of the new managerial ideology in the welfare state. But there is no one book which provides an up-to-date survey of the organization of welfare delivery and the developments of recent years. In discussing these important developments, and the issues which they raise, *Delivering Welfare* brings together a range of material by drawing upon current thinking and research. Although the discussion of the details of recent changes in the arrangements for the delivery of welfare, and the accompanying legislation, will focus essentially on England and Wales, the issues raised are applicable to the whole of Britain.

The book has been written mainly for students of social policy and administration, and of public administration, at undergraduate level. It is also likely to prove useful for students undertaking postgraduate courses in social policy: indeed, the book was partly inspired by a series of lectures given on the core course of the successful MA Social Policy and Administration programme run by the Department of Social Policy and Politics at Goldsmiths' College since 1984. The book should also be of use to students following courses of professional training in the area of social policy and administration.

As will be apparent from the References and the text, the book draws heavily on the work of the many writers who have contributed to current thinking and research in the various areas covered by this wide-ranging and important subject. In collecting and organizing material for the book, I have been greatly helped by a number of people. I am grateful to librarians at the British Library of Political and Economic Science and the, now sadly defunct, Royal Institute of Public Administration. I would also like to thank Gavin

Drewry of Royal Holloway College for his comments on my final draft. The growing demands of university life have meant that the latter stages of completing this book have taken far longer than originally anticipated and I am grateful to my publishers, especially Pat Lee, for their patience in the face of a number of broken deadlines.

One of the consequences of working in higher education in the 1990s is that research and writing have increasingly to be undertaken at times which eat heavily into family life. Accordingly, I would like to thank my family for tolerating my long absences in my study, especially at those times when I should have been fulfilling my responsibilities for delivering their welfare.

Tony Butcher

Abbreviations

ACC	Association of County Councils
AHA	Area health authority
CAG	Comptroller and Auditor General
CCT	Compulsory competitive tendering
CHC	Community Health Council
CPRS	Central Policy Review Staff
CSA	Child Support Agency
CTC	City technology college
DEmp	Department of Employment
DES	Department of Education & Science
DFE	Department for Education
DHA	District health authority
DHSS	Department of Health & Social Security
DoE	Department of the Environment
DoH	Department of Health
DSS	Department of Social Security
FAS	Funding Agency for Schools
FEFCE	Further Education Funding Council for England
FHSA	Family health service authority
FMI	Financial Management Initiative
GLC	Greater London Council
GP	General Practitioner
HAT	Housing Action Trust
HEFCE	Higher Education Funding Council for England

HMI	Her Majesty's Inspectors of Education
HSC	Health Service Commissioner
ILEA	Inner London Education Authority
JASP	Joint Approach to Social Policy
JCC	Joint Consultative Committee
JCPT	Joint Care Planning Team
LMS	Local management of schools
MNI	Ministry of National Insurance
MoH	Ministry of Health
MPNI	Ministry of Pensions and National Insurance
NAB	National Assistance Board
NCT	New Control Total
NHS	National Health Service
OFSTED	Office for Standards in Education
OS	Operational Strategy
PAR	Programme Analysis and Review
PCA	Parliamentary Commissioner for Administration
PESC	Public Expenditure Survey Committee
QAP	Quality Assessment Package
RAWP	Resource Allocation Working Party
RHA	Regional health authority
RMI	Resource Management Initiative
RSG	Rate Support Grant
TEC	Training and Enterprise Council
UAB	Unemployment Assistance Board
UDC	Urban Development Corporation

1

Introduction

The welfare state that was created in the years immediately after the Second World War, and which was consolidated and expanded in the following three decades, was deliberately set up under a form of state organization which placed a great deal of emphasis on the bureaucratic ideal of efficient and impartial administration. It was what has been called an 'administrative model' of welfare delivery characterized by the familiar bureaucratic features of hierarchical structure, clearly-defined duties, and rule-based procedures, in which tasks which could not easily be controlled by rules were carried out by professionally qualified staff who were given what has been referred to as 'bounded discretion' in the performance of their work (Hadley and Young 1990: 12). Such an approach to the delivery of welfare was a deliberate move away from the provision by voluntary and charitable organizations that had been such an important feature of welfare provision for much of the nineteenth and early twentieth centuries. The Labour Government which came into office in 1945 and established the apparatus of the welfare state as part of the post-war settlement, 'turned [their] backs on philanthropy and replaced the do-gooder by highly professional administrators and experts' (Crossman 1976: 278). In the brave new world of post-war Britain, the public sector was entrusted with the primary responsibility for the delivery of social welfare. Faith was placed in the public sector as 'a way of guaranteeing provision that was comprehensive and universal, professional and impartial, and subject to democratic control' (Webb et al. 1976: 7).

The post-war Labour Government regarded the state and its administrative apparatus as the main instruments of social change (Hadley and Hatch

1981: 15). The institutions of public administration – central government departments, elected local authorities and the newly created National Health Service (NHS) – were seen as the most effective means of delivering the core social services of social security, health care, education and housing, together with the various local authority health, welfare and children's services which were later to be consolidated as the personal social services in the early 1970s.

What can be described as the public administration model, with its emphasis on the efficient and impartial administration of services, characterized the organization of the delivery of welfare in Britain for most of the post-war period. Not only was the system created in the years immediately following the Second World War based upon this approach, but, as Hadley and Young (1990: 13) have shown, subsequent re-organizations of local government, local authority personal social services and the NHS in the 1960s and early 1970s took many of the principles of this model for granted. In recent years, however, the public administration model, and the institutions associated with it, have been the subject of critical debate, particularly since the election of the Conservative Thatcher Government in 1979. This debate has been joined by critics on all sides of the political spectrum, ranging from the group of thinkers described as the New Right, through the welfare pluralists with their advocacy of the voluntary sector, to the so-called New Urban Left. But it is the first group who have been particularly influential: indeed one commentator has argued that the general agreement that there is a case against large state welfare bureaucracies is among the New Right's 'most striking intellectual achievements' in the field of social policy (Deakin 1987: 177). Since the election of the first Thatcher Government, the welfare state has been passing through an era in which traditional assumptions about the organizational arrangements for the delivery of welfare have been fundamentally questioned and in which major changes have been made in the organization and management of the delivery agencies concerned.

The organization of welfare delivery and recent important developments will be discussed in greater detail in later chapters. Meanwhile, the aim of this introduction is to outline the main characteristics of the public administration model and to provide a brief review of the major criticisms which have been made of the traditional institutions and processes of welfare delivery.

The public administration model of welfare delivery

The traditional public administration model which has underpinned the delivery of welfare in Britain since 1945 has several distinctive characteristics:

- a bureaucratic structure;
- professional domination;
- accountability to the public;
- equity of treatment;
- self-sufficiency.

These will be described in the following sections.

Bureaucratic structure

A major characteristic of the public administration model of welfare delivery is the emphasis on bureaucratic organization. Associated with the classic account outlined by the German sociologist Max Weber (1964) in the early years of the century, bureaucracy is a term used to describe a form of organization which in its 'ideal type' exhibits a number of characteristics, such as the hierarchical structure of offices, the clear specification of functions, rule-based procedures, and staff who act impartially without favouritism (see, for instance, Albrow 1970).

Bureaucratic structure has been a major feature of the traditional pattern of organization in the delivery agencies of the welfare state. The traditional organization of the delivery of social services by both central government departments and local authorities has been characterized by the principle of hierarchy, the emphasis upon uniformity of treatment, and the division of responsibilities around particular tasks such as education and housing (see, for example, Stewart 1986: 12–15). Thus the giant social security system operated by the Department of Social Security (DSS) has been described as 'the most bureaucratized, routinized and therefore "clericalized"' of the major social services (Pollitt and Harrison 1992: 10). Writing in the mid-1980s about local authorities, the major delivery agencies of the welfare state, Stewart (1986: 15) argued that the principles of the bureaucratic mode had become 'written into the thought processes' of those who worked in local government. In his view, they had become not principles but assumptions that were rarely challenged. The form of bureaucratic structure traditionally found in the local authority departments concerned with the delivery of welfare has been what has been described as that of a 'professionalised bureaucracy', the professional staff of such organizations being allowed a certain amount of freedom in the way they deliver services (Taylor-Gooby and Dale 1981: 206). As we shall see, this latter form of bureaucracy has also been a characteristic of the organization of the NHS.

The advantages of a bureaucratic system of organization are well documented: they are said to include such virtues as consistency, reliability and susceptibility to political control. A bureaucratic form of organization is also supportive of what we will later identify as two other key features of the public administration model, the values of accountability and equity (see Pitt and Smith 1981: 139). By allowing for the detailed control of subordinate staff within a hierarchical structure, bureaucracy provides a means by which large organizations can carry out their functions in accordance with the requirements of public accountability (Greenwood and Wilson 1989: 25). Bureaucracy's emphasis on the depersonalization of administration also means that the users of a bureaucratic organization's services are subject to 'formal equality of treatment' (Weber 1964: 340).

Professional domination

Another major characteristic of the public administration model of welfare delivery has been the important role played by professionals in the delivery of social services. Although the biggest spending social service, social security, is a clear exception to this general rule, professionals have dominated the delivery agencies of the welfare state. As we shall discuss in Chapter 3, elected local authorities and the institutions of the NHS are dominated by professionals. It is doctors, teachers, social workers and other welfare professionals – described by one writer as the 'trusted instruments' of the welfare state (Donnison 1982: 21) – who deliver welfare and, in many cases, make key decisions about resource allocation and other important issues. As Klein (1973: 4) has observed: 'The Welfare State is, in many respects, also the Professional State.'

The development of welfare professionalism was an inevitable concomitant of the expansion of state social services in the post-war period. As Wilding (1982: 14–15) puts it in his discussion of the nature of professional power in the field of social welfare:

> A commitment to welfare by government means a need for professionals – to advise on the organisation of services, to manage, man and mediate services, to decide questions of eligibility and need, to individualise justice, to raise standards of health and child care.

The three decades following the end of the Second World War represented what has been described as 'the high tide of professionalism' in the welfare state, with professionalism becoming 'the dominant occupational paradigm' (Laffin and Young 1990: 17, 32). The two well-established welfare professions – medicine and education – consolidated their positions: indeed, as we will discuss in Chapter 3, the medical profession were given substantial representation in the administrative structure of the NHS established in 1948, as well as being allowed to continue to enjoy considerable professional autonomy in the way they delivered health care. Although not enjoying the same degree of influence and autonomy as the medical profession, the teaching profession were also given a substantial amount of freedom in the running of the post-war education system.

Other welfare professions developed within local government as local authorities were given responsibility for those services requiring what has been described as face-to-face 'professional style' involvement with the users of services (Cochrane 1993: 14). Thus the new welfare responsibilities imposed on local authorities by the post-war legislation dealing with domiciliary and residential care, child care and community care 'pointed the way' for the growth of the social work profession in the 1950s and 1960s (Marwick 1982: 62–3), culminating in the creation of a single professional social work organization, the British Association of Social Workers, in 1970. This particular process of professionalization was reinforced by the setting up of unified local authority social services departments a year or two later. While the development of professionalization in the sphere of local authority housing was not nearly as rapid as in the other two major local authority social services, the commitment of successive post-war governments to municipal housing did result in an acceleration in the development of housing management, which had begun to establish itself as a profession by the late 1970s (Rhodes 1988: 221–2). In the closely related area of town planning, the post-war package of land use planning established by the Attlee Government, and developed by later administrations, increased the power of another professional group – town planners – in decisions about housing and urban problems.

Thus, in the words of one commentator: 'Professional power has marched hand in hand with public welfare' (Wilding 1982: 70). Although it is difficult to generalize about the nature and extent of such power in the delivery of welfare, it is possible, using the typology constructed by Wilding (1982), to identify the different types of power exercised by welfare professionals. Firstly, welfare professionals exercise power in both the making of welfare policy and its administration. Secondly, the power of welfare professionals is underpinned by their generally accepted right to define the needs and problems of their clients. Thirdly, welfare professionals exercise power and influence in the allocation of resources, not only at the level of general planning decisions by central and local government, but also at the organizational level – hospitals, schools, etc. – and in routine decisions affecting the individual client. These last two forms of power both affect the way services are delivered and are examples of the way in which welfare professionals exert power over people – the fourth type of power. Finally, welfare professionals have power to control their area of work, through such devices as self-regulation of the profession.

These powers clearly derive in part from the expertise of welfare professionals and the important role that they play in both the making and implementation of social policy, but, as Wilding (1982: 67) observes, professional power is also buttressed by the bureaucratic nature of welfare delivery agencies. Being part of a bureaucratic organization releases welfare professionals from many of the constraints encountered if they work on their own in the private sector. Thus Wilding usefully quotes Klein (1973: 5): 'To the extent that the professional becomes part of an administrative machine . . . so his command over resources, and his ability to affect the consumer, is magnified.'

Accountability to the public

Another important characteristic of the public administration model of welfare delivery is accountability. The concept of accountability is an elusive one and we shall encounter it, in its various guises, throughout this book. One important aspect of what Day and Klein (1987: 1) describe as this 'chameleon word' is the existence of public accountability to elected representatives, at both the national and local level. As one textbook on public administration puts it: 'At its most elementary, public accountability simply requires that public bodies give an account of their activities to other people and provide a justification for what has been done' (Smith and Stanyer 1976: 30–1). Thus the Secretary of State for Social Security is accountable to Parliament for the operations of the DSS, whilst his Cabinet colleague, the Secretary of State for Health, is accountable to Parliament for everything that happens in the NHS. At the local government level, the directors of the local authority departments responsible for the delivery of education, housing and the personal social services report to committees of the elected local authority.

The accountability of the delivery agencies of central government, local government and the NHS is not confined to the political dimension. The armies of bureaucrats and professionals employed by the delivery agencies of the welfare state are also subject to what has been referred to as 'administrative accountability': the duty to account to non-political bodies which examine the fairness and reasonableness of administrative procedures – administrative tribunals and the various ombudsmen who operate at the level of central government, local government and the NHS (Oliver 1991: 27). This particular form of accountability also includes the duty of local authorities and health authorities to account to the Audit Commission with regard to efficiency and value for money. Like other public bodies, the delivery agencies of the welfare state are also accountable to the courts, having to make sure that their activities conform to the requirements of legality.

Thus, as one distinguished writer on post-war social policy, Richard Titmuss (1974: 55), observed, public accountability is a distinguishing feature of the public administration of the social services, the agencies delivering social services being subject to 'quality controls' through Parliament and other procedures. In addition, the welfare professionals employed by local authorities and the NHS, who, as we have seen, play a major role in the delivery of welfare, are also accountable to their peers and professional associations. We will discuss these various forms of accountability in more detail in Chapter 5.

Equity of treatment

Another characteristic of the public administration model, with its emphasis on impartial administration, is that the personnel responsible for the delivery of social and other public services are, in the words of Greenwood and Wilson (1989: 9), 'expected to treat members of the public fairly without showing partiality to one at the expense of another'. Or as Glennerster (1992a: 32) has put it: 'Public organisations must be seen to be dealing fairly with all those who use the service. Like cases must be treated alike.'

Many of the services and benefits provided by the delivery agencies of the welfare state are specified in detail in legislation and there is a public expectation that delivery agencies and their staff will treat everybody equally and fairly. This value of equity 'puts a premium on stability, consistency and accuracy' in the operation of public bodies (Smith and Stanyer 1976: 31). As we shall discuss in Chapter 5, in parts of the social security system, this expectation is actually institutionalized in the form of the adjudicatory machinery provided by administrative tribunals. A range of ombudsmen also operate in an attempt to ensure that the users of social services are treated reasonably in their dealings with the various delivery agencies of the welfare state.

Self-sufficiency

Finally, another characteristic of the public administration model is what Stewart and Walsh (1992: 509), speaking of the public services in general, refer to as the assumption of self-sufficiency. Where a public organization is responsible for a function, it has normally carried out that function itself and employed those who deliver the service. As Pinker (1992: 273) has observed, it was 'taken for granted' in the years following the creation of the welfare state that the state had a dominant role to play as both the funder and provider of social services.

The two roles were not always combined. Before the emergence of a developed welfare state, government intervention in both education and housing had involved the separation of the funder and provider roles. Thus, in the nineteenth century, central government gave grants to voluntary societies to provide local education, whilst immediately after the First World War, government subsidies were given to private builders to provide working-class housing. But the need for closer quality control, together with demands for stronger financial and political accountability and equity in service provision, resulted in the fusion of the roles of funder and provider (Glennerster 1992a: 32–3; 1992b: 15–16). The 'accepted way of thinking' about the delivery of welfare in the system that developed in the post-war period was that social services should be both financed and provided by an agency of the state (Glennerster 1992a: 31). Thus welfare delivery agencies fulfilled the role of both funder and provider of most social services. The state provided and financed the core social services of education, housing, the personal social services, social security and health care.

The public administration model under challenge

The public administration model of welfare delivery has long been the subject of criticism, but the traditional methods of delivering welfare, and the key assumptions underpinning them, have been the subject of particular debate since the election of the first Thatcher Government in 1979. The debate has revolved around a number of specific, though interrelated, concerns. It is possible to identify four main themes: firstly, that the delivery agencies of the welfare state are inefficient, wasteful and unbusiness-like, with a lack of concern for efficiency and value for money; secondly, that welfare delivery agencies are provider dominated and pay insufficient attention to the needs and wants of the users of their services; thirdly, that the institutions of welfare delivery and their personnel are not close enough to their users or customers; and, fourthly, that the delivery agencies of the welfare state are not sufficiently accountable. The remainder of this chapter will discuss these concerns.

Inefficiency and waste

Contrary to the classic Weberian notion of bureaucracy as a form of organization which operates more efficiently than other forms of body, there has long been a popular view which associates public sector bodies with inefficiency and waste. Indeed, Albrow's examination (1970: 89–91) of the various usages of the term includes one definition of bureaucracy as 'organizational inefficiency', and writers on bureaucracy have long pointed to such imperfections as duplication of effort and unnecessary red tape. Since the early 1980s, criticisms about inefficiency and waste in the delivery agencies of the welfare state have been part of a wider debate about the size and efficiency of the public sector, a topic which we will discuss in greater detail in Chapter 8.

All three major types of delivery agency of the welfare state have been the subject of concerns of this kind, particularly in the context, since 1979, of the Conservative Government's commitment to the reduction of public spending. Central government's administration of what is by far the most expensive part of the welfare delivery system – the huge social security benefits operation – has long been the target of criticism regarding its inefficiency and wasteful procedures. The House of Commons Public Accounts Committee, charged with the oversight of the spending of government departments, has regularly commented on the overpayment of social security benefits resulting from administrative errors (see, for example, Public Accounts Committee 1971), as well as the high costs of administering the social security system (see, for example, Public Accounts Committee 1978). One survey in 1984 discovered that 40 per cent of social security benefit claimants were not receiving their correct entitlement to benefit because of errors by the (then) Department of Health and Social Security (DHSS) (McKnight 1985: 35), whilst, two years later, evidence on the same Department's efficiency indicators showed that over 10 per cent of supplementary benefit payments were wrongly calculated (see MacPherson 1987: 142). In 1987, the National Association of Citizens Advice Bureaux actually sought an action for judicial review against the DHSS for the Department's failure to meet its target times for processing benefit claims.

There has also been a widespread belief that local authorities, the major delivery agencies of social services, are inefficient and wasteful, despite the fact that there is little real evidence to prove or disprove such claims (Newton and Karran 1985: 17–18). Concern about value for money in local authorities figured prominently in the evidence given to the Layfield Committee on local government finance in the mid-1970s (Layfield 1976: 90). There has been particular concern about the management of local authority housing. For example, in the early 1980s, the former chief housing officer of one London borough, Alex Henney (1984: 216, 260), argued that local authorities had 'spent a great deal of money producing unpopular housing slowly and expensively, without knowing what it cost'. He further maintained that the problem of waste and the lack of concern for value for money was not confined to local authority housing: it was widespread and also included education and the personal social services.

Neither has the third major welfare delivery agency, the NHS, been immune from such criticisms. A study undertaken for the Royal Commission on the National Health Service in 1979 referred to criticisms about the quality of management in the service, a view supported by research undertaken for the Commission, which concluded that the NHS's system of financial management did little to ensure that resources were efficiently and effectively used (Merrison 1979: para. 4.19). Parliamentary select committees have also charged the NHS with inefficiency in the use of resources, highlighting defects in the financial control exercised by health authorities and stressing the need to increase the commitment to value for money (see, for example, Public Accounts Committee 1976). Criticisms of the lack of efficient management and value for money in the NHS have also come from the right-wing Adam Smith Institute, the director of which has referred to the costs of the service being unknown and waste remaining unchecked (Butler 1988).

One critic actually referred to the NHS in the late 1980s as 'the land of waste', alleging that it wasted several billion pounds every year, examples of which ranged from an inefficient use of property to the lack of controls on the purchase of certain types of medical equipment (see Coleman 1989: 122). Evidence of widespread variations in levels of spending on similar services between different health authorities have also raised questions about efficiency and value for money in the NHS. Official figures published in the late 1980s revealed that the average cost of treating acute hospital in-patients in 1986–87 varied by as much as 50 per cent between different health authorities (Department of Health 1989a: 3).

These kinds of complaints about the inefficient and wasteful nature of welfare delivery agencies have been given intellectual respectability by the New Right. Thus public choice theory argues that the inefficiencies of public sector bureaucracies are located in what has been referred to as the 'property-rights structure' of such organizations, in which there is no incentive to closely monitor organizational slack (Dunsire and Hood 1989: 147). We will discuss the views of the public choice school further in our discussion of provider domination in the next section.

Provider domination

Another major theme in the contemporary debate about the traditional arrangements for delivering welfare has been the concern about provider domination. Critics on both the right and the left of the political spectrum have argued that the delivery agencies of the welfare state are provider dominated and driven by the needs and wants of the providers of services – welfare bureaucrats and professionals – rather than by the needs and wants of the users of those services.

There are a number of strands to this particular argument. From the perspective of the ideology of the New Right, public choice theorists argue that welfare delivery, and other public sector, organizations promote the growth of their activities and tend to 'oversupply' their services in an attempt to maximize their budgets, responsibilities, status and job security (see, for example, Niskanen 1971). Not only is it argued that what is seen as the tendency of public bureaucracies to oversupply services results in waste and lack of value for money, but it is also claimed that it leads to the preferences of the consumers of services being ignored in favour of narrow sectional interests. Thus, writing in the early 1980s about welfare administrators, Nigel Lawson, then Financial Secretary to the Treasury, argued that far from being 'the selfless Platonic Guardians of paternalistic mythology', the providers of social services were 'a major powerful interest group in their own right' (Lawson 1980: 9). In 1973, one of Lawson's colleagues in the Thatcher Government, Nicholas Ridley (1973: 87), the minister in charge of the restructuring of council housing in the late 1980s, had described the work of one leading public choice theorist as 'of devastating importance'.

Twenty years later, another Conservative Cabinet Minister, William Waldegrave (1993: 9–10), writing about the post-war reforms of the public sector, argued that:

> it turned out that we had designed public services where the interests of the providers systematically outweighed those of the users, and which, driven only by the natural tendency of all provider organisations to claim that they can only do better with more money, contained an over-whelming dynamic for increasing cost which was bound to end in con-flict with reality.

Concerns about provider domination in the welfare state are not, of course, confined to critics on the right of the political spectrum. Critics on the left have expressed similar worries, although, as we shall see in later chapters, the solutions offered by the two sides are very different. Thus, a Fabian pamph-let of the late 1980s claimed that welfare bureaucracies were unresponsive to public demands, having taken it upon themselves to 'designate what the public needs rather than responding to its demands'. It argued that the delivery agencies of the welfare state 'see the public as a passive receiver of services rather than as citizens who have obligations to and rights over public institu-tions' (Corrigan et al. 1988: 10).

Arguments of this kind overlap with long-standing criticisms of the role of welfare professionals in the making and implementation of decisions about the delivery of welfare. Since the late 1960s, there has been a growing chal-lenge to the right of welfare professionals to define needs and problems and to the view that professional solutions are the best responses to the kinds of problems found in such areas as housing and health care. As Pollitt (1984b: 29) has argued, the 'heroic, uncritical image' of welfare professionals as highly educated experts with the interests of their clients and the public good at heart, has come under attack. Thus Wilding (1982: 23) has observed that:

> professional influence means that in many issues the decisions made serve professional interests rather than the public interest . . . it leads to services organised according to professional skills and ideas rather than according to client need.

The provider domination critique has been applied to a number of welfare delivery agencies. Thus the criticisms of the state education system made by the right wing Adam Smith Institute (1984: 2–3) in the mid-1980s referred to 'producer capture', arguing that the local authority education system had been 'captured' by producers – the teachers and administrators – whose objective was not to respond to the wishes of the consumers, but to impose their own wishes on the educational system. Ranson and Thomas (1989: 56) encapsulate the issue in their summary of this particular critique:

> The professionals create a technical language which serves only to bamboozle ordinary people and they organise the system for their convenience rather than to respond to the demands of the consumers.

Local authority housing is also an area in which critics claim that provider definitions of needs and problems have been accepted by policymakers rather than the definitions of those directly affected by the outcomes of policies (Wilding 1982: 30). One element of the New Right critique of state housing is that the design and management of post-war housing has been dominated by professional and bureaucratic self-interest, unwilling to adapt to consumer demand (see Cole and Furbey 1994: 192–3).

Such strictures are not confined to the social services delivered by local authorities. Similar criticisms about provider domination were made about the NHS before the reforms of the early 1990s. Thus Alain Enthoven (1991: 62–3), the North American health economist, whose notion of an internal market was so influential in the debate leading up to the recent NHS reforms (on which see Chapter 8), argued that 'Behind the rhetoric of caring for patients, the NHS was provider-dominated', with each district health authority being a monopoly supplier of health services to people in its particular area. As Enthoven (1991: 63) observed:

> consultant physicians had lifetime contracts with Regional Health Authorities, with merit pay determined by professional recognition, not service to patients. Nobody was seriously charged with the responsibility to measure and prioritize patients' needs and wants and then to use resources as effectively as possible in response.

Consumerism and being closer to the customer

Closely related to criticisms about provider domination has been the growing concern about the relationships of the delivery agencies of the welfare state and their staff with the consumers of services. Writers on private sector management emphasize the importance of listening to the customer: the best run private sector organizations are seen as those who, *inter alia*, take the customer seriously (see, for example, Peters and Waterman 1982; Osborne and Gaebler 1992). But recent years have been dominated by criticisms that unlike the best run private sector organizations, organizations in the public sector are not 'close' enough to their 'customers'. While the term 'customer' might not be the most appropriate term to describe the users of social services, the gulf between the delivery agencies of the welfare state and the users of their services has been at the forefront of debate since the late 1980s. The importance attached to the users of such services has been reinforced by the advent of the Major Government's Citizen's Charter and the subsequent publication of individual charters for most of the core social services.

Laffin and Young (1990: 43) have described the whole issue of consumerism as a 'major new addition' to the political agenda. Speaking of consumerism within local government, they argue that:

> The rise of consumerism . . . challenges the bureaucratic or professional definition of citizens' needs. Consumerism reflects the disillusionment with the paternalistic welfare state which is increasingly seen as large and bureaucratised and as insensitive to individual requirements.

As we shall discuss in our examination of this issue and recent developments in Chapter 9, consumerism and the concept of being 'closer to the customer' have a number of different dimensions. One important dimension is the geographical accessibility of service providers to the users of their services. Another dimension is what has been described as 'social accessibility' (Hambleton and Hoggett 1988: 22) – whether the staff responsible for delivering welfare are sensitive enough to the needs of the users of their services. Getting closer to the customer also involves finding out about the needs of service users, generating consumer feedback on service delivery and providing more information on services.

An excellent example of the way in which the welfare delivery system has been said to demonstrably fail to reflect the principle of being close to the customer has been central government's arrangements for the delivery of social security benefits, primarily the responsibility of the DSS, but also involving the Department of Employment (DEmp), which acts as an agent for the DSS in the payment of unemployment benefits. The administration of the social security system has long been the target of complaints, critics arguing that high levels of staff turnover, inadequate staff training, poor pay and low levels of staff morale have all combined to create a climate which has not been conducive to giving sufficiently high priority to the 'sympathetic administration' of the benefits system (Alcock 1987: 117). As Metcalfe and Richards (1990: 96) have observed of the arrangements for paying benefits to the unemployed: 'Few claimants felt that the system worked in a way that made any concessions to their convenience or their interests.'

The government department responsible for the delivery of social security benefits has long been aware of its poor relations with the public. As long ago as 1983, the then DHSS acknowledged that it was not fully complying with its statutory duty to provide 'a prompt, accurate, courteous and humane income maintenance service'. In a revealing phrase, the Permanent Secretary in charge of the social security side of the Department stated that its staff had to recognize that 'doing business with one of our local offices must often seem a less agreeable experience than approaching many other undertakings' (quoted in MacPherson 1987: 131). In 1988, research comparing 20 organizations providing services to the public showed that although the customers of the social security system rated it as providing a better service than the courts and the police, and on a par with local authorities and some other bodies, it was ranked lower than 14 other organizations with which the public had contact (Moodie *et al.* 1988: para. 20).

It is not only central government departments which have been criticized for failing to take the consumers of their services seriously. Criticisms have also been made about the gap which exists between the local authority departments responsible for the delivery of local social services and the users of their services. High on the agenda have been concerns about the geographical inaccessibility of the departments responsible for housing and the personal social services. Concern has also been expressed that local authorities have tended to provide services *to* the public rather than *for* the public, with service providers believing that they know what the public wants or needs (Stewart and Clarke 1987: 167). Research conducted for the Association of Metropolitan Authorities in the mid-1980s found that nearly one-third of those members of the public who had attempted to contact a local authority official had experienced difficulty in getting hold of the right person, with a similar proportion finding officials to be uninterested in their problems (quoted in Gyford *et al.* 1989: 245).

Concern about the lack of sensitivity to service users has also been an important theme in criticisms of the NHS. Since its inception in the late 1940s, the NHS has been pervaded by the medical model of health, in which the medical profession has a pre-eminent position in matters of health care (see, for example, Ham 1992: 225). The general acceptance of this particular model has been used to justify not only the dominant role of the medical profession in the delivery of health care, but also the profession's failure to take sufficient account of the needs of patients and to involve the public in the running of the NHS (Hogg 1990: 154–5). In the words of one commentator writing in the 1970s, there has been a tendency within the NHS to assume that 'what is good for medicine is also good for the patient' (Brown 1973: 84). As a result, the NHS has been seen as a producer orientated organization which makes little attempt to discover the reactions of the public to its activities. Such arguments were given official respectability in the early 1980s in the critique of the Griffiths Report (1983: 10), which concluded that, unlike the private sector, it was not clear that the NHS was meeting the needs of its customers.

Accountability

Another major strand in the contemporary debate about the delivery agencies of the welfare state and their personnel has been concern about their lack of accountability. This concern has several dimensions, one of which is the accountability of delivery agencies for the money which they spend. Particular concern has been expressed about the financial accountability of the NHS, with the House of Commons Public Accounts Committee during the late 1970s and early 1980s highlighting the lack of financial control exercised by various health authorities over spending from the funds provided through the DHSS (see, for example, Public Accounts Committee 1976, 1977 and 1981). The recessionary economic climate of the 1970s and 1980s also saw a growing concern on the part of central government with ensuring that delivery agencies such as the NHS and local authorities – widely viewed, as we saw earlier, as inefficient and wasteful organizations – were answerable for the efficient use of resources.

The debate about accountability has not been confined to concern about the control of spending and the efficient use of resources by welfare delivery agencies. It has also included worries about the professionalization of welfare delivery, which has, in the words of one observer, the potential to become a mechanism for avoiding not only control from the centre but also accountability to the consumer (Means 1993: 16). In a similar vein, Elcock (1983: 25) has argued that local government professionals are resistant to outside control, suggesting that what he refers to as 'accountability outwards' to colleagues within the professions and relevant local authority departments has been strengthened at the expense of 'accountability upwards' to elected local councillors and 'accountability downwards' to the users of services. Welfare professionals such as social workers, teachers and doctors – who interact with members of the public and exercise a high degree of discretion in their work – are examples of what have been termed 'street-level bureaucrats' (Lipsky 1979: 17). Such groups are difficult to control, especially the medical profession – described as 'the ultimate example' of 'street-level' power (Lowe 1993: 47) – which has traditionally operated on the basis that doctors have 'clinical freedom'.

A key theme in New Right criticisms of the welfare state has been that unless welfare delivery agencies and other public organizations are limited by stronger systems of accountability, they will put their own interests before those of service users (Oliver 1991: 15). This particular argument has been an important element in the development of Conservative policy towards the public sector, it being argued that there is an 'implied mistrust' of traditional forms of public accountability as a means of controlling the performance of public services (Oliver 1991: 14). Consequently, the Conservative Government since 1979 has introduced a number of initiatives in an attempt to enable the consumers of social services to exercise greater influence over the delivery of welfare.

Plan of the book

The remainder of this book is divided into two parts. Part I describes and discusses the structure and organization of welfare delivery – the 'public face' of welfare. Chapter 2 focuses on the central government departments responsible for the provision of social services. It identifies the main social service departments and their functions, highlighting the important distinction between those government departments which are directly involved in the delivery of social services and those who perform what is essentially a policymaking, resource allocation and supervisory role. The chapter goes on to explore the break-up of the DSS – the biggest spending government department – into semi-autonomous executive agencies operating at arm's length from the policymakers who remain in the core of the Department in Whitehall.

The discussion of the organization of welfare delivery is continued in Chapter 3, which examines the other public bodies responsible for the delivery of welfare – elected local authorities, the institutions of the NHS and various quasi-governmental bodies. This chapter also discusses the problems encountered by central government departments in attempting to ensure that the organizations making up what has been described as 'sub-central government' successfully implement centrally determined welfare policies. An important issue raised by the number and range of bodies involved in the delivery of welfare is that of coordination, which is the subject matter of Chapter 4. The coordination and planning of social services is essential to the delivery of welfare, and the chapter discusses the major obstacles to the successful coordination of social policies and assesses the various mechanisms intended to overcome these barriers. In Chapter 5 we turn to a discussion of the procedures for accountability and the redress of individual grievances, as well as discussing the various arrangements for involving the users of social services in the processes of welfare delivery.

Having discussed the framework and institutions of welfare delivery, Part II leads to a discussion of recent important developments. Chapter 6 considers the changes which have taken place in the role of elected local authorities as delivery agencies of the welfare state. It begins by looking at the role of local authorities and their relationships with central government in the post-war years before the election of the Conservative Government in 1979. It then considers developments since 1979, particularly the transformation of local authorities from front-line delivery agencies of the welfare state into what have been described as 'enabling authorities'. Chapter 7 moves on to an examination of the privatization of welfare delivery, focusing in particular on the privatization of council housing, contracting out, the encouragement of the private sector, and the introduction of quasi-markets into the operation of the NHS and the personal social services. The chapter also examines the expanding role of the voluntary sector in the context of the privatization of welfare delivery. Closely related to questions of privatization and marketization is the whole issue of managerialism and the search for efficiency and value for money in the operations of the delivery agencies of the welfare state, and this is the subject matter of Chapter 8. As we shall see in this chapter, all three main types of welfare delivery agency – central government's social service departments, local authorities and the NHS – have been greatly affected by the Government's attempts to encourage value for money and more business-like methods, a process seen by many observers as conflicting with the traditional values of the public administration model of welfare delivery. Chapter 9 looks at attempts to bring the delivery agencies of the welfare state closer to what are increasingly described as the 'customers' of social services, as manifested in such initiatives as the increasing emphasis on consumerism and customer care in the delivery of welfare and the geographical decentralization of local authority housing and the personal social services to area and neighbourhood offices. This chapter also examines the principles of 'charterism' being implemented in the major social services following the introduction of the Conservative Government's Citizen's Charter.

The final chapter returns to the public administration model discussed in this introductory chapter and considers how it has been affected by the developments of the 1980s and 1990s.

Part I

The public face of welfare

2

Central government and welfare

A key feature of the organization of the major social services in Britain – the 'public face of welfare' – and a theme which will run throughout this and Chapter 3, is that most of these services are not delivered by central government departments, but by other forms of public sector organization. Apart from the social security benefits system, the delivery of the major social services is the responsibility of non-departmental organizations. It is the organizations making up what Rhodes (1988) refers to as the 'sub-central governments' of Britain – elected local authorities in their various forms, the institutions of the NHS and a range of quasi-governmental bodies operating on the fringes of both central and local government – that are the major executants of welfare policy. As we shall see later, this gap between the making of welfare policy and its delivery has important implications for central government's control of the implementation of its welfare policies.

Thus there are two 'public faces' of the government of welfare in Britain. One face is made up of a small number of central government social service departments who are not normally delivery agencies of welfare, but are, as we shall see later, primarily concerned with the functions of policymaking, resource allocation and supervision. The other public face of welfare consists of a range of non-departmental organizations, notably local authorities and health authorities. This latter face of welfare – the world of welfare delivery outside the Whitehall departments – will be the subject of Chapter 3. The purpose of this chapter is to examine the organization and role of central government departments in the delivery of welfare.

Central government's social service departments

When discussing the central government departments responsible for the social services in Britain, one immediately comes up against problems of classification. Which central government departments are concerned with the social services? Where does one draw the line between social service departments and the rest?

Writing about central government in the late 1950s, Chester and Willson (1957: 139–40) maintained that what they referred to as the 'social services' formed what had come to be thought of as a coherent group of governmental functions. This 'coherent group' consisted of four major service areas: education, health, 'cash payments' (i.e. pensions, health and unemployment benefits, family allowances and assistance) and environmental conditions such as public housing. Since the late 1950s, there has, of course, been a rapid expansion and consolidation of local authority personal social services, sometimes described as 'the fifth social service'. Thus a useful starting point nearly 40 years after Chester and Willson's analysis is to take the government departments responsible for the five core social services – education, health care, social security, housing and the personal social services – which most commentators agree make up what is called the 'welfare state' in Britain (see, for example, Lowe 1993).

On this basis, the major Whitehall social service departments today are the Department for Education (DFE), the Department of Health (DoH) – responsible for the personal social services as well as the NHS – the Department of Social Security (DSS) and the Department of the Environment (DoE), which has responsibility for social housing. The pattern of social service departments is based upon the functional principle enunciated by the Haldane Report in 1918, whereby the responsibilities of government are allocated between departments according to the services to be performed rather than the clientele to be dealt with. A departmental structure built upon this 'philosophically ambiguous' concept (Pollitt 1980: 95) has – as we shall see in Chapter 4 – important implications for the coordination and planning of related services.

Another approach to the classification of social service departments is to update the scheme drawn up in 1970 by the then head of the home civil service (Armstrong 1970). This categorization divided the major government departments into five segments: overseas and defence; financial, economic and industrial; physical; social; and law and order (see Table 2.1). The DFE, the DoH and the DSS clearly fall within the 'social' sector. The fourth major social service department, the DoE, with its responsibility for social housing, can be placed on the dividing line between the 'social' and the 'physical' sectors.

Two other departments also have 'social' responsibilities. Thus the Home Office, with its responsibility for coordinating government action affecting the voluntary social services, can be placed on the dividing line between the 'social' and the 'law and order' sectors. In addition, although the Department of Employment (DEmp) – with its responsibilities for employment initiatives and

Table 2.1   Main central government departments 1994

Overseas and Defence	Ministry of Defence
	Foreign and Commonwealth Office
Financial, Economic and Industrial	Department of Trade and Industry
	Treasury
	Department of Employment
	Ministry of Agriculture, Fisheries and Food
Physical	Department of Transport
	Department of the Environment
Social	Department for Education
	Department of Social Security
	Department of Health
Law and Order	Home Office
	Lord Chancellor's Department

Source: Adapted from figure in Armstrong (1970).

industrial relations – is located firmly in the 'financial, economic and industrial' sector of the categorization, its responsibilities also include the administration of the payment of unemployment benefit, the running of the Job Centre network, and aspects of education and training. Indeed, the vast majority of the DEmp's staff are concerned with these latter responsibilities and the Department is clearly an important part of central government's arrangements for the delivery of welfare.

Although our discussion of central government's arrangements for the delivery of welfare will concentrate on the four major social service departments of the DSS, DoH, DFE and the DoE (with some discussion of the DEmp), we should also note the special cases of Scotland and Wales. Apart from social security, responsibility for their major social services is not divided between functional departments like Education and Health, with headquarters in Whitehall, but is in the hands of territorial departments in the form of the Scottish and Welsh Offices. The Scottish Office, which dates from 1885, comprises five main departments, three of which are involved with social services – the Home and Health Department, which has responsibility for the NHS in Scotland; the Education Department, which is responsible for education and social work services; and the Environment Department, which has responsibility for social housing. The Welsh Office, a relatively new addition to the list of central government departments – having been set up as recently as 1964 – does not have such wide ranging responsibilities for social services as its Scottish counterpart, but is responsible for housing, health and personal social services, which are brought together under its Housing, Health and Social

Table 2.2   Central government social service departments and responsibilities

• Department for Education	Policies for education; Goverment relations with the universities
• Department of Health	National Health Service; personal social services provided by local authorities
• Department of Social Security	Social security system
• Department of the Environment	Policies for local government; housing; inner cities
• Department of Employment	Employment Service; employment training; youth education; vocational education
• Home Office	Voluntary services
• Scottish Office	Local government; housing; National Health Service and social work services; education, excluding universities
• Welsh Office	Health, community care and personal social services; education; local government; housing; Urban Programme
• Northern Ireland Office	Education; housing; health and personal social services; social security; employment service and training schemes

Services Policy Group. The Welsh Office's Education Department is responsible for schools and further and higher education in the Principality. Northern Ireland also has its own territorial department, the Northern Ireland Office, with overall responsibility for all social services in the province.

Having identified the social service departments of central government, let us look at each of them in more detail (see Table 2.2).

The Department of Social Security

The DSS, which from 1968 to 1988 formed part of the giant Department of Health and Social Security (DHSS), is Whitehall's biggest spending department, disposing of just over 30 per cent of total government spending. Its major executive responsibilities were 'hived off' to a number of semi-autonomous agencies in the early 1990s as part of the Conservative Government's attempts to improve the efficiency of central government. The most important of these agencies, the Benefits Agency, is responsible, through its nationwide network of 159 district offices, for the operation of the social security benefits system. One of the DSS's predecessors, the Ministry of National Insurance, was only responsible for six major social security benefits when it was set up in 1948: its modern-day equivalent has responsibility for about 20 such benefits. We will examine the history and structure of this key Department in more detail later (p. 27–9).

The Department of Health

The DoH originated in 1919 as the Ministry of Health, a department which absorbed the Local Government Board, as well as taking over the powers exercised by a number of other bodies. It started life concerned with local government, housing and public health, together with the supervision of health insurance and some pensions work. Although it lost its insurance and pensions responsibilities to the newly formed Ministry of National Insurance in 1945, it retained its responsibility for housing until 1951. In 1948 it became responsible for the newly created NHS. The Ministry of Health was amalgamated with the then Ministry of Social Security in 1968 to form the DHSS, although it regained its separate status in 1988. In addition to its responsibility for the NHS, the DoH is also responsible, through its Community Services Division, for the oversight of the personal social services delivered by local authorities.

The Department for Education

The third major Whitehall social service department, the DFE, originated in 1899 as the Board of Education, although its origins can be traced back to a Privy Council committee set up in 1839 to administer government grants made to church voluntary societies which provided elementary schools. Following the pioneering Education Act 1944, the Board of Education became a Ministry. Twenty years later, the Ministry of Education became the Department of Education and Science, its responsibilities being enlarged to include the financing of the universities and various aspects of civil science. It kept this new title up until the aftermath of the Conservative victory in the 1992 General Election, when its responsibilities for sport and science were transferred to other departments, and it was renamed the Department for Education. Although long regarded as a 'Cinderella' department (Hennessy 1990: 428), it is one of the largest spending Whitehall departments. It has, however, very little direct involvement in the day-to-day spending of these vast amounts of money, state education being delivered by local education authorities and other non-departmental organizations.

The Department of the Environment

Central government responsibility for the key social service of housing, along with aspects of the associated policy area of urban policy, lies with central government's fourth major social service department, the DoE. The DoE was founded as recently as 1970, being the result of the merger of the Ministry of Housing and Local Government (itself only formed in 1951 as a result of the hiving off of certain functions from the Ministry of Health) and the Ministry of Public Building and Works. The DoE's core functions are concerned with local government and housing, but, as Hennessy (1990: 439–40) observes, the Department is 'a bit like a Whitehall holding company' in the range of activities it supervises at arm's length. Indeed, he describes it as 'the classic quangoid department', working through a network of quasi-governmental bodies such as the Housing Corporation and the Urban Development Corporations (Hennessy

1990: 440). We will have more to say on these quasi-governmental bodies and their involvement in the delivery of welfare in Chapter 3.

The Department of Employment

The DEmp, one of the two other central government departments involved with aspects of the social services (the other being the Home Office), has its origins in the Ministry of Labour founded in 1916. It is primarily responsible for policy on employment, training and industrial relations. Its Training, Enterprise and Education Division is responsible for the development and delivery of training and vocational education programmes, operating through a nationwide network of Training and Enterprise Councils (TECs). The DEmp also administers the Technical and Vocational Education Initiative (TVEI), which was introduced in the early 1980s in an attempt to emphasize work-related courses in schools and colleges of further education. Important-antly, the Department also acts as an agent of the DSS for the payment and administration of unemployment benefit. The vast majority of the DEmp's staff are involved in this area of its activities, which, together with its job placement service and other programmes for unemployed people, is the day-to-day responsibility of the Employment Service, a semi-autonomous agency within the department.

The Home Office

The Home Office, one of the oldest government departments, dating from 1782, is what one commentator has referred to as the 'ragbag of Whitehall' (Fowler 1967), being responsible for a variety of domestic functions of government which have not been given to other departments. Although it lost its responsibilities for child care to the former DHSS following the implementation of the Seebohm Report on the re-organization of local authority social services in the early 1970s, it is still involved in the welfare sphere through its Voluntary Services Unit, which is responsible for the coordination of central government interests in the voluntary sector.

A federation of departments

It can be seen that central government responsibility for the social services is distributed amongst a variety of departments, some of which are clearly major social service departments, while others are only concerned with the delivery of welfare amongst a range of other responsibilities. Why are welfare respon-sibilities distributed in the way summarized in Table 2.2? Why, for example, does the list of social service departments not include a Ministry of Social Welfare, as discussed by some observers in the late 1960s (see, for example, Lapping 1968), instead of related functions being distributed between separate departments like Health, Social Security, Education and Employment? Why are the organizational arrangements for the payment of social security benefits not linked with the Inland Revenue to form a new department? (see, for example, Wicks 1987: 242). Why does Britain not have a single government department to deal with the needs of elderly people (shared mainly between the DSS, the DoH and the DoE)? The answer to these questions can be found in the fact that the pattern of social service departments owes more to political considerations and changing needs than to administrative theory (see, for example, Pollitt 1984a). In the words of two commentators on this issue, the process of distributing responsibilities between central government departments has been 'a continuous process of creation, fission, fusion and transfer, rapid at some times, slower at others' (Hanson and Walles 1984: 139). As we shall see in the next section of this chapter, one clear expression of the *ad hoc* nature of this process has been the changing arrangements for the distribution of functions relating to social security.

One of the consequences of this essentially incremental process of allocating departmental functions is that the boundaries of central government's social service departments are arbitrary. Even what might appear to be an obviously functional department – the DoH – overlaps with other departments. Thus health in the armed forces comes under the wing of the Ministry of Defence, whilst health care in Scotland, Wales and Northern Ireland is, as we have already seen, the responsibility of the three territorial departments. We have already noted that government policy for the elderly is shared between at least three social service departments (the DSS, the DoH and the DoE). As we shall see in Chapter 4, such overlap creates serious problems for the coordination and planning of welfare delivery.

Within this collection of departments, there is no such thing as a 'typical' Whitehall social service department. The size, functions and characteristics of social service departments vary enormously. Social service departments vary considerably in their size, ranging from a very large department like the DSS, with some 87 000 full-time staff, to very small departments like the DFE, with only about 2000 civil servants, and the DoH with just under 4700 staff. The DoE has just over 7000 staff. The small size of these last three departments reflects the fact that they are not directly responsible for the delivery of major services. Between these extremes, we find the DEmp and the Home Office, both with about 50 000 staff, although the vast majority of those who work for the Home Office are not engaged in work affecting the delivery of welfare.

Social service departments not only vary in size, but also in the extent to which they are concerned with the direct administration of welfare policies. Dunleavy's analysis of the British central state (1989: 254–5) includes three major types of government department: delivery agencies, transfer agencies and control agencies. 'Delivery' agencies are departments which directly undertake the delivery of public services to citizens using their own staff to implement policies. 'Transfer' agencies are 'money-moving' organizations, handling payments of some kind made by government to private individuals. Finally, central government includes 'control' agencies, whose primary role is to pass government funds to other public sector organizations in the form of grants and to supervise the activities of those organizations, while having no major responsibilities for service delivery of their own.

The DSS, in Dunleavy's terminology, is a 'transfer' agency, with most of its staff responsible for the administration of the huge social security benefits system. It is Whitehall's biggest spender, with a budget of about £87 billion per year, equivalent to just over 30 per cent of total government spending. The payroll of the DSS's stablemate, the DEmp, includes nearly 45 000 staff who administer unemployment benefit on behalf of the DSS and work in local Job Centres.

The other three major social service departments are 'control' agencies, whose core budgets absorb only a very small proportion of their programme budgets. Spending on their own activities is small. Thus the DFE spends less than 2 per cent of its budget on its own activities – administration, research and miscellaneous services – the remainder going to such delivery agencies as local education authorities, grant maintained schools, city technology colleges, further education corporations in charge of sixth form colleges and further education colleges, and universities. The DoH is also primarily a 'control' agency. It is the institutions of the NHS which deliver health care services. The DoH also acts as a 'control' organization – through its Community Services Division – for the personal social services provided by local authorities. The Department's core health budget – spent on the cost of administration and other central services – is only just over 3 per cent of its total budget, the bulk of its expenditure on health care being spent by health authorities and family practitioners (family doctors, dentists, opticians and pharmacists). The DoE is also primarily a 'control' agency, operating through local authorities and a network of quasi-governmental bodies such as the Housing Corporation and the Urban Development Corporations in the implementation of its social housing and urban policies.

Thus the only central government social service departments directly involved with the delivery of major services are the DSS and the DEmp, and in both cases day-to-day responsibility for the delivery of their main executive services is actually in the hands of semi-autonomous agencies operating at arm's length from departmental headquarters – the Benefits Agency and the Employment Service. Both agencies operate under the direction of chief executives who work within the parameters of policy and resources frameworks set by their parent departments. Although the creation of executive agencies has been a key feature of the development of central government since the late 1980s, the process has proceeded very much further in the DSS and the DEmp – which have responsibility for the direct provision of services – than in traditional 'control' departments like the DFE and the DoH, where the scope for 'hiving off' is limited. Thus the Benefits Agency is fundamental to the mainstream policy and operations of the DSS, as is the Employment Service to the DEmp. The agencies which have been established within the other major social service departments, however, are not concerned with mainstream policy and operations, but with providing services to their departments using particular specialist skills. Thus although the DoH has four executive agencies, they all deal with technical activities, such as controlling the standards of medicines (Medicines Control Agency) and managing NHS estate and property (NHS Estates). Similarly, the only executive agency created in the DFE is the Teachers' Pensions Agency, responsible for the administration of the teachers' superannuation scheme. We now turn to a fuller discussion of the impact of the agency concept on central government's largest social service department, the DSS.

The changing face of the Department of Social Security

As we have seen, in terms of both spending and numbers of staff, the major social service department is the DSS. This Department has a chequered history, culminating in the transfer of most of its functions and staff to executive agencies in the early 1990s. A brief examination of the history of the DSS, and its predecessor departments, will throw further light upon the changing arrangements for the grouping of departmental responsibilities for the social services.

The antecedents of the DSS are complicated, but its origins can be traced back at least as far as 1916 and the establishment of the Ministry of Pensions, which was set up to administer the war pensions scheme introduced during the First World War. However, the administrative arrangements for the delivery of income maintenance in the inter-war period were complicated by the fact that contributory pensions were administered by the Ministry of Health, non-contributory pensions by the Board of Customs and Excise, the workmen's compensation scheme for industrial injuries by the Home Office, and the unemployment insurance scheme by the Ministry of Labour. In 1934 the Unemployment Assistance Board (UAB), under the direction of the Ministry of Labour, was set up to administer a means-tested unemployment assistance scheme. In the early 1940s, the UAB was renamed the Assistance Board and also took over responsibility for supplementing the income of old age pensioners.

Thus by the time of the publication of the influential Beveridge Report on Social Insurance in 1942, a number of government departments were involved in the delivery of income maintenance. The beginnings of the administrative rationalization of the system emerged soon after Beveridge, with the establishment in 1944 of a Ministry of National Insurance (MNI) to superintend the administration of the new system of social security adopted by the war-time Coalition Government. The Ministry of Labour continued to administer unemployment insurance on an agency basis and in 1948 the renamed National Assistance Board (NAB) took over responsibility for administering the national assistance scheme. The reasoning behind this particular division of functions was the importance attached by the Government to preserving the distinction between insurance and assistance (Minister of Reconstruction 1944: para. 161).

Although the creation of the MNI helped to rationalize the administrative arrangements for the delivery of social security, the Government did not merge the Ministry of Pensions with the new Department, as had been recommended by the Beveridge Report, probably because it was thought politically important to treat war pensioners as a separate group (Chester and Willson 1957: 180). But the Beveridge proposals did not disappear, and in 1953 the Ministry of Pensions was dissolved and its functions amalgamated with the MNI to form the Ministry of Pensions and National Insurance (MPNI). The rationale behind the merger of the two departments was to eliminate the duplication of administrative arrangements for the payment of pensions and national insurance benefits.

Thirteen years later, in 1966, the Labour Government decided that a merger of the MPNI and the NAB would make for even greater administrative simplification, as well as the elimination of stigma, in the delivery of benefits (Brown and Steel 1979: 283). Described by one writer as 'a piece of obvious administrative streamlining' (Pollitt 1984a: 69), the merger of the two departments resulted in the creation of the Ministry of Social Security.

The fusion process asserted itself again in 1968, when the recently formed Ministry of Social Security was amalgamated with the Ministry of Health to form the DHSS. The unification of the two departments was part of a wider trend towards the establishment of giant departments, the creation of the DoE – another social service department – in 1970 being another example of the process. The reasoning behind the establishment of the DHSS was the potential advantages offered by the wider application of resources and a more coherent approach to the priorities of social care (Nairne 1983: 247). In the event, however, as we shall discuss in Chapter 4, health and social security were administered in the new Department in two separate wings, the two sets of activities having little in common (Brown 1975: 285). In due course, the forces of fission reasserted themselves. In 1988, as part of the Thatcher Government's attempts to demonstrate its commitment to the NHS, the DHSS was split into two separate departments, with the Department of Social Security (DSS) emerging as a separate department.

Since the early 1990s, the newly created DSS has undergone a major upheaval, with most of its functions being transferred to semi-autonomous Next Steps agencies, operating within the terms of framework documents defining goals and setting targets. The decision to adopt the agency model for most of the executive functions of the DSS was announced in May 1989 (House of Commons Debates 17 May 1989, cols 318–32), and followed a study initiated the previous year which concluded that virtually all the operational tasks of the DSS could be run more effectively as executive agencies. The Resettlement Agency was subsequently established soon afterwards to administer the DSS's hostels for single homeless people without a settled way of life. In April 1990, the Department established the Social Security Information Technology Services Agency to develop and support the computing and communication technology services required by the DSS and its agencies. The

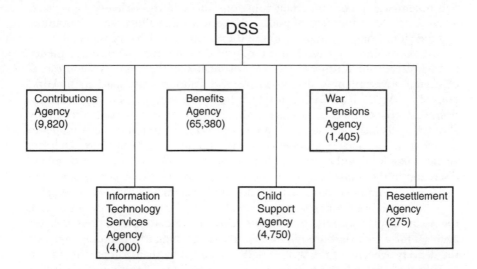

Figure 2.1   The Department of Social Security and its agencies. Staff numbers at April 1994 are given.

main work of the agency involves the calculation, recording and payment of social security benefits and it is linked to terminals in local social security offices and the local offices of the Employment Service. But the jewel in the crown of the establishment of executive agencies in the DSS was the setting up in April 1991 of the Benefits Agency, which currently employs just over 65 000 staff, nearly one-eighth of the total non-industrial civil service, and is responsible for the efficient and effective delivery of the Government's social security benefits scheme through a nationwide network of local offices. The same month saw the establishment of the Social Security Contributions Agency, which operates the National Insurance scheme. In April 1993, the Department set up the Child Support Agency, which is responsible for the operation of the child support maintenance system. A sixth executive agency followed a year later, with the establishment of the War Pensions Agency reponsible for the delivery of services to war pensioners.

As a result of these developments, by the end of 1994 some 97 per cent of DSS staff were working in executive agencies, with only a small number of staff located in headquarters offices in Whitehall (see Figure 2.1). The creation of executive agencies raises important questions and we will return to this key development in Chapters 8 and 9.

The role of government departments

Despite the fact that most social services are delivered by non-departmental agencies like local authorities and health authorities, and, in the case of the DSS and the DEmp, by semi-autonomous executive agencies, central government departments carry out important functions affecting the delivery of welfare. These are the development of policy, the securing and allocation of resources, and the monitoring and supervision of the activities of delivery agencies.

Policymaking is central to the role of central government departments. Indeed, Webb and Wistow (1987: 131) maintain that the 'primary significance' of central government is that it 'shapes and elaborates the legal framework, created by Act of Parliament, in which local authorities, voluntary organizations and private services operate'. Although they were writing specifically about the personal social services, Webb and Wistow's argument also applies to the other major social services of education, housing and health care. Delivery agencies like local authorities and health authorities may retain a fair degree of discretion in the implementation of central government's welfare policies, but the legislative framework clearly lays down the parameters for their activities.

A second important role undertaken by central government departments is the securing of resources, which they then allocate to the various delivery agencies for which they are responsible. By far the bulk of the money spent by the delivery agencies of the welfare state is acquired by their parent departments in Whitehall through the system of public expenditure allocation. Over half of local authority spending is now financed by grants from central government and health authorities are almost entirely financed from Exchequer funds. Since 1961, government decisions about the total level of public spending and the allocation of funds between different spending programmes have been taken in the context of the Public Expenditure Survey system (commonly known as PESC). Each year, central government's social service departments and other individual spending departments calculate the costs of their programmes for the following three years, with final departmental allocations being decided after detailed negotiations have taken place between the Treasury and Ministers and senior civil servants from the relevant departments. As we shall discuss in Chapter 4, technical changes to the PESC system in the 1970s and 1980s have seriously affected the ability of Whitehall's social service departments to plan effectively. The experience of the PESC system since its creation in the early 1960s has also highlighted the difficulties of persuading social service departments and their Ministers to act collectively when making decisions about spending priorities.

The third major role of central departments is monitoring and supervising the agencies which deliver welfare. Whitehall's social service departments possess a range of instruments enabling them not only to monitor and supervise the activities of local authorities and health authorities, but also to intervene in their operations. We discuss these instruments, and the relationship between the two sides, in the remainder of this chapter.

Controlling the delivery agencies

Before we come to discuss the instruments available to central government departments in their dealings with the major delivery agencies of the welfare state, we first need to examine the justifications for central intervention.

One important justification given for central intervention is the major role played by local authorities and health authorities as delivery agencies of the welfare state and the enormous amounts of money involved in their operations. Local authority spending in Britain on the three major social services delivered by local government – education, housing and the personal social services – amounted to something in the order of £45 billion in the financial year 1992–93. The NHS spent nearly £35 billion in the same financial year. This level of spending – representing nearly a third of total government spending – allied to the importance of the services involved, helps to account for what Smith and Stanyer (1976: 124) refer to as the demand for 'efficient and honest government', a demand which has been reflected in the attempts by the Conservative Government since the early 1980s to encourage a greater emphasis on efficiency and value for money in the public sector (see Chapter 8).

A second factor in the case for central intervention in the affairs of both local and health authorities is the need to promote what has been described as 'territorial justice' – the notion that the users of a particular service in one area of the country should receive the same standard of service as people in another area (see, for example, Byrne 1990: 248; Davies 1968). As the Labour Government stated in 1977, one of the roles of central government is to ensure that local services such as education, housing and personal social services 'are provided at broadly comparable standards' (Department of the Environment 1977: para. 2.2). Similar arguments were used in the context of the attempts to ensure a more equitable distribution of resources between the various regions in the NHS, based on the RAWP (Resource Allocation Working Party) formula introduced in the late 1970s. The RAWP system allocated resources based on such factors as population size, population profile and morbidity patterns. Although RAWP was replaced by a new approach to resource allocation with the NHS reforms of the early 1990s, its underlying principles have been retained.

A third important factor in the case for central government intervention arises from the undeniable fact – however unpleasant it may be to many localists – that the social services provided by local authorities often have a party political dimension. Central governments, of both major political parties, periodically commit themselves to national policies in fields where the delivery of services lies in the hands of elected local authorities, many of which are often under the control of a political party of a different persuasion. Thus, for example, as we shall discuss in more detail in Chapter 6, the Labour Government in the 1960s attempted to promote the concept of comprehensive education through the famous Circular 10/65, whilst the Conservative Government in the 1980s attempted to privatize local authority housing through the introduction of the controversial Housing Act 1980, which gave council house tenants the right to buy their homes. Governments also attempt to promote particular lines of service development in the NHS. Thus, for example, the 1974–79 Labour Government attempted to fulfill its objective of giving priority to spending on services for client groups like the mentally ill and mentally handicapped by publishing guidance to health authorities on priorities for service development (Department of Health and Social Security 1976). It is hardly surprising that central government will attempt to ensure that such policies – invariably included in election manifestos – are successfully implemented by delivery agencies at the local and sub-national level.

Finally, and crucially in the context of developments since the election of the Conservative Government in 1979, there is the economic case for central intervention in the affairs of local government. Successive post-war governments have argued that no central government, with its responsibility for macroeconomic policy, can allow local government spending to remain completely free from central control or influence. Thus, in 1977, the Labour Government argued in a Green Paper that because of its responsibilities for the management of the economy, central government had to concern itself with total local government expenditure and taxation. Consequently, the role of central government was to 'ensure that, in aggregate, local government's spending plans are compatible with the Government's economic objectives' (Department of the Environment 1977: para. 2.2). The economic case for central intervention has become even more significant since the election in 1979 of the Conservative Government, which argued that 'overspending' local authorities damage the health of the national economy. It further stated in 1986 that '[b]ecause Governments are responsible for the overall management of the economy they have to be concerned with the amount of local authority expenditure, borrowing and taxation' (Department of the Environment 1986: para. 1.13). Such a view is not without its critics, it being argued that the case for central government control of local government spending is 'built on shaky theory and lacks empirical support', and that local government current spending has little impact on aggregate national demand (Newton and Karran 1985: 124; see also Jackman 1982).

The instruments of central intervention

Using the typology developed by Stanyer (1976: 221), it is possible to discuss the relationships between central government and the delivery agencies of local government and the NHS in terms of two main types of central intervention – *methods of influence* and *methods of control*. Whereas the latter methods presume a confrontation between central government and its delivery agencies and allow for any conflict to be resolved in favour of central government, methods of influence are intended to prevent such a conflict arising in the first place by encouraging consensus between the two sides. We will first look at the weapons enabling central government departments to intervene in the affairs of local authorities, before turning to an examination of central government's controls and influences over health authorities.

At the heart of the apparatus for controlling the welfare delivery agencies of local government is legislative and judicial control. Local authorities are creatures of legislation, deriving their powers from Acts of Parliament. The limits of a local authority's powers in education, housing and the personal social services are set by the doctrine of *ultra vires*, according to which no local authority is allowed to carry out any activity unless permitted to do so by an Act of Parliament. The doctrine is enforced by the courts, and a local authority which attempts to exceed its legal powers may be prevented from doing so by a court order. Legislation also imposes certain statutory duties upon local author- ities – for example, the Housing Act 1980 requires local housing authorities to sell council houses to tenants who request it. Such duties are often reinforced by provisions which give government Ministers the power to issue a directive ordering a local authority to carry out, or refrain from carrying out, a particular action. Legislation sometimes also contains default powers enabling the rele- vant minister to take over the responsibilities of recalcitrant local authorities. This 'big stick' of default power is rarely used. It was used in the famous Clay Cross affair in 1974 (see Chapter 6) and in the early 1980s over Norwich City Council's slow progress in selling council houses, but it always remains in the background as an indicator of potential central power.

What Byrne (1990: 261) describes as 'the closest and most continuous form of control' over local authorities is the range of specific administrative controls given to government Ministers by various statutes. Thus the Secretary of State for Health must approve the appointment of local authority directors of social services. The same Minister can also issue regulations prescribing how local authorities should perform duties as various as the arrangements for the fostering of children or charges in old people's homes. Similarly, local housing authorities are required to seek the permission of the Secretary of State for the Environment for capital allocations. Government Ministers can also require local authorities to prepare plans for the development of a particular service: thus in 1972 local authorities were asked by the Secretary of State for Social Services to prepare ten-year plans for the development of their personal social services. These, and other types of administrative controls, have been described by one commentator as setting up 'gates' or 'bottlenecks' through which individual local authorities must pass certain proposals before they can be implemented (Dunsire 1981: 176).

Each of the methods of intervention described so far has a statutory basis and is therefore, in the terminology used by Stanyer (1976: 221), a form of 'control'. In addition, central government departments possess a range of other methods whereby they can attempt to 'influence' the affairs of local authorities. One major form of administrative influence is the use of departmental circulars, described nearly twenty years ago by the then Department of Education and Science (DES) as 'the main instrument of formal communication with local authorities' (Central Policy Review Staff 1977: para. 2.7). The content of circulars varies from technical advice to such major policy pronouncements as DES Circular 10/65, which requested local education authorities to submit plans for the re-organization of secondary schools in their areas on comprehen- sive lines. DES Circular 2/81 asked local education authorities for information about surplus school places and their plans to remove them, a request which was seen as a way of putting pressure on local education authorities to begin the rationalization of schools (Ranson 1985: 196).

In two of the major social services, education and the personal social services, the central government departments charged with responsibility for the oversight of these services maintain inspectorates whose duties are to visit local authorities and report on standards of efficiency. The use of such inspectorates is one of the oldest forms of central government intervention, going back at least to the Poor Law Inspectorate of the mid-nineteenth century, and make up what one writer has called a system of central government 'quality control' (Glennerster 1992a: 80). The Education Act 1944 imposed a duty on ministers to ensure inspection of every educational establishment, and Her Majesty's Inspectors of Education (HMIs) were given responsibility for monitoring and advising local education authorities. Following the establishment of the Office for Standards in Education (OFSTED) in 1992, the number of HMIs has been reduced and private teams led by registered inspectors tender for school inspection work. The DoH's Social Services Inspectorate, which monitors the efficiency and effectiveness of local authority social services departments, is a much more recent innovation, having only been established in 1983.

A third form of central government influence over the activities of local authorities is through finance. As we saw earlier, the bulk of local authority revenue comes from central government grants. Although a significant proportion of central support is given through specific grants – which must be spent on a particular service or project – since 1958 most central government financial support has been distributed to local authorities in the form of a general grant which is not allocated to specific services (formerly Rate Support Grant, now Revenue Support Grant). As Byrne (1990: 267) points out, both forms of grant enable central government to exercise a form of influence. Specific grants help to encourage the provision of a particular service. General grant brings with it the power to exercise a general 'influence', since local authorities can be encouraged or discouraged from spending by changes in central government grant. Thus an increase in the amount of central grant can be used to encourage local authorities to increase spending, whilst, conversely, a government wishing to encourage a decrease in local government spending can reduce the amount of central grant. Since local taxation – whether it be in the form of local authority rates, community charge or council tax – is unpopular with those who have to pay it, it is argued that local councils would probably be reluctant to impose extra costs on local tax payers in order to maintain spending levels. As we shall see in Chapter 6, large increases in central government grants played a major part in influencing the rapid expansion of the various local authority social services during the post-war development of the local government welfare state.

Thus central government departments have a variety of methods through which they may attempt to control or influence the activities of local authorities. It is, however, difficult to generalize about the relationship between the two sides. As Griffith (1966: 528) has pointed out, each government department has its own philosophy about the way in which local authorities should be treated. The balance of power between the two sides has also varied over time. Thus, historically, local housing authorities have been used to a higher degree of autonomy than other local social services (Karn 1985: 163), although the situation has changed over the last 30 years or so. Thus Karn (1985: 163–5) has identified three main phases in the central–local relationship in this particular area: a period of *laissez-faire* from 1919 to the 1960s, where local authorities were left to define the extent of local housing need and how far it should be met; the period from the 1960s to the late 1970s, which was characterized by a more interventionist concern with the quality, scope and cost of local authority housing; and the period since the election of the Conservative Government in 1979, which has been characterized by financial cuts, privatization and increased centralization. The relationship between central government and local education authorities has also been marked by change, in this case a movement away from a period of local dominance in the late 1960s and early 1970s to one of increasing centralization (see Ranson 1985). We will discuss developments in these two areas since 1979 in more detail in Chapter 6.

Like its sister departments in their relations with local authorities, the DoH also has a range of influences and controls available to it in its relations with regional and district health authorities. Thus the DoH provides guidelines to health authorities through circulars, (e.g. the circular on competitive tendering issued in 1983) and consultative documents and White Papers spelling out priorities for the development of particular health services (e.g. the document on priorities for 'Cinderella' services issued in 1976; Department of Health and Social Security 1976). Since the early 1980s the Department has also monitored the NHS through an annual review process which assesses the performance of each region in the previous year (see Chapter 8).

The DoH also exercises administrative influence within the NHS through its power to issue regulations on a range of matters. In addition, the Secretary of State has the power to appoint, and to dismiss, the chairmen and non-executive members of regional health authorities and the chairmen of other health authorities. Financial sanctions are also available to the DoH, which can penalize health authorities through reductions in their financial allocations. Ultimately, as in the case of the relationship between central government departments and local authorities, the Secretary of State for Health has the power to direct health authorities to comply with the Department's wishes, and has the ultimate power to suspend individual health authorities. Although Brown (1979: 10) has argued that these drastic powers 'are about as usable in practice as nuclear weapons', they were used in 1979 when, after threatening to overspend its budget, the Lambeth, Southwark and Lewisham Area Health Authority was suspended and replaced by a team of centrally appointed commissioners.

A study of central–local relations in the mid-1960s concluded that the Ministry of Health had a *laissez-faire* attitude towards local health authorities (Griffith 1966: 515), but since the creation of the giant DHSS in 1968 central government has developed a more interventionist approach (Hunter and

Wistow 1987: 49). In particular, as we shall see in Chapter 8, the NHS has witnessed a marked change in central–local relations since the early 1980s.

Given the battery of weapons available to central government departments in their relations with local authorities and the institutions of the NHS, it is not surprising that some observers have characterized the relationship between the centre and both these types of welfare delivery agency as that of principal and agent (see, for example, Robson 1966 on local government and Powell 1966 on the NHS). As we shall see in later chapters, however, this view is a misleading one. Both types of welfare delivery agency – elected local authorities and appointed NHS authorities – possess important resources and central government is dependent on them for the implementation of centrally determined social policies (see Rhodes 1979; Ham 1992: 176).

3

The government of welfare outside Whitehall

As we saw in Chapter 2, the social service departments of central government are mainly concerned with the functions of policymaking, resource allocation and supervision. With the exception of the DSS and the DEmp, government departments are not usually involved in the day-to-day delivery of welfare, and, even in the case of the DSS and the DEmp, the delivery of services has been hived off to semi-autonomous agencies operating at arm's length from the policymaking core in Whitehall. Leaving aside executive agencies like the Benefits Agency and the Employment Service, for most people what might be termed the 'public face' of the statutory social services consists of the organizations which make up the system of 'sub-central government', consisting of local authorities, the institutions of the NHS, and the various quasi-governmental bodies associated with the delivery of welfare (Rhodes 1988; Stoker 1990). It is these non-departmental organizations, and the part that they play in the delivery of welfare, which form the subject matter of this chapter.

The local government welfare state: from the cradle to the grave

The major delivery agencies of the welfare state are local authorities, consisting of unpaid, locally elected councillors who are accountable to their local electorates. The fact that local authorities are elected is an important part of the traditional case for local government, the localist tradition arguing that this particular delivery agency of the welfare state contributes to local democracy by enabling people not only to express the views of the local community, but

Table 3.1 Local authority social services current expenditure and staff, England and Wales 1992–93

Sector	Spending (£m.)	Staff ('000)
Education	22,908	760
Housing (includes housing benefit)	7,397	69
Personal social services	5,309	242
Total local authorities	52,182	1,823

Sources: H.M. Treasury (1993a); *Employment Gazette*, January 1994.

also to participate in the delivery of local services through election as local councillors. Localists also claim that local government helps to spread political power, thereby contributing to a pluralistic system of government (see, for example, Widdicombe 1986: 47–52; Jones and Stewart 1983: 5–8). For many, however, the major justification for local government is that it is an efficient means of providing for the welfare of the population (Hampton 1991: 5). As multi-functional bodies, local authorities can respond to local needs and conditions and coordinate the provision of such services as education, housing and the personal social services (see, for example, Sharpe 1970: 166).

Although local authorities are responsible for a wide range of services, the major category, in terms of both expenditure and staff, is what has been termed the 'personal' group – education, housing and the personal social services – defined by Byrne (1990: 69) as the services which seek to enhance personal welfare. In the financial year 1992–93, this group of services accounted for over 68 per cent of local government current expenditure in England and Wales and over 58 per cent of local authority staff (see Table 3.1). These three services are sometimes referred to as 'collective consumption' services – those services which are used by people in order to live and bring up their families (Kingdom 1991: 480). Consequently, local government has often been described as influencing people's lives 'from the cradle to the grave' or 'from womb to tomb' (Chandler 1991: 32; Redcliffe-Maud and Wood 1974: 15), although this description has been slightly less applicable since the transfer of local authorities' health functions to the NHS in 1974.

The most important of these three services, education, was brought under local authority control in England and Wales following the Education Act 1902. The 1902 Act abolished the elected local school boards established under the Education Act 1870 to superintend the provision of elementary (what would now be called primary) education and transferred their powers to the counties and county boroughs set up as part of the restructuring of local government at the end of the nineteenth century. These newly designated local education authorities were also given powers to provide secondary or 'higher' education beyond the elementary level. The larger county districts were also given powers to provide elementary education. Local school boards in Scotland were not abolished until 1918, when counties and the largest burghs became local education authorities.

Further important changes followed the Education Act 1944, a piece of pioneering legislation which was to form the basis of the local authority education system until the Education Reform Act 1988. As a result of the 1944 Act, the counties and the county boroughs were made the sole local education authorities, with responsibility for ensuring the provision of primary and secondary school education in their areas. Local education authorities were also given responsibilty for the provision of further education, an area of activity which included some of the colleges which were later transformed into polytechnics during the rapid expansion of higher education in the late 1960s and 1970s and which later became the 'new' universities in the early 1990s. The 1944 Act created what has been described as a 'partnership' between central and local government, with central government having the duty to 'promote' the education of school children, while local education authorities provided and operated the schools.

Education is by far the costliest local authority service, accounting for almost a third of total local authority spending. It is little wonder that it has been regarded by many as being a semi-autonomous local authority service (Jennings 1977: 124), with one writer on local government describing it as constituting 'almost an authority within each council' (Elcock 1986a: 119). As we shall discuss in Chapter 6, the position of local education authorities as monopolistic providers of state education in their areas is being transformed following legislation in the late 1980s and early 1990s which has had the effect of removing a large number of schools from local authority control, together with polytechnics, colleges of higher education and further education institutions.

Local authority involvement in the second major social service, the provision of housing, dates back to the end of the nineteenth century when local authorities were given powers by the Housing of the Working Classes Act 1890 to build housing for general needs. Local authorities, however, were not obliged to build such housing, and this limitation, together with the absence of central government subsidies, meant that only a few local authorities, notably the London County Council, built houses under this legislation. It was not until the Housing and Town Planning Act 1919 (the Addison Act), which followed Lloyd George's famous promise to build 'homes fit for heroes' for the servicemen returning from the First World War, that central government provided local authorities with subsidies encouraging them to build housing to let at affordable rents.

During the inter-war period, 1.5 million council homes were built. Since then, local government involvement in housing has increased substantially with the extension of the policy of government subsidies, notably by the post-war Labour Government through the Housing Act 1946, which trebled the monetary value of subsidies compared with 1939 (Malpass and Murie 1990: 74). The Attlee Government saw local authorities as the main means of meeting the serious housing shortage created by the bomb damage of the Second World War, and the majority of building licences in the immediate post-war years were given to local authorities rather than to private builders, a decision which was justified on the grounds that local authorities could be trusted to honour planning agreements (Lowe 1993: 245). In the words of Aneurin Bevan, the Minister responsible for the Attlee Government's housing programme: 'If we are to plan, we have to plan with plannable instruments, and the speculative builder, by his very nature, is not a plannable instrument' (quoted in Hamnett 1993: 151). As a result, over 80 per cent of all new dwellings constructed between 1945 and 1951 were built by local authorities.

Local authorities continued to play an important role in the provision of social housing after 1951. By 1979, the zenith of local authority housing, some 31 per cent of all dwellings in Britain were in the local authority sector. Like local authority education, local authority housing has been the subject of much criticism since the election of the first Thatcher Government in 1979, with council tenants being encouraged to purchase their homes or to transfer to alternative landlords in the private and housing association sectors.

The third major social service delivered by local government, the personal social services, is much more recent, dating, in its present form, from the 1970 Local Authority Social Services Act. The antecedents of the modern-day personal social services, however, go back much further. Some of the personal social services – those dealing with the elderly, children and the mentally ill, for example – have their roots in the nineteenth-century Poor Law. Others – the home help service, for instance – developed as offshoots of other local services such as health, education and housing (Seebohm 1968: paras 52–3). What Hill (1993: 38) describes as 'the foundations' of the development of the personal social services were laid in the late 1940s by the Attlee Government. With the dismantling of the Poor Law, local authorities were given responsibility for providing services for elderly and handicapped people by the National Assistance Act 1948. They were also given significantly increased responsibilities in the field of child care by the Children Act of the same year, and, as part of the tripartite structure set up to run the new NHS, were given charge of community health services. Until 1970, administrative responsibility for these various services was divided between separate local authority departments for welfare, children's and local health services.

It was not until the late 1960s and the early 1970s that the personal social services really 'leapt from the margins to the centre' of social welfare (Young-husband 1978: 35), and it was the fastest growing of the five major social services in the 1960s (Gould and Roweth 1980: 349–50). Following legislation in 1970, which closely followed the proposals of the Seebohm Committee two years earlier, the three separately organized services of welfare, care for deprived children and local health care were brought together under the wing of self-contained local authority social services departments.

The new social services departments' responsibilities for local health services were later transferred to area health authorities (subsequently replaced by district health authorities) in 1974, as part of the unification of the NHS (see p. 47). Despite this loss of functions, local authority social services departments are still responsible for a variety of important services, notably the provision of residential care for the elderly, children, the mentally ill and handicapped and the physically disabled, but also including the protection of children and various forms of social work. Like the other two major social services provided by local authorities, the organization and management of local authority social services departments has also been the subject of substantial change in recent years, with the separation of the roles of purchaser and provider in the area of community care (see Chapters 6 and 7).

The development of the local government welfare state

As we saw in the last section, education and housing emerged as major functions of local government well before the Second World War. During the inter-war years, as a result of the abolition of the boards of guardians and the transfer of their duties to counties and county boroughs in 1929, local authorities also played a key role in poor relief and in the running of the majority of hospitals. Such was the growing importance of local government in the provision of social welfare during this period that in 1935 one eminent authority wrote that local government was firmly established as 'the most effective instrument of social welfare in our national life' (Robson 1935: 464). But, despite its involvement in welfare delivery in the immediate pre-war years, local government during this period was mainly concerned with what have been described as 'production-orientated' services – trading services, such as gas and electricity, and public goods, such as highways and street lighting, that benefitted all local residents (Loughlin 1986: 6). In 1935, spending on the collective consumption services of education, housing, poor relief and hospitals only totalled just over 40 per cent of total local government current expenditure in England and Wales (see Table 3.2).

The local government welfare state only really took off in the post-war period, with the launching of the welfare state by the Labour Government after the 1945 General Election. Although the late 1940s saw the handing over of local authority hospitals to the newly established NHS and the transfer of poor relief to the new National Assistance Board as part of the establishment of a national social security system, local government was given new responsibilities

Table 3.2 Local authority current expenditure on social services in England and Wales 1935 and 1980 (percentage of total current expenditure)

Sector	1935	1980
Education	19.1%	36.1%
Housing	9.8%	21.8%
Poor relief	8.0%	–
Hospitals	5.0%	–
Personal social services	–	6.9%

Source: Jackman (1985: 151).

in the field of social welfare, while some existing responsibilities were expanded. As we have seen, local authorities were given wider powers in the area of child care, as well as being given responsibility for providing services for the elderly and handicapped. The role of local education authorities was expanded by the introduction of universal free state secondary education up to the age of fifteen in the Education Act 1944. Local authorities were also given a major responsibility for implementing the state's policy of housing reconstruction.

As a result of these developments, local government became what Stoker (1991: 5) has called a 'prime vehicle' in the post-war drive to create the welfare state. The 30 years following the end of the Second World War witnessed a substantial development of the local authority education service in the 1950s and 1960s, a massive growth – fuelled by central government subsidies – in the rate of council house building, and a major expansion of the personal social services in the 1960s and early 1970s. By 1980, the three major social services of education, housing and the personal social services made up nearly two-thirds of local government current expenditure in England and Wales (see Table 3.2).

The welfare state character of local government was also manifested in the redistributive nature of central government's grant aid to local authorities, whereby the general grant (later renamed Rate Support Grant and then Revenue Support Grant) which made up the bulk of central government's financial support to local government took account of the needs and resources of individual local authorities (Pickvance 1991: 52). To use Pickvance's terminology (1991: 49), the post-war period saw the creation of a 'welfare state' model of local government, in which local authorities were responsible for the delivery of a range of services and relied on a mixture of central and local finance, supported by a grant equalization system, which paid grant to those authorities whose financial means were below the national average. This latter component was specifically intended to secure a degree of territorial justice, uniformity between local authority service provision being, as we saw in Chapter 2, a key part of central government's concern with the activities of local government.

The structure of the local government welfare state

The structure of the local government welfare state in Britain is a complex one. Responsibility for providing local government's three core social services rests with 514 main local authorities. In the non-metropolitan counties of England and Wales, responsibility for social services is split between two tiers, a system which was established with the re-organization of local government structure in 1974. Forty-seven county councils, ranging in population from just under 119 000 (Powys) to nearly 1.6 million (Hampshire), have responsibility for the provision of education and personal social services. At the lower tier, 333 district councils, ranging in population from 23 500 (Radnor) to 376 000 (Bristol), are responsible for housing. It had been argued in the reform process of the early

1970s that the accurate assessment of housing requirements and the provision of housing and housing advice to individuals is of such 'paramount importance' that the housing service should be operated as close to the citizen as possible (Department of the Environment 1971: para. 23). There is also a two-tier system throughout most of Scotland, with the nine upper-tier authorities, known as regions, responsible for education and social work, and the lower tier of 53 district councils responsible for housing. Three all-purpose authorities operate in the Scottish islands, covering Orkney, Shetland and the Western Isles.

The local government system in Greater London and the six metropolitan areas of the West Midlands, Greater Manchester, Merseyside, West Yorkshire, South Yorkshire and Tyne and Wear is very different from that of the rest of the country. Before 1986, responsibility for education in Greater London was divided between the 20 Outer London boroughs and the Inner London Education Authority (ILEA), which provided education for the twelve Inner London boroughs. Responsibility for housing was divided between the Greater London Council (GLC) and the 32 London boroughs. Of the three major social services, only the personal social services was the unfettered responsibility of each of the London boroughs. This division of functions had been in place since the reform of London government in 1965. With the abolition of the GLC in 1986, and the winding up of the ILEA two years later, each of the London boroughs is now responsible for all three major social services in its area. (The City of London also has responsibilities for the three major social services in its area, but with a population of only about 6000 people, it is not one of the main local authorities.) A similar single-tier system exists in the six metropolitan areas, where, since the abolition of the metropolitan counties in 1986, 36 metropolitan districts serve as multi-purpose authorities with responsibility for the provision of the three social services (see Table 3.3).

Thus, although all three major local authority social services are the responsibility of a single tier – in effect unitary authority – system of local government in each of the London boroughs, the 36 metropolitan districts and the three Scottish island authorities, this is not the case in the remainder of Britain. The three social services are divided between two tiers of local government in the non-metropolitan counties of England and Wales and on the Scottish mainland. This two-tier system, which dates from 1974 in England

Table 3.3   Local authorities and the social services

Function	NMC	NMD	MD	LB	SR	SD	SI
Education	×		×	×	×		×
Housing		×	×	×		×	×
Personal social services	×		×	×	×		×

Key: NMC, Non-metropolitan counties; NMD, Non-metropolitan districts; MD, Metropolitan districts; LB, London boroughs; SR, Scottish regions; SD, Scottish districts; SI, Scottish islands.

and Wales (and 1975 in Scotland), is the product of many years of debate and conflicts with the principle put forward by various official bodies in the 1960s that all three major local government social services should be provided by the same local authority.

The shortcomings of the two-tier system were recognized in 1991 by the Conservative Government which initiated a process to reshape the structure of local government in England outside Greater London and the metropolitan areas, the underlying assumption being that unitary authorities could often be the best form of structure (Department of the Environment 1991a). In 1992, a Local Government Commission embarked upon a review of the structure of local government areas in England and has made a series of proposals advocating the creation of unitary authorities in many parts of the country. In the meantime, the Government had announced that the Welsh counties and districts will be replaced by a system of 21 unitary authorities in 1996 (Welsh Office 1993; Boyne and Law 1993) and that 28 single-tier local authorities will replace the local authorities in Scotland in the same year. We will return to this issue in Chapter 4. Meanwhile, as one observer has pointed out, we should be aware that structural change is already 'coming in through the back door' as evidenced by the breaking up of local authority housing and the reductions in the role of local education authorities (Wilson 1993: 32) (see Chapter 6).

Managing the local government welfare state

Responsibility for decisions about local authority social services rests with the full council, made up of all the elected members. In practice, however, the full council meets infrequently and generally ratifies decisions made elsewhere, its powers and functions being devolved to committees covering the various responsibilities of the authority. Local authorities are required by law to appoint committees dealing with the personal social services and, until 1993, were required to do the same for education. Many local housing authorities also have housing committees.

The staff responsible for the planning and delivery of local authority services are organized hierarchically in departments which, like those of central government, are organized on the functional principle – departments of educa tion, housing and personal social services. The chief officer of each department is accountable to a committee of the council. As Brown (1975: 113) has described in his discussion of the management of the personal social services, the committees and the departments *are* the local authority for all practical purposes, and it is rare for decisions made by a service committee to be overturned by the full council.

Most of the senior positions in local authority departments are held by professionally qualified staff. Unlike their central government counterparts, local authority education and social services departments are what Stanyer (1976: 157) refers to as 'professional organizations', in which the most senior positions are held by those who have qualifications in the activity being under-taken by the organization, while those staff who have general educational qualifications occupy positions lower down the departmental hierarchy. Thus a local authority social services department will be headed by a director of social services, a deputy director and probably two or three assistant directors, all of whom are generally qualified social workers. Local authority administrators generally work as 'subordinates of the specialist', relieving the professionals of those tasks which do not require specialist experience and qualifications (Poole 1978: 43). Most local education authorities expect their directors of education to have considerable experience of teaching and a high proportion of education officers begin their careers in the teaching profession: indeed, it has been suggested that those who do not are hindered in their career in educational administration (Regan 1977: 28). As we saw in Chapter 1, the development of professionalism has not been nearly as rapid in the local authority housing service as it has been in education and the personal social services, and membership of the appropriate professional organization is not as important in housing departments as in the other two local authority social services (Laffin 1986).

As Laffin and Young (1990: 21) observe, professionalism has been the dominant organizational principle within local authorities since the end of the Second World War. But the role of local government professionals has come under serious challenge since the late 1960s, when questions began to be asked about the compartmentalized way in which local authority services had de-veloped (Laffin and Young 1990: 21). While welfare professionalism within local government has undoubted strengths, it can result in tunnel vision, with the compartmentalization of professionals into separately organized depart-ments leading not only to problems in the coordination and integration of related activities, but also to allegations that individual local authority services, such as education, promote themselves with the purpose of satisfying the aspirations of particular local authority professionals rather than meeting the needs of the local community (Poole 1978: 44). As a consequence, there has been an increasing emphasis on the importance of viewing local government as being responsible for the social, economic and physical well-being of its com-munity as a whole (Bains 1972). We will turn to these important issues in Chapter 4.

Delivering health care

Collective consumption services are not only delivered by elected local author-ities. Another major delivery agency of the welfare state is the National Health Service (NHS). The second most expensive of the social services, after social security, the NHS cost nearly £35 billion in 1992–93, over 13 per cent of total public expenditure, and employed nearly one million staff.

The structure of the NHS is very different from that of central govern-ment departments and local authorities. Indeed, the service has been aptly described as 'an administrative oddity' (Carter *et al.* 1992: 103). Although overall policy and the allocation of funds are the responsibility of the DoH in Whitehall, the day-to-day administration of the NHS is in the hands of regional health authorities (RHAs), district health authorities (DHAs), NHS trusts, family health services authorities (FHSAs) and special health authorities, acting on behalf of the Secretary of State for Health. The various health authorities are governed by boards of appointed lay members and employ non-civil service staff.

The NHS has a unique organizational form. In the words of one writer, it was the first large public sector organization concerned with a universally available welfare service in which 'a different kind of democracy from that traditionally understood was introduced by a form of direct delegation from a Minister to chosen individuals representing a wide sweep of special and professional interests' (McLachlan 1979: x). This particular form of organization was the result of a deliberate decision taken by the post-war Labour Government not to entrust responsibility for the day-to-day administration of the NHS to either a central government department or to elected local authorities.

The decision not to place responsibility for the day-to-day running of the NHS in the hands of a central government department with its own regional and local structure staffed by civil servants, and with clear lines of accountability between the responsible Minister and NHS staff, was based on the desire to avoid a centralized service run directly by the then Ministry of Health (MoH). As one commentator on these events has observed, the MoH lacked both 'the experience and the inclination' for operating the new service – as we saw in Chapter 2, the Ministry's major functions involved housing and local government. It was a department 'with a tradition of regulatory rather than executive functions, reluctant to take on direct administrative responsibilies for a complex service' (Klein 1989: 9, 12). Although responsibility for the running of the majority of hospitals was already in the hands of elected local authorities – the Poor Law hospitals having been transferred to county councils and county boroughs in 1929 – and a municipally controlled health service had originally been favoured by the MoH, the suggestion that the new system of health-care delivery be entrusted to local government was also rejected. Concern was expressed about the suitability of existing local authority areas for the administration of the new service, but the main reason for the rejection of this particular alternative was the fierce opposition of the medical profession to local government control of hospital and general practitioner (GP) services. The medical profession has always been hostile to the idea of local government control of its activities, fearing that this would somehow encroach upon its cherished clinical freedom. One study of the creation of the NHS actually referred to the medical profession's 'hatred' of local government control of their services (Willcocks 1967: 95), and the medical profession has repeated its opposition to the possibility of local government control ever since.

Thus, when the NHS was launched in 1948, responsibility for the administration of the new service was decentralized to regional and local bodies. In what became known as the tripartite structure, one set of institutions (appointed regional hospital boards and hospital management committees) were responsible for hospital services; another set of institutions (executive councils, responsible to the Minister) ran the services provided by GPs, dentists, pharmacists and opticians; local authority medical officers of health and their departments provided a range of local community health services, thereby ensuring that some health responsibilities remained with local government. Representatives of local authorities, together with members of the medical profession, were also included in the membership of the first two sets of institutions.

As with so many areas of the British administrative system, the NHS structure which emerged in 1948 was the result of compromise, in this case between the Cabinet Minister involved, Aneurin Bevan, and the medical profession (see, for example, Willcocks 1967). As one senior official involved in the early planning of the NHS was later to observe, the structure set up in 1948 'was as far as we could reasonably expect to go at the time' (Godber 1975: 61). Or as Brown (1973: 120) put it, it was an administrative structure 'which seemed to combine the best prospects for success with the minimum of disturbance to existing arrangements'.

It was over a quarter of a century before a unified administrative structure was created for the NHS. In 1974, following criticisms of the tripartite structure (the lack of a single body with overall responsibility for the provision of health services; the difficulty of securing coordination in a system deliberately built upon fragmentation; and the absence of proper machinery for local medical planning; Brown 1975: 142), it was replaced by a unified structure which brought the whole of the NHS under RHAs and area health authorities (AHAs). Despite the emphasis upon integration, however, GPs retained the freedom to work as independent contractors which had been awarded to them in 1948. Nor did the 1974 re-organization go nearly as far as the reforms introduced the year before in Northern Ireland, where responsibility for the delivery and management of both health and personal social services was given to area health and social services boards.

Important changes have taken place in the structure of the NHS since 1974. In 1982 AHAs, which were seen as being too large for the proper delivery of services, were abolished and replaced by DHAs as part of the Conservative Government's wider attempts to create a 'slimmer and fitter' public sector (see Chapter 8). Following the recommendations of the Griffiths Report in 1983 (see also Chapter 8), changes also took place in the central management of the service, with the establishment of a central NHS Supervisory Board (now the NHS Policy Board) and, below it, a NHS Management Board (now the NHS Management Executive), responsible for the central management of the NHS. Even more radical changes to the machinery for the delivery of health care were introduced in 1991, with the creation of NHS trusts as part of the newly created internal market (see Chapters 7 and 8), which was followed by further streamlining in 1994. As a result of these changes, the

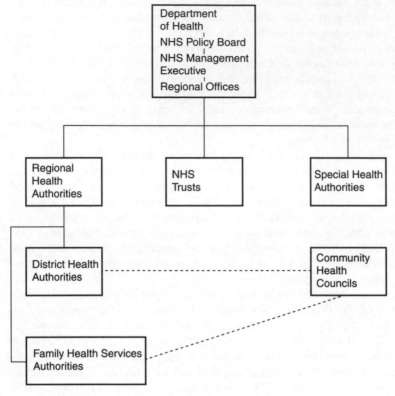

Figure 3.1   Structure of the NHS in England 1994

present structure of the NHS in England consists of a three-tier system (Figure 3.1). (This discussion focuses on the organization of the NHS in England, although there are some differences in Scotland and Wales.)

The new National Health Service

At the top of the NHS structure is the DoH, which is responsible for setting national policies and priorities and for allocating resources to the regions. The Secretary of State for Health is assisted by the NHS Policy Board in determining the strategy, objectives and finance of the health service. Chaired by the Secretary of State, the Policy Board consists of Ministers and senior civil servants from the DoH, the Chief Executive of the Management Executive, a leading clinician from the NHS and a number of outside businessmen. Since April 1994, the Policy Board has also included non-executive directors to cover each of the eight regions.

Under the Policy Board is the NHS Management Executive, chaired by the Chief Executive and responsible for implementing the Government's policies for the NHS. The Management Executive is distinct from the DoH's policy-making machinery, a dichotomy symbolized by the geographical separation of the two different parts of the Department, the Management Executive being based in Leeds, whereas the policymaking core of the department remains in Whitehall. Despite suggestions that it might be hived off from the DoH to become a Next Steps agency on the lines of the executive agencies operating within the DSS and DEmp (see, for example, Klein 1990), the Government has made it clear that the Management Executive will remain an integral part of the DoH as the 'headquarters' of the NHS (Department of Health 1993: para. 17). To enable it to carry out this important role, the Management Executive was re-organized in 1994 to include eight regional offices, each headed by a regional director, the intention being that the regional offices will replace the existing Regional Health Authorities with effect from April 1996. The role of the regional offices will be to oversee the development of the purchasing function in the NHS's internal market and to monitor NHS trusts.

In the middle of the NHS structure are the RHAs, who are responsible for planning, resource allocation, quality improvement, and monitoring the performance of the DHAs and FHSAs in their regions. RHAs also play an important part in the process of establishing NHS trusts, overseeing the funding systems for GPs and DHAs, and developing contracts between purchasers and providers in the newly created internal market. Each RHA is run by a board consisting of a chairman and five non-executive members, all appointed by the Secretary of State, together with five executive members, including the general manager and the director of finance. The day-to-day running of each RHA is in the hands of its own full-time administrative and professional staff, headed by the general manager. The NHS re-organization of 1974 originally set up 14 RHAs for England, but since April 1994 the number has been reduced to eight, sharing common boundaries with the Management Executive's regional offices which will replace them in 1996.

At the bottom of the NHS structure are DHAs and FHSAs. Each region includes a number of DHAs, totalling some 111. DHAs are responsible not only for the management of hospitals and other directly managed provider units, but also for the purchase of health care for the residents in their areas from these units and other providers (see Chapter 7 for a more detailed discussion of these arrangements). Like RHAs, each DHA consists of 11 members, comprising a part-time chairman appointed by the Secretary of State, five full-time executive members, who include the general manager, and five non-executive members, who include local businessmen and are appointed by the RHA. When they were first set up in 1982, DHAs (like the AHAs they replaced) included local authority representatives, but these were removed in the 1991 reforms. Each DHA has its own full-time administrative and professional staff, with executive responsibility resting in the hands of a district general manager.

There are curently 92 FHSAs, responsible for the purchase and management of the services provided by the family practitioner services – GPs, dentists, pharmacists and opticians. Each FHSA consists of a chairman appointed by the Secretary of State, nine non-executive directors and the authority's general manager. As part of what it describes as its 'unfinished business' from the 1991 reforms, the Government is committed to the introduction of legislation enabling mergers between FSHAs and DHAs, thereby establishing one single authority at local level with responsibility for the implementation of national health policy, as well as integrating health-care purchasing across primary and secondary care boundaries.

The NHS organizational jigsaw is completed by three other types of body. Special Health Authorities include the body responsible for the running of the three high-security mental hospitals, and the Health Education Authority. NHS trusts are self-governing units within the NHS which have opted-out of DHA control – mainly hospitals or groups of hospitals – and are run by boards of directors directly accountable to the Secretary of State. Trusts have considerable managerial freedoms, including the freedom to employ their own staff on their own conditions, borrow capital, and acquire and dispose of assets. Most of their income is derived through contracts that they, as health-care providers, negotiate to provide services to the purchasers of health care – DHAs and those GPs with large practices who have been given control of their own budgets and can buy care for out-patients. By April 1994, 440 trusts had been established, with responsibility for some 90 per cent of NHS services.

The representation of user views within the NHS (especially important with the removal of local authority representation from DHAs in 1991) is the function of Community Health Councils (CHCs). Each district has a CHC, which is funded by the RHA. Although local authorities no longer have representation on DHAs, they appoint half of the members of each CHC, with one-third being appointed by local voluntary groups and the remainder by the RHAs. We will discuss CHCs in more detail in Chapter 6.

The NHS is thus characterized by what has been described as a 'baroque administrative structure' (Carter et al. 1992: 103). In the words of another observer, from the top it resembles 'a mountain range rather than a pyramid' (Rose 1989: 325). Within this complicated organizational structure, the medical profession has traditionally played a dominant role. Indeed, writing in the late 1980s, Rhodes (1988: 78) stated that the NHS was the most cited example of a 'professionalized policy network', in which professional, rather than managerial or political, influences had been dominant. The creation of the NHS in 1948 was underpinned by the establishment of what has been described as an 'underlying concordat' between the state and the medical profession, an agreement which not only gave doctors power over the allocation of resources within the NHS, but also representation as of right on policymaking bodies at all levels of the service (Elston 1991: 67). As we shall discuss, in later chapters, the development of managerialist and consumerist challenges within the NHS since the early 1980s has brought this concordat into question, and what has been referred to as 'the frontier of control' between doctors and managers has been shifted in favour of the latter (Harrison 1988).

The arm's length administration of welfare

In addition to the NHS and local authorities, there are a number of quasi-governmental bodies which perform important tasks at arm's length from central government departments and local authorities. Quasi-governmental bodies are not elected and have a certain degree of independence from central and local government control. They play an important part in the organization of the welfare state and the delivery of its services.

The use of such bodies outside the traditional structures of central government departments and local authorities has been an important feature of the development of the welfare state in the post-war period. Indeed, one writer has referred to the post-war period as the 'era of quangocracy' (Rhodes 1988: 54). Quasi-governmental bodies are, of course, not new. Such bodies, in their various guises, have been a feature of the British administrative landscape since the nineteenth century: for example, the Poor Law Commission, which supervised the activities of the Poor Law Guardians, played an important part in the delivery of welfare in the nineteenth century. However, the importance of quasi-governmental bodies has grown markedly in the post-war period.

The whole area of quasi-governmental bodies is surrounded by definitional uncertainty. Various terms have been used to describe such organizations, including non-departmental public bodies, independent public bodies, fringe bodies, arm's length agencies, extra-governmental organizations and quasi-autonomous non-governmental organizations – popularly known as 'quangos'. Attempts to classify such bodies are difficult because of the wide variety of functions, methods of financing and degree of independence accorded to them. According to Rhodes (1988: 180), the only real generalization that can be made about such bodies is that 'there is no uniformity'.

Thus some quasi-governmental bodies are promotional bodies which channel funds to other organizations. One such promotional body in the field of welfare is the Housing Corporation, which was established by the Housing Act 1964 to promote the development of housing associations as a 'third force' in the housing market (Harden and Lewis 1986: 169). Following the Housing Act 1974, there was a major expansion of the Housing Corporation, and since the early 1980s it has come to play a major role as the Conservative Government came to see housing associations as an alternative to local authorities in the delivery of social housing.

Another example of a promotional body in the field of the social services is the Higher Education Funding Council for England (HEFCE), the successor body to the University Funding Council (itself a successor to the University Grants Committee) and the Polytechnics and Colleges Funding Council, which is responsible for the channelling of public funds to the universities and other institutions of higher education. (There are comparable bodies for Scotland and Wales.) Similar bodies – the Further Education Funding Council for England (FEFCE) and its Scottish and Welsh counterparts – are responsible for the channelling of public funds to further education colleges and sixth-form colleges, which now have the status of further education corporations and are independent of local education authority control.

Other quasi-governmental bodies carry out important managerial functions, a notable example being the various Urban Development Corporations (UDCs), including the London Docklands Development Corporation, first set up in the early 1980s to oversee the economic and physical regeneration of certain inner-city areas. Funded by central government, and accountable directly to the Secretary of State for the Environment, UDCs are controlled by government-nominated boards. They are based upon another form of quasi-governmental body, the New Town Development Corporations, the first generation of which were set up in the early post-war years to plan and develop the new towns which were part of the reconstruction plans of the Attlee Government. The New Town Development Corporations were a 'major vehicle' for meeting housing needs in the post-war period (Malpass and Murie 1990: 144), and it is the Conservative Government's intention that UDCs play as important a role in the revival of the inner cities.

The reasons for the creation of quasi-governmental bodies are several (Hague 1971). In some cases, this kind of body is set up in an attempt to take a particular policy area 'out of politics' – thus the Housing Corporation has been seen as a way of channelling money directly to housing associations rather than government subsidy becoming enmeshed in what has been described as 'the politically sensitive morass of central–local government relations and financial controls' (Cole and Furbey 1994: 216). Quasi-governmental bodies are also often used to bypass existing public sector organizations, government department or local authority procedures being seen as inappropriate. The need to avoid the perceived pathologies of public sector organizations – the 'escape theory' – has been an important consideration in recent Conservative Government initiatives in the inner cities, where UDCs have been established to escape the constraints associated with local authorities, especially those controlled by the Labour Party. The creation of grant maintained schools and City Technology Colleges (CTCs) are other examples of the use of a form of quasi-governmental body to bypass local government. Another important reason for the creation of such bodies has been to draw upon expertise and experience which would not normally be available in a government department or local authority. The Housing Corporation has been seen as a quasi-governmental body with some of these characteristics (Lewis 1985: 206).

The use of quasi-governmental bodies in the post-war period has been the subject of much debate, with concern being expressed over their alleged erosion of democratic accountability and control. The Conservative Government elected in 1979 was especially critical of such bodies, and the early 1980s saw a cull of quasi-governmental bodies – described by one commentator as the blood sport of 'quango-hunting' (Dunsire 1982: 15). But, although originally hostile towards this arm's length approach to the delivery of public services, the potential benefits of quasi-governmental bodies as vehicles of welfare delivery were soon recognized by Conservative governments, notably in the fields of education, housing and health care. The creation of quasi-governmental bodies has been a major feature of the Government's reforms in the delivery of welfare since the late 1980s.

Thus, as we shall discuss in more detail in Chapter 6, a central plank of the Government's policy in the field of education since the Education Reform Act 1988 has been the creation of grant maintained schools managed by governing bodies free from local education authority control. Although such bodies do include a small number of elected parent governors, they consist mainly of non-elected 'first governors', including representatives of the local business community. The payment and monitoring of grants to grant maintained schools is in the hands of another quasi-governmental body, the Funding Agency for Schools (FAS), and the DFE has the power to set up appointed local education associations to take over schools identified as failing to provide an acceptable standard of education. Further education colleges and sixth-form colleges are now run by appointed further education corporations, as well as being funded by a quasi-governmental body – the FEFCE. The Government has also established a number of CTCs, managed by appointed governing boards, in parts of the country.

In a related area, 82 Training and Enterprise Councils (TECs) were set up in the early 1990s in England and Wales with responsibility for the development of training in their local areas, including arrangements for the delivery of Youth Training and work-related further education. Two-thirds of their membership is reserved for business people. The concept of the quasi-governmental body has also been introduced into the field of local housing. Following the Housing Act 1988, Housing Action Trusts, consisting of boards appointed by the Secretary of State for the Environment, have been set up in parts of the country to take over and renovate designated run-down local authority council estates. As we saw earlier in the chapter, reforms in the recent delivery of health care included the creation of independent NHS Trusts, run by appointed boards of directors and accountable directly to the Secretary of State for Health. It has been predicted that almost all NHS hospitals and community health services will eventually be controlled by such bodies. One consequence of the growth of these kind of non-elected bodies in the NHS, housing, education and elsewhere (what some observers refer to as 'the quango state') has been to revive the debate about their democratic accountability and control (see, for example, Weir and Hall 1994).

The sub-central government of welfare delivery

Our survey of the government of welfare here and in Chapter 2 shows that most government policies involving the social services in Britain are not delivered by central government departments but by organizations outside the Whitehall department system, by a system of 'sub-central government'. There is a clear distinction between the small groups of social policymakers in Whitehall and the delivery agencies of the welfare state. This division clearly has

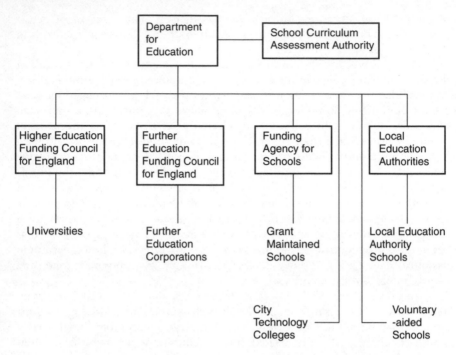

Figure 3.2   The pattern of education delivery in England (adapted from table in Weir and Hall 1994: 50)

important consequences for the social service departments of central government. In the words of Stoker (1990: 127):

> central government may legislate, regulate and exhort but it does so in the context of a system of sub-central government in which day-to-day control and the scope for innovation and initiative is in the hands of a range of other elected representatives, appointees and full-time officials and managers.

Thus the organization of the British welfare state is characterized by a complex pattern of delivery agencies. As Hood (1982: 66) has observed, government departments, local authorities and other governmental bodies are increasingly operating in 'complex and dense networks or cross-cutting territorial, functional and hierarchical organisational relationships' and within the context of an increasingly 'money moving' style of administration – government by grants and by indirect administration. The delivery of education provision in England is a particularly good example of this complex pattern, with its complicated network of local education authorities, further education corporations, grant maintained schools and CTCs, together with the bodies responsible for funding – HEFCE, FEFCE and FAS – not to mention the School Curriculum Assessment Authority and other quasi-governmental bodies (Figure 3.2).

One obvious issue created by the existence of what has been described as a system of 'multi-bureaucratic' government (Hood 1982: 67), is the weakening of central government's ability to ensure the successful implementation of centrally determined welfare policies. The literature on policy implementation describes several preconditions for 'perfect implementation', one of which is the requirement that the dependency relationships involved in the implementation process are minimal (Hogwood and Gunn 1984: 202):

> that there is a single implementing agency which need not depend on other agencies for success, or if other agencies must be involved, that the dependency relationships are minimal in both number and importance.

As we have seen, the implementation of policies involving such major social services as education, housing, health care and the personal social services do not involve just the central government department concerned. Instead, there is an interlocking network of non-departmental organizations.

The history of central–local government relations in the post-war period is littered with examples of local authority resistance or tardiness in implementing centrally determined social policies, and we will examine a couple of well-known episodes in Chapter 6. One of these concerns education, where, as we have already seen, the implementation of centrally determined policy is not in the hands of the responsible central government department, the DFE, but in the hands of local education authorities and other non-departmental organizations. As one ex-minister, who became Minister of Education after having served as First Lord of the Admiralty, put it:

> In the Admiralty you are a person having authority. You say to one person 'Come' and he cometh, and another 'Go' and he goeth. It is not so in the Ministry of Education. You suggest rather than direct. You say to one man 'Come' and he cometh not and to another 'Go' and he stays where he is.
>
> (Lord Hailsham quoted in Kogan 1971: 31)

It is not only the delivery agencies of local government which are beyond the day-to-day control of central government. There have also been occasions when the institutions of the other major delivery arm of the welfare state, the NHS, have frustrated the implementation of central policies. As Ham (1992: 172) observes:

> The fact that NHS authorities actually provide service and have day-to-day management and planning responsibilities means that the (DoH) has to work through and with those authorities to achieve its goals.

According to Haywood and Elcock (1982: 139), the history of the NHS shows that health authorities have not been 'particularly zestful' in applying central government policies. Indeed, there has been resistance to the implementation of central policies that 'challenge established professional hierarchies and priorities' (Elcock 1986a: 283). For example, central government attempts in the 1960s and 1970s to draw up health service priorities were often frustrated by the opposition of the medical profession, a well-documented example being the inability of central government to shift resources away from the 'glamour' areas of acute hospital medicine to such 'Cinderella' services as those for the mentally handicapped (see, for example, Ham 1992: 208–11). Writing in the early 1980s, Day and Klein (1983: 1813) described the NHS as being rather like a 'feudal society' in which independent authority was exercised by a number of groups, notably the medical profession. As we shall discuss in more detail in Chapter 8, recent organizational reforms in the NHS have been introduced in an attempt to reduce what has been described as 'the risk of organizational anarchy' by strengthening lines of accountability and imposing checks and balances within the service (Levitt and Wall 1992: 319).

Another major issue raised by the number and range of organizations responsible for the delivery of welfare is that of coordination. The problem of departmentalism and its implications for coordination and planning at the national level are well documented. Thus Whitehall has been described as 'a seething mass of discrete departmental interests' where Ministers are expected to fight their corners in the battle for scarce resources (Drewry and Butcher 1991: 84). Problems of coordination and social planning are also a feature of the world of welfare delivery beyond Whitehall. We have referred earlier in this chapter to the fragmented nature of local government throughout most of the country, with responsibilities for the delivery of social services being divided between different types of local authority. This particular feature of the local government system, together with the division of the related functions of the personal social services and health care, makes a coordinated approach to the local management of welfare delivery difficult. We turn to a discussion of these problems, and to some of the arrangements which have been set up in an attempt to resolve them, in Chapter 4.

4

The coordination and planning of welfare

It has long been recognized that there is a need for a coordinated approach to social policy and the delivery of welfare. The fact that the people affected by welfare policies are often very dependent upon the social services places a 'heavy responsibility' on those concerned with delivering services to ensure that their activities are coordinated (Webb 1991: 229). Thus the coordination and planning of social services is central to welfare delivery. A group of academic researchers who undertook a study of the practice of coordination in welfare policy in the late 1980s saw effective coordination as an essential part of a collective, rational approach to the making of policy, with an emphasis on the existence of a systems-wide viewpoint, a well-developed capacity for policy analysis, and 'organizational arrangements appropriate to the analysis of problems and the implementation of solutions' (Challis et al. 1988: 33).

A major problem arising from the arrangements for delivering welfare is that social problems and client groups do not always fit conveniently within the organizational and professional boundaries of the welfare state. As Webb (1991: 229) has pointed out, the public services are all too often 'a jumble of services fractionalised by professional, cultural and organisational boundaries and by tiers of governance'. Many social problems cut across the boundaries of the public bodies responsible for welfare policy and its delivery. Examples include the needs of one-parent families, the care of the elderly and other dependent groups, the problems of the homeless and the social conditions of the inner cities. Professional defensiveness and cultural differences may also be barriers to effective coordination.

A lot of time and effort has been spent since the early 1960s in attempts to construct structures and procedures designed to improve the coordination and planning of welfare delivery. But before we discuss these arrangements and their impact, we need to look more closely at some of the obstacles to coordination.

Agency fragmentation and welfare delivery

A major characteristic of the structure of both central and local government in Britain is the fragmentation of the agencies responsible for welfare delivery and its planning. This is particularly the case at the level of central government, which has been described as being plural and not singular (Central Policy Review Staff 1977: 21).

As we saw in Chapter 2, the activities of central government have been generally grouped together according to the services performed rather than according to the particular client groups dealt with. The organization of central government departments on the basis of what is known as the 'functional principle' – affirmed by the Haldane Report as long ago as 1918 – is reflected in the major social service departments of social security, education, and health, which are responsible for providing particular services to the community as a whole rather than a range of services limited to particular groups in the community. As Haldane (1918: para. 19) itself recognized, one disadvantage of such a pattern of departmental organization is the inevitable overlapping between departments. Many client groups cut across the boundaries of government departments. For example, policies for the care and support of the elderly – pensioners currently make up over 18 per cent of the population – are served by three different social service departments, the DSS, the DoH and the DoE, with the result that it is sometimes unclear which particular government department is actually responsible for certain policy issues of importance to this client group.

Uncertainty about which department has the major responsibility for a welfare problem or particular client group has not been confined to policy issues affecting the elderly. Critics of housing policy in the post-war period have highlighted the inadequacy of organizational arrangements for dealing with the problem of the homeless. Thus up to the enactment of the Housing (Homeless Persons) Act 1977, the legislative powers for providing temporary accommodation for the homeless were not in the hands of the government department responsible for housing, but in those of the department responsible for social security. As a result, there was what has been described as an 'uncertain division of responsibility' between the DoE and the then DHSS, and their predecessor departments (Raynsford 1986: 37).

Another example of the fragmentation of organizational responsibility for a particular welfare problem is that of fuel poverty policy. The split of responsibility between the DoE and the DSS, together with the former Department of Energy (since incorporated within the Department of Trade and Industry), seriously inhibited the development of appropriate fuel policies for low-income families in the 1980s (Boardman 1991: 229). There has long been ambiguity about whether fuel poverty policy is part of housing, social or energy policy, and a former chairman of the now defunct Supplementary Benefits Commission has referred to the immense obstacles that the DHSS and the DoE placed in the way of proposals for a fuel subsidy system in the late 1970s (Donnison 1982: 151).

The lack of coordination in Whitehall is not confined to the problem of drawing together the activities of different social service departments. On occasions the separate divisions of individual departments may fail to harmonize their policies. A good example of such a failure of inter-departmental collaboration occurred in the DHSS in the 1980s, when the Department's policy of financing places in private sector residential and nursing homes through the supplementary benefit system clearly conflicted with its other policy of attempting to persuade elderly people to stay in the community by continuing to live in their own homes. There was inevitably criticism that the social security, health and personal social services divisions of the DHSS had failed to coordinate their policies, with the result that they were 'pulling against each other' (Challis et al. 1984: 32).

The problems created by overlapping functions and departmental fragmentation are compounded by the notorious departmentalism of Whitehall. British central government is characterized by a culture in which the loyalty of departments is upwards to ministerial and departmental interests rather than outwards to the government as a whole. The now defunct Central Policy Review Staff – itself set up in an attempt to overcome the problems engendered by departmentalism in British central government (see later in this chapter) – accurately described central government as 'a federation of separate departments with their own Ministers and their own policies' (Central Policy Review Staff 1977: para. 5.1).

As a result, competition between departments is a major characteristic of the Whitehall system. Central government departments constantly compete with each other for scarce resources, and during the annual negotiations on the PESC allocations (which we will discuss later in this chapter) Ministers are expected to fight their departmental corners, either in seeking additional financial resources or keeping what they already have under the pressure to make cuts. Thus social service Ministers come to Cabinet to fight for their departmental budgets, and not as Cabinet Ministers with a collective view about spending priorities. In the words of two American observers of the process – 'The minister who appears to give up without a fight loses credibility all around' – Margaret Thatcher was being cited as a classic example of a Minister who fought hard for more money when she was in charge of the DES in the early 1970s (Heclo and Wildavsky 1981: 135–7).

Competition between social service departments is not confined to rivalry over their share of the public expenditure cake. Each central government department has a notion of its own territory, what has been described as 'policy ownership' (Challis *et al.* 1988: 109), with departments fiercely resisting any invasion of their territories by other departments. Thus an attempt to transfer the (then) Children's Department of the Home Office to the newly created DHSS in 1968 led to a strong and successful protest by the (then) Home Secretary, James Callaghan (Crossman 1977: 146–8, 150; Callaghan 1987: 235). The DES strongly resisted the threatened invasion of its territory by the Department of Trade and Industry in the mid-1980s, when the latter Department attempted to acquire more influence over education policy (Jordan and Richardson 1987: 167–8). More recently, it was reported in early 1994 that the DSS and the DEmp were at loggerheads over which of their two Departments should administer the job seeker's allowance due to replace unemployment benefit in 1996. The DSS argued that as the unemployed often receive other social security benefits, it would be more efficient for it to administer the new benefit, an argument which was opposed by the DEmp, which was concerned to protect jobs in its depart-ment (*The Sunday Times*, 2 January 1994).

These examples show that, in the words of a former senior civil servant (Ponting 1986: 102):

> Much of the work of Whitehall is institutionalised conflict between the competing interests of different departments. Each department will de-fend its own position and resist a line that, while it might be beneficial to the government as a whole or in the wider public interest, would work against the interests of the department.

Thus the concept of 'central government' is 'an abstraction which con-ceals reality' (Central Policy Review Staff 1977: para. 5.1). Central govern-ment is, in fact, a collection of separate departments, with unfortunate consequences for the coordination and the planning of social services.

The fragmentation of welfare delivery at the local level

The fragmentation of responsibilities for welfare provision and the pheno-menon of departmentalism are also features of welfare delivery at the local level. Like their central government counterparts, local authority departments are organized on the basis of the functional principle, with separate depart-ments for such services as education, housing and the personal social services (although the dramatic decline of local authority housing since the early 1980s has meant that some local authorities have amalgamated their housing and social services departments). The fact that there used to be a legal requirement for local authorities to set up separate committees for both education and personal social services – the requirement to have education committees was abolished in 1993 – has also helped to create barriers between the two closely related services.

Within the London boroughs and the metropolitan districts – which are most-purpose authorities – coordination between the different departments responsible for education, housing and the personal social services takes place within the individual authorities. Outside Greater London and the major conurbations, however, responsibility for the three services in England and Wales is divided between two tiers of local government, with education and the personal social services being a county responsibility and the housing service being administered by the districts. This division has been the subject of much criticism, and as long ago as 1968 the Seebohm Committee argued (1968: paras 676 and 681) that an effective 'family service' could only be fully effective if education, housing and the personal social services were the undivided responsibility of the same local authority.

The same conclusions were reached a year later by the majority report of the Redcliffe-Maud Commission on local government in England and Wales (1969: para. 249). After endorsing Seebohm's view that it would be wrong to divide responsibility for education and the personal social services between different local authorities, the report went on to say that the ties between housing and the personal social services were equally strong. Housing was an 'essential part of social policy' and much of the work of the personal social services stemmed directly from housing conditions, with the people and families most likely to make the greatest demands on the personal social services also being those most likely to suffer from severe housing problems. In the report's opinion (1969: para. 250):

> An authority responsible for the personal social services but not for housing lacks an essential means of dealing with the difficulties of those people and families who need its help; and a housing authority which does not administer the personal social services will not be aware at first hand of the social needs that should receive priority in its management policies and building programmes.

The interdependence of the two services was also stressed by the Wheatley Commission on local government in Scotland, which also reported in 1969, its report arguing that the personal social services were 'linked intimately' with house building, allocation and management (Wheatley 1969: para. 472).

The division of responsibility for housing and the personal social services in many parts of the country has been seen as a major barrier to the efficient delivery of welfare, professionals on both sides arguing that it is difficult to separate the 'social' and 'housing' parts of individual cases (Alexander 1982b: 69). There are many areas in which the two services are linked, including the allocation of housing, the problem of tenants with rent arrears and the needs of the disabled. One major area of shared concern which has been a particular problem is the issue of homelessness, what one writer has described as a personal social services 'condition' with a housing 'remedy' (Alexander 1982b: 59). According to Alexander (1982a: 55), in metropolitan districts, where housing and the personal social services are both departments of the same local authority, local councillors and officers have not seen any financial advantage in attempting to pass responsibility for tackling the problem of homelessness from one department to the other. However, he suggests that the situation seems to have been the reverse in the non-metropolitan counties, where the two services are the responsibility of different local authorities, because there has been seen to be some advantage in shifting part of the responsibility from one local authority to the other, particularly when the local authorities concerned are controlled by different political parties.

It was partly to deal with these kinds of problems that Redcliffe-Maud recommended the establishment of unitary (i.e. all-purpose) local authorities for England and Wales outside the Greater London area and the three very large metropolitan areas around Birmingham, Liverpool and Manchester. According to Redcliffe-Maud, a major strength of the unitary authority is that it can see the full extent of the relationships between different services, the developments in the services needed to meet people's needs, and the gaps between services that need to be filled (1969: para. 253). It's Scottish counterpart, the Wheatley Commission, had also recognized the value of integrating the major local authority social services, recommending that the three key services of education, housing and social work should be the responsibility of the same local authorities (1969: paras 419, 453). Nearly a quarter of a century later, in 1992, the Conservative Government established a Local Government Commission to recommend changes in the structure of English local government, believing that there should be a move towards unitary authorities in the non-metropolitan counties. The Government argued that one benefit of such a development would be better coordination of services, which would not only improve quality but also reduce costs (Department of the Environment 1991a: para. 25). As we saw in Chapter 3, unitary authorities are already due to be introduced in Scotland and Wales in 1996.

Despite these developments, it would be naive to believe that the widespread creation of unitary authorities would automatically result in the better coordination of local social services, particularly between housing and the personal social services. Like their Whitehall counterparts, local authorities are afflicted by the phenomenon of departmentalism, with local authority officials perceiving that they are in competition with other local authority departments for scarce resources. According to Stoker (1991: 102), such perceptions have three main sources: the 'bureaucratic rivalry' stemming from the wish of officials to protect and extend their departmental empires; the 'professional jealousies' which exist between rival departments over such issues as 'territory'; and the 'value clashes' between different departments.

Examples of such competition can be readily found in the field of local authority welfare. Thus Stoker's study of the politics of a housing renewal programme in a Manchester suburb in the mid-1970s found that, in an attempt to pacify departmental interests, responsibility for the programme was divided between three departments – housing, environmental health and architects (1991: 101). Other studies of local authority housing have provided examples of inter-departmental conflict (see, for example, Paris and Blackaby 1979), while Challis and her colleagues (1988: 214) found rivalry between local authority education and social services departments over policy for the under-fives, with social services departments being regarded as 'empire builders'. As we shall see in a later section of the chapter, collaboration between housing and the personal social services within the same local authorities is restricted by the problem of conflicting professional attitudes and priorities.

The fragmentation of responsibility for service delivery has also been a feature of the NHS. Thus the delivery of primary care has been criticized for its fragmented nature, responsibility being divided between FHSAs, responsible for services provided by GPs, and DHAs which are responsible for community health services. Although primary health care teams, including professionals from both sides, were established in the early 1960s to enhance coordination, their proceedings tended to be dominated by GPs 'much to the annoyance of the other professions' (Baggott 1994: 203).

The delivery of welfare at the local level is not only characterized by the fragmentation of services within local government and the NHS, but also by the separation of related services between local authorities and health authorities. There is a clear interdependence between the personal social services provided by local authorities and those services provided by health authorities (see, for example, Merrison 1979: para. 16.2). Patients discharged from hospital, particularly the elderly, often need to be referred to local authority social services departments for such support services as domiciliary care. The provision of such services might even help to support certain people in the community and thereby keep them out of hospital. The increasing attention given to the policy of community care since the late 1980s has helped to emphasize the links between the two groups of services. We will discuss the arrangements for collaboration between local authorities and the NHS later in this chapter.

The Treasury and social planning

The centrepiece of attempts to improve coordination and social planning at the level of central government is the public expenditure survey system. Before 1961, central government decisions on public spending were taken for a single year only, with little attention being paid to the long term. Following the famous Plowden Report of 1961, the Government set up the PESC system – an acronym for the inter-departmental Public Expenditure Survey Committee – presided over by the Treasury, the department responsible for coordinating and overseeing the whole public expenditure process. The aim of the system was to provide government Ministers with a projection of departmental spending commitments in the medium term (originally five years, but now three years), together with a forecast of economic prospects. The idea was that this information would then enable Ministers collectively to take spending decisions and determine priorities. PESC was based on what Jordan and Richardson (1987: 206) have referred to as the notion of 'a rational, considered, collective allocation' of public expenditure. Between 1970 and 1979, the PESC exercise was reinforced by a system of Programme Analysis and

Review (PAR), enabling spending departments to assess the effectiveness of current departmental programmes in achieving their objectives and to review other available options. Spending programmes which were evaluated under this system included higher education and school building, but, in the absence of ministerial backing and a strong central organization, PAR was abandoned in 1979 (see Gray and Jenkins 1982).

The PESC system, however, has survived and remains the basis for decisions on the spending programmes of central government's social service, and other, departments. Nevertheless, the system has had its problems. Firstly, what Glennerster (1992a: 55) refers to as 'the rules of the game' have changed. When it was first set up in the early 1960s, PESC was based on volume planning rather than cash planning. This approach meant, for example, that governmental spending programmes for the NHS provided for a volume of hospitals, doctors, nurses, equipment, etc. which was costed in constant prices and thus insulated from the effects of inflation. Thus, the spending programmes for education, housing, the NHS and the other major social services were protected from any rises in pay and prices for four years ahead, thereby allowing social service managers a degree of confidence in the short term (Glennerster 1992a: 57).

Although this system worked well in a period of low inflation, in the early 1970s underestimations of costs, together with increases in pay and prices, meant that the actual cost of a particular volume of services turned out to be far greater than had originally been planned. The turning point in the PESC system came in 1975, when inflation reached 25 per cent. The out-turn for the 1974–75 financial year was some £6.5 billion more than had been planned – what became known as the 'missing billions'.

The response of the Labour Government to what has been called the 'crisis of control' (Wright 1977) was to change the whole basis of the PESC system. In 1976, cash limits (which included an allowance for inflation) were placed on the amount spent on certain programmes for the coming financial year, which meant that, whatever the volume of services provided for in their spending plans, departments could not spend above the limit specified. (The social security programme, which is determined by demand, and therefore difficult to forecast, was not covered by this new system.) Further changes to the system were introduced by the Thatcher Government in the early 1980s. The planning period was reduced from five to three years and, from 1982, volume planning was replaced by cash planning, with spending programmes being laid down in terms of the cash which will actually be available for the next three years. Cash plans include an allowance for estimated inflation.

Cash planning clearly has significant implications for spending on social services. If the Treasury underestimates the level of inflation, then spending programmes will effectively be cut in real terms. Thus the spending plans announced each year by the Government are 'unhelpful for long-term planning purposes' (Glennerster 1992a: 60), as social service departments like the DoH and the DFE will be uncertain about the cash that they will be able to actually spend on doctors and hospital equipment, teachers and school equipment, etc. The result of the introduction of cash planning and other changes is that the emphasis of the PESC exercise shifted from its original concern with medium-term planning to an emphasis on short-term control.

The framework provided by PESC also does not appear to have persuaded spending Ministers to adopt 'a rational, considered and collective' approach in their discussions about public spending. Indeed, as Challis and her colleagues (1988: 75) observe, the main determinant of public-spending decisions has often been 'the relative political weight and forensic skill of the individual ministers struggling to defend their departmental budgets against the Chancellor'. This has been confirmed by a former insider, Joel Barnett (1982: 59), Chief Secretary to the Treasury in the Labour Government of the late 1970s, who has stated that public-spending decisions were never thought through as to their relative priority in either economic or social terms. Instead, they were often made 'on the strength of a particular spending minister and the extent of the support he or she could get from the Prime Minister'. Clearly, the politics of the public expenditure process have been more important than the procedures of the PESC exercise (Jordan and Richardson 1987: 209).

Former Secretaries of State for the Social Services have recorded their battles to defend departmental spending. The flavour of the process has been nicely captured by Barbara Castle, Secretary of State in the Labour Government of the mid-1970s, who was particularly astute at 'fighting her corner'. Thus she records in her *Diaries* (1980: 641) how the 1976 public expenditure White Paper 'demonstrated vividly how much more successful I have been than some of my colleagues in defending my programmes'. Castle's successor at the (then) DHSS, David Ennals, appears to have been less successful in his battles with the Treasury, and was apparently actually prevented from arguing the case against a cut in the health programme because the Prime Minister was annoyed with the way in which Ennals had handled an NHS dispute (Barnett 1982: 59–60). More recently, a former Conservative Secretary of State for the Social Services during the 1980s, Sir Norman Fowler, has also referred to his 'battles' with the Treasury (1991: 206–7).

Important changes in the PESC system were introduced in 1992. What has been described as the 'bottom-up' approach, in which the total level of public expenditure tended to be the consequence of the compromises negotiated between the Treasury and spending Ministers, was replaced by a new 'top-down' approach in which the total level of public expenditure is to be limited in advance by setting annual ceilings for the New Control Total (NCT). The PESC system now involves the allocation of resources from within the NCT, the hope being that this will allow for a more collective approach to the setting of spending priorities, with a Cabinet committee making recommendations to the full Cabinet on its preferred allocation of resources (H.M. Treasury 1993b: 6–7).

The search for joint planning

In addition to the introduction of the system of public expenditure planning, governments have experimented with various other measures in an attempt to achieve better coordination of welfare delivery and the policy planning which underpins it. Developments at the level of central government have included the creation of huge departments such as the DHSS and the DoE, the setting up of the Central Policy Review Staff, and the Joint Approach to Social Policy (JASP) initiative. As we shall see in the later sections of this chapter, there have also been some important developments at the local level, both within local authorities and between them and health authorities.

One approach to improving coordination at the level of central government's social service departments involved the amalgamation of the separate Ministries of Social Security and Health to form the DHSS in 1968. The rationale behind the merger was that the new Department could develop a more coherent approach to dealing with social care and apply resources on a larger scale (Nairne 1983: 247). In the event, however, coordination and planning within the DHSS was fragmented and *ad hoc*. The different parts of the new Department had little in common. As a former Permanent Secretary to the DHSS was later to point out, the tasks of the two main sides of the Department were very different: whereas the social security side was derived from legislation and was directly under the control of the Department, the health side was concerned with allocating resources to health authorities, which involved a great deal of discretion (Expenditure Committee 1977, question 897). The Department remained 'a conglomerate' (Nairne 1983: 255), being divided essentially along the lines of its three main responsibilities, health, social security and the personal social services. There was little strategic planning and the Department was criticised for its failure to adopt a coherent policy strategy across it (see, for example, Social Services Committee 1980). In 1988, on its twentieth anniversary, the DHSS was split into its two former departments, Health and Social Security.

However, as Malcolm Wicks (in a letter to *The Times*, 8 July 1983) pointed out, social planning is far too important to be left to spending departments alone or to the Treasury. An important attempt to overcome the departmentalism of central government and strengthen its capacity for collective strategic policy planning was the creation of the Central Policy Review Staff (CPRS) by the Conservative Government of Edward Heath in 1970. A small, multi-disciplinary unit located in the Cabinet Office, the CPRS's major purpose was to tackle problems that crossed departmental boundaries and to extend the perspective of individual spending Ministers beyond their narrow departmental briefs. Like PAR, which was introduced at the same time, the CPRS was a deliberate attempt to break down the notorious departmentalism of Whitehall.

From the very beginning, the CPRS invested a great deal of time and attention to social policy, the authors of one history of the unit maintaining

that its main contribution in this particular area was in seeing 'the interrelation-
ship between different parts of the jigsaw' (Blackstone and Plowden 1988:
199). Reports were published on such subjects as population and the social
services, services for young children with working mothers, and the inter-
actions between housing and social services (see Blackstone and Plowden 1988:
Appendix I). But probably the most important initiative in this area was the
CPRS's attempt in 1975 to introduce a joint approach to social policy. Fully
aware that the most intractable problems of social policy are often the concern
of more than one government department and that there existed no framework
within which to effectively formulate coherent and consistent social priorities,
the CPRS advocated a joint approach to social policy (JASP). JASP promised
better coordination between related social services, improved analysis of (and
prescriptions for) complex problems, especially where these were the concern
of more than one government department, and the development of collective
views on policy priorities (Central Policy Review Staff 1975: para. 8).

Although JASP made a promising start, with six-monthly meetings of
Ministers in the major social service departments and follow-up studies by
CPRS staff (including a report which recommended that central government
departments should act more inter-departmentally in their dealings with local
authorities; Central Policy Review Staff 1977) the exercise fizzled out in 1977.
Perhaps its demise was inevitable: as Drewry (1988: 178) has observed, its
failure could have been predicted from the outset – as we saw earlier, fighting
one's departmental corner is one of 'the most deeply engrained features of the
Whitehall culture'.

Coordinating welfare delivery at the local level

The importance of coordinating welfare delivery is not confined to the central
government level. Criticism of the traditional separatist approach of local authorities has led to a growing recognition of what has been described as an
'integral' view of local authorities. This approach emphasizes the close relations
between local authority services and argues that they should be planned as a
programme rather than as a combination of separate activities (Greenwood et
al. 1980: 15). A series of official reports in the late 1960s emphasized the
interdependence between the various social services delivered by local authorities and the consequent need for a more integrated approach to their planning
and provision. Thus the Plowden Report 1967 on primary schools highlighted
the impact of the local environment upon schools and educational standards
(Plowden 1967), whilst, a year later, the Seebohm Report on local authority
personal social services pointed to the complexity of social problems and the
need for a more coordinated approach by interdependent local authority departments (Seebohm 1968).

The turning point in the development of structures for a more coordinated and planned approach to local authority services was the report of the
Maud Committee in 1967. Highly critical of the absence of coordination and

what it referred to as the 'loose confederation of disparate activities' which existed within local authorities, the report concluded that while there might be unity in the different parts of individual local authorities, there was 'disunity in the whole' (Maud 1967: paras 97 and 130). A key recommendation in Maud's proposals for a more integrated approach to the management of local services was a reduction in the number of local authority departments and committees and the creation of a management board, which would serve as the focal point for the management of the affairs of each local authority and oversee the work of the authority as a whole. Although the overall reaction to Maud has been described as negative (Haynes 1980: 48), many local authorities did streamline their departmental and committee structures. Notable changes took place in the personal social services, which, following the Seebohm recommendations, have been administered since the early 1970s by unified social services departments and committees, rather than by the fragmented system developed in the late 1940s. Subsequently, with the decline in local authority housing stock since the early 1980s, some local authorities have amalgamated their social services and housing departments.

However, despite the developments following Maud, the importance of coordination really found expression in the Bains Report of 1972, which argued that the traditional departmental attitude found within many local authorities had to give way to a wider-ranging corporate outlook (1972: para. 2.11), underpinned by policy and resources committees, chief executives and management teams of chief officers. There was widespread adoption of the structures of corporate planning within local authorities following the reorganization of local government in 1974 (see Greenwood et al. 1980: 50).

Despite such developments, however, there has been criticism that although local authorities have adopted the structures of corporate planning, not all have adopted its processes. Thus research by Challis and her colleagues (1988) into the coordination by local authorities of policies for elderly people and the under-fives found that while each local authority studied had established corporate machinery, a few had never even attempted to develop corporate processes, and what enthusiasm there was for such processes in the other local authorities studied had disappeared. As with central government, departmentalism was a dominant phenomenon and local authority departments 'largely went their own way with little apparent regard to the wider local authority context' (Challis et al. 1988: 160). One issue highlighted by the study was the defensiveness of local education authorities as an obstacle to coordination. Education departments regarded themselves as being more 'professional' than other services, with their own 'professional territory' (Challis et al. 1988: 214, 240). The researchers referred to the 'paranoia' about the effects of service integrity being diluted, a concern which outweighed any estimation of wider benefits (1988: 240).

What has been termed 'strategic collaboration' over the development of local services and the allocation of resources (Sargeant 1979: 173) is seen as being particularly necessary in the case of local authority housing and social services departments. As Hudson (1986: 56), echoing Seebohm, states, 'clearly many clients of (social services departments) have housing problems, and many tenants of housing authorities have social problems'. As we saw earlier in the chapter, the problems of housing allocation, rent arrears and homelessness have been identified as particular candidates for collaborative activity (Hudson 1986: 54). Observers, however, have criticized the tradition of limited collaboration between housing and social services departments (see, for example, Challis *et al.* 1988: 162–3). As Hudson (1986: 61) notes, there is little capacity for strategic planning in either type of department.

Housing and social services departments have been characterized not only by the absence of strategic collaboration, but also by the absence of what has been termed *ad hoc* case coordination regarding the treatment of individual clients (Sargeant 1979: 173). Effective coordination of this kind between the two services has been hindered by their different professional ideologies, one group of writers on housing policy pointing out that while the major concern of housing management is with the administration of standardized procedures, social work has a much more client-based perspective (Clapham *et al.* 1990: 220). It has also been suggested that communication between the two sides is inhibited by the existence of a hierarchical structure in which social workers often find that their opposite numbers in the housing service are at different levels of seniority (Barclay 1982, quoted in Hudson, 1986: 58).

Although such problems might be alleviated by the merger of the housing service and the personal social services into single departments – as has occurred in some metropolitan local authorities – there is still the problem of the non-metropolitan counties, where the two services are delivered by different types of local authority. The creation of a system of unitary authorities would bring responsibility for housing and social services in the non-metropolitan counties under the same authorities, but, as we saw earlier, attitudinal obstacles are still an important barrier to successful coordination.

Notwithstanding the difficulties involved in achieving effective strategic collaboration, and the problems associated with *ad hoc* coordination, there have been several examples of what Sargeant (1979: 173) has termed 'operational coordination' between housing and social services departments, whereby formal structures have been set up in an attempt to integrate complementary services. Thus some local authorities have decentralized the delivery of both services to neighbourhood and area offices, part of a process which is replacing what has been described as the 'top-heavy' system of corporate management in many local authorities (Hudson 1986: 63; see also Clapham *et al.* 1990: 218–20). We will discuss this particular development in the local delivery of welfare in our discussion of local authority decentralization in Chapter 9.

Collaboration between local authorities and health authorities

As Greenwood and Wilson (1989: 170) remind us, the corporate approach found within local authorities is only one variable in securing the efficient delivery of social services within a local community. The other major delivery agency of the welfare state at the local level – the NHS – is also responsible for the provision of key services. It is therefore important to develop collaboration between local authorities and health authorities.

Although the NHS was deliberately set up to operate outside local government control, there are, as we saw earlier, clear interdependencies between the services delivered by health authorities and local authorities. In recent years, the growing importance attached to the policy of community care has emphasized the interrelationships between the two types of authority. In the words of one writer on local government: 'It is clearly unsatisfactory if the right hand of the welfare state does not know what the left is doing' (Kingdom 1991: 61). The importance of collaboration between local authority social services departments and health authorities was explicitly recognized when local government and the NHS were both re-organized in 1974 and a formal system of 'strategic collaboration' over service development and resource allocation between the two sides was introduced (see Sargeant 1979).

Legislation imposed a duty on health authorities and local authorities to cooperate in the planning and operation of health and related social services. Collaboration between the two sides was facilitated by the drawing up of common boundaries between the operational tiers of the NHS – the then AHAs – and those local authorities responsible for providing personal social services. Joint Consultative Committees (JCCs), made up of members of the matching authorities, were established to advise on cooperation and planning. In order to develop detailed planning arrangements, the two sides were required to establish Joint Care Planning Teams (JCPTs) of senior officers, a development described as 'the keystone' of joint strategic planning (Challis *et al.* 1988: 172). In 1976, joint planning was encouraged by the introduction of a system of joint finance enabling NHS funds to be used on projects of benefit to both sides.

However, despite the various structural arrangements introduced to facilitate strategic collaboration, the history of joint planning has been much criticized. In the words of Hunter and Wistow (1987: 130), its progress has been 'limited and uneven'. Criticisms have been made that the whole concept was based upon unrealistic assumptions. In the event, JCCs have tended to be 'talking shops' and JCPTs have been criticized as 'clumsy and ineffectual' (Challis 1988: 181). The experience of joint planning has been described as at best a form of 'parallel planning' based on consultation and the exchange of information (Hunter and Wistow 1987: 113).

Various reasons have been suggested for the limited impact of joint planning. Allsop (1984: 114) has stated that both local authorities and health authorities are 'micro-political systems' which operate in different environments with 'their own organisational imperatives, system of financing and professional and political perceptions of priorities'. An official report in the late 1980s pointed to the major differences of planning timescale, management structure and geographical boundaries between the two types of authority, coterminosity having disappeared with the NHS re-organization of 1982 (National Audit Office 1987: para. 3.7). One academic study concluded that joint planning bore little resemblance to the official model, but 'was essentially a local professional power game' (Glennerster *et al.* 1983: 90).

The need for coordination between the two types of delivery agency was a central theme of the Griffiths Report (1988a) on the arrangements for community care in 1988. As we shall discuss in greater detail in Chapter 6, Griffiths recommended that local authorities should take the leading role in the development of community care, but as enablers and not necessarily as direct providers of services. The Government's response to Griffiths was contained in the National Health Service and Community Care Act 1990, which spelt out the new arrangements for community care. Under these arrangements, local authorities are required to prepare and publish plans for the provision of community care services. DHAs and FHSAs are also expected to prepare plans laying out the arrangements they propose for securing community care. If these new planning arrangements are to work, joint planning between the different types of authorities will be essential, and the DoH has recommended that, wherever possible, there should be planning agreements which include agreed policies on such areas as hospital-discharge arrangements and care management. Even where joint planning is difficult (as, for example, in areas where authorities have different boundaries) the two sides are expected to ensure that their separate plans are complementary (Department of Health 1990: paras 2.3 and 2.12). As we have already seen, the attitudes and behaviour of those involved in these kind of arrangements are crucial. The experience of earlier attempts to achieve coordination between local authority personal social services and health services, not to mention the difficulties in securing corporate links between the different social services delivered by local authorities, shows only too clearly that the personnel of welfare delivery agencies do not easily change their behaviour and perceptions when required to develop new approaches to the delivery of welfare.

5

Accountability and the public

We turn in this chapter to a discussion of the relationship between the delivery agencies of the welfare state and the users of their services. What are the arrangements for ensuring that the providers of social services are held account-able? What mechanisms exist to enable the users of social services – now increasingly described as 'customers' – to participate in decisions about the delivery of those services?

At the heart of the traditional framework of public accountability is the accountability of service providers to democratically elected representatives. But, as we shall discover, accountability upwards to elected representatives is only one part of a complex system through which the delivery agencies of the welfare state are held accountable and controlled. Welfare delivery agencies are also accountable downwards to the consumers of their services. In addition, the welfare professionals involved in the delivery of social services are also account-able outwards to their colleagues (Elcock 1991: 16); indeed it has been argued that the growth of professionalism in the welfare state has resulted in what has been termed the 'privatization of accountability' (Day and Klein 1987: 1), with welfare professionals claiming that their work can only be judged by their peers. The delivery agencies of the welfare state are also subject to legal and financial accountability. A further dimension to accountability has been intro-duced by demands for user participation in the making of decisions about, and the delivery of, social services.

The accountability of the delivery agencies of the welfare state has been the subject of much political debate in recent years, culminating with the publication in 1991 of the Conservative Government's Citizen's Charter, a document which was followed by the issue of a series of individual charters for such groups as NHS patients, parents of school children, council house tenants and those receiving benefits from the social security system. The development of 'charterism' and other initiatives has emphasized the importance of consumer accountability in the arrangements for delivering the social services. We will turn to a discussion of these more recent developments in Chapter 9. Meanwhile, the focus of this chapter is on traditional methods of accountability and user participation in the social services.

Holding welfare delivery agencies accountable

Traditionally, the delivery agencies of the welfare state have been held accountable through the mechanisms of political accountability. There is a line of accountability running from service deliverers to elected representatives at both the national and local levels, who are responsible to elected assemblies. To paraphrase the description of the situation given by one writer some 20 years ago, there is a chain of command leading from the local social security office and the hospital bed to the relevant Ministers in the House of Commons. In the case of the three major social services provided by local authorities, the chain leads first to the relevant committee room in the county hall or town hall and then, because of the overall responsibility of government Ministers for the development of these services, to the appropriate Minister in Whitehall (Brown 1975: 247).

Through its elected representatives, the public is given the opportunity to question the working of the delivery agencies of the welfare state. Thus the government Ministers in charge of a department like the DSS can be questioned by Members of Parliament at question time and during adjournment debates in the House of Commons. Ministers and their senior civil servants, including the chief executives of the Benefits Agency and other executive agencies, appear before the House of Commons Public Accounts Committee and the various departmental select committees, such as the Select Committee on Social Security, where they can be questioned about their policies and actions. These parliamentary mechanisms are supplemented by less formal procedures, such as ministerial replies to letters from MPs on behalf of aggrieved constituents. In certain circumstances, an MP might also pass a constituent's grievance to the Parliamentary Commissioner for Administration.

But although the constitutional theory of ministerial accountability might be clear-cut, its practice is not. Although Ministers have to accept responsibility for all the work that is done in their name, given the size and scale of government departments, especially a giant department like the DSS, it is impossible for them to be aware of everything that goes on. In the case of the delivery of social security, the problem has been compounded by the hiving off of responsibility for the delivery of benefits to the Benefits Agency and other executive agencies, all operating at arm's length from their parent departments in Whitehall and given certain freedoms in the way that they deliver services.

Complaints concerning social security benefits have long formed a major part of what has been described as the 'welfare officer' role performed by individual MPs (Richards 1972: 164). Indeed, research in the late 1970s revealed that the then DHSS received more letters from MPs than any other government department, the bulk of them being case-related and involving social security matters (see Norton 1982: 62). One consequence of the hiving off of responsibility for the delivery of social security benefits to the Benefits Agency is that letters from MPs to DSS Ministers concerning constituents' complaints about social security matters are now passed on to the Agency's chief executive, who deals with the matter. Although it can be argued that, being involved with the day-to-day delivery of services, the Agency is best placed to deal with such complaints, concern has been expressed that this procedure undermines the right of direct access to Ministers traditionally enjoyed by MPs.

At the local government level, education, the housing service and the personal social services all conform to the traditional model of political accountability. All three services are controlled by elected local councillors directly accountable to the public at the polls. But the whole concept of local authority accountability is undermined by the detailed controls exercised by central government departments (see Chapter 3): as Day and Klein (1987: 164) put it in their discussion of accountability and the local education service, the members of local education authority committees operate in 'conditions of constrained freedom'. There are also problems in attempting to control services delivered by welfare professionals, who, as we have seen, exercise discretionary powers in the delivery of services. Thus the elected members of the local authority education committee interviewed by Day and Klein (1987: 188) expressed serious doubts about their ability to control the education service, seeing themselves as being 'enmeshed in a web of powerlessness spun by the professionals actually running the service'.

The constitutional position on accountability is also clear-cut in the case of the third major delivery agency of the welfare state, the NHS. The Secretary of State for Health is supposed to be accountable to Parliament for everything that happens in the service. In the words of Aneurin Bevan, the Cabinet Minister responsible for the setting up of the NHS, 'when a bedpan is dropped on a hospital floor, its noise should resound in the Palace of Westminster' (quoted in Day and Klein 1987: 76). Like her counterpart at the Department of Social Security, the Secretary of State for Health is held accountable to Parliament through such traditional parliamentary processes as question time and adjournment debates, as well as having to appear before the Public Accounts Committee and the Select Committee for Health. But, despite this well-developed institutional apparatus of parliamentary control, as the Royal Commission on the National Health Service (Merrison 1979: para. 19.2) noted in 1979, 'detailed ministerial accountability for the NHS is largely a constitutional fiction'. As with government departments like the DSS, the sheer size and complexity of the NHS makes any degree of detailed ministerial supervision impossible.

Responsibility for the day-to-day running of the NHS is in the hands of appointed health authorities and, since 1991, NHS Trusts. Studies in the 1980s found that members of the old-style health authorities appeared 'not to be accountable to anyone' (Hunter 1984: 44) and that they saw accountability upwards to the Secretary of State as a low priority, their primary concern being their accountability downwards to the local community (Day and Klein 1987: 101). But in attempting to fulfil this latter responsibility, health authority members felt powerless, being too dependent on the managers of the authority for information (Day and Klein 1987: 97). The removal of local authority representatives from the new-style health authorities set up in 1991 has led to criticisms that health authorities are now less accountable to the local community (Ashburner and Cairncross 1993: 371).

The traditional framework of accountability in the public sector also includes procedures for enforcing legal and financial accountability. Thus the delivery agencies of the welfare state are duty-bound to obey the law and not act *ultra vires*, and can be required by the courts to fulfil their statutory obligations and to refrain from acting in a manner which is beyond their powers. The development of the welfare state in the post-war period has witnessed a number of cases where the courts have become involved: the Norwich case in 1982, where the Court of Appeal agreed that the Secretary of State for the Environment could invoke powers contained in the Housing Act 1980 enabling his Department to take over the running of the City Council's sale of council houses, is just one well-known example. Aggrieved members of the public also occasionally resort to the use of judicial review, one notable example being the case of the controversial regulations made in 1985 by the Secretary of State for Social Services, concerning board and lodgings allowances payable to unemployed people, which were declared *ultra vires* by the courts.

Although changes in the system of judicial review have made the courts more accessible to members of the public wishing to question the legality of the actions of welfare delivery agencies, the courts are generally of limited value for individuals attempting to require public bodies to conform to their legal obligations. Judicial proceedings are not only complex, but also time consuming and expensive. In the view of one writer on public law, judicial review has done nothing for the management of local authority housing waiting lists, the treatment of NHS patients, or claimants in local social security offices (McAuslan 1983: 5). The use of the courts by individuals who are in dispute with welfare delivery agencies is also very much a last resort, disputes over many social services being entrusted, as we shall see in the next section, to internal review procedures and administrative tribunals.

Welfare delivery agencies are also constrained by the requirements of financial accountability. The accounts of central government departments are audited by the Comptroller and Audit General (CAG), whose findings are reported to the prestigious Public Accounts Committee of the House of Commons, which summons the permanent secretaries of departments, and the chief executives of executive agencies, to answer points raised in the reports. The original concept of audit concentrated on the narrow technical concern of legality and regularity, ensuring that departmental expenditure had been upon approved services and in accordance with statutory authority. In recent years, however, the CAG has extended his investigations to broader questions of efficiency, effectiveness and value for money, a process reinforced by the transformation of his department, the Exchequer and Audit Department, into the National Audit Office in the early 1980s. As we shall see in Chapter 8, this increasing concern with efficiency and value for money is part of a wider search for efficiency in central government departments.

Financial regularity has also been a major concern of local authorities. Evolving out of the system set up to check the Poor Law accounts in the nineteenth century (Keith-Lucas and Richards 1978: 153), the local government audit system requires the accounts of local authorities to be audited on an annual basis by either the district auditor or an approved auditor from the private sector. Overlapping with the doctrine of *ultra vires*, local government audit has traditionally been concerned with ensuring that local authorities are able to show legal authority for all their expenditure. Like audit at the national level, however, local government audit has progressed from its traditional concern with regularity and legality to include a far greater concern with value for money and effectiveness.

Financial accountability is, of course, part of a framework of accountability which was established long before the development of the post-war welfare state. As Johnson (1974: 7) has observed, what really matters to the consumer of social services is the quality of those services, the way in which they are delivered, and the accessibility of the agencies which deliver them. It is not surprising, therefore, that it has been suggested that traditional approaches to accountability have become less relevant. Political accountability, in particular, has been seen as 'too blunt an instrument' in the context of the kind of services delivered by the welfare or service state (Johnson 1974: 7). Traditional approaches to accountability are now supplemented by a number of other methods through which members of the public can attempt to control the social services. An important aspect of these methods are mechanisms which help to enhance user participation. Before we turn to these, however, we need to discuss the procedures for the handling of complaints and enabling individuals to obtain redress for grievances, all of which help to make up what has been described as 'accountability downwards' (Elcock 1991: 16).

Complaining if things go wrong

Most delivery agencies of the welfare state have internal procedures for dealing with formal complaints before such external mechanisms as tribunals and ombudsmen are brought into action. Thus appeals against decisions on many social security benefits are reviewed by DSS and DEmp adjudication officers before going to a social security appeals tribunal. Complaints about the refusal of a local office of the Benefits Agency to provide a discretionary grant or loan under the Social Fund are the subject of an internal review, with a further review by a Social Fund inspector. Appeals on disability benefits and decisions of the Child Support Agency are dealt with first of all by internal reviews. All local offices of the Benefits Agency have customer service managers to deal with complaints, as do the centres of the Child Support Agency.

Internal complaints procedures also exist within the NHS. Under the Hospital Complaints Act 1985, DHAs are required to designate a senior officer to deal with complaints for each hospital or group of hospitals. The system has been criticized for its lack of independence and specialist knowledge (Hogg 1990: 162), and recommendations for reforming it were made by a review committee in 1994 (Department of Health 1994). The broad principles of the recommendations, involving a two-stage process involving a relatively informal internal procedure followed by appeal to an independent panel, were accepted by the Government.

At the local authority level, individuals who are unhappy with the delivery of a particular service can, of course, ask a local councillor to pursue their complaint. Local authorities also have their own internal complaints procedures. Thus, social services departments are required to establish complaints procedures. Complaints about housing benefit, which is administered by local authorities, are the subject of internal reviews. Since 1978 local authorities have also had a voluntary code of practice for handling complaints from the public, produced jointly by the local authority associations and the Commission for Local Administration (the local ombudsmen). However, the code has been criticized as being aimed at internal management efficiency rather than consumer needs, 'ensuring that a local authority is not "caught out" by making elementary mistakes' (Birkinshaw 1985: 61–2).

The existence of formalized complaints procedures seems to vary across the three main local authority social services. Thus a research study into complaints handling in local government carried out in the mid-1980s found that few local authority education departments had formalized procedures, while only just over one-quarter of housing departments had procedures for all areas of their work. Although social services departments had more formalized procedures than the other two departments, only a minority of local authorities publicized them and they seemed to be used as 'protection' for social workers, who were very conscious of 'the necessity of making their decisions accountable in an increasingly critical environment' (Seneviratne and Cracknell 1988: 185).

Challenging the delivery agencies: the tribunals of the welfare state

In addition to internal complaints procedures, there are also external mechanisms through which the users of social services can make complaints about the delivery of welfare. At the heart of these arrangements are the various

Table 5.1   The main tribunals of the welfare state (numbers of cases decided in 1992*)

Social Security Appeals Tribunals	75,325
Education Appeal Committees	23,687
Medical Appeal Tribunals	16,370
Mental Health Review Tribunals	4,935
Pensions Appeal Tribunals	2,801
Disability Appeal Tribunals	2,276
Family Health Services Authority Service Committees	1,974

* Figures refer to tribunals under the direct supervision of the Council of Tribunals.
Source: Council on Tribunals (1993).

administrative tribunals which are able to determine disputes if individuals feel that they have been the victims of unfair decisions by a welfare delivery agency. The creation of such bodies has been an important by-product of the many social services and benefits introduced by the post-war welfare state, the delivery of which often give rise to disagreement.

This particular form of redress procedure can be found in all three types of delivery agency of the welfare state (see Table 5.1). Thus in the NHS, Service Committees of the FHSAs – consisting of three lay and three professional members and a chairperson – operate as tribunals in investigating complaints from patients against general practitioners, dentists, opticians and pharmacists. Mental Health Review Tribunals hear appeals against cases of compulsory detention of the mentally ill. Local education authorities are required by the Education Act 1986 to set up appeal committees giving dissatisfied parents the opportunity to appeal against decisions on the allocation of secondary school places. Similar committees have been set up by the grant maintained schools which have been established following the Education Reform Act 1988.

But the area of the welfare state which gives rise to most disputes is social security, where a number of tribunals adjudicate on the application of – often very complex – rules to individual cases. Thus Medical Appeal Tribunals adjudicate on claims arising from industrial injuries. Pensions Appeal Tribunals determine appeals from ministerial decisions on war and military service pensions. Appeals against decisions on disability benefits and against decisions on child support maintenance also include an independent tribunal. But the type of tribunal in this field of welfare delivery which receives by far the greatest number of complaints is the Social Security Appeals Tribunal, a body which has its origins in the tribunals established to settle disputes arising out of the health and unemployment insurance schemes introduced by the National Insurance Act 1911, and which was formed as the result of the merger of the separate supplementary benefit appeal tribunals and national insurance local tribunals in 1984. Described as 'one of the most important forms of civil justice in the modern legal system' (Wikeley and Young 1992: 242–3), social security appeals tribunals decided over 75 000 cases in 1992.

The delivery of social security benefits is dependent on those claiming benefits meeting certain rules. Thus some 15 000 adjudication officers working in the local offices of the DSS's Benefits Agency take millions of decisions each year concerning the entitlement of claimants to income support and contributory benefits. Over 5 million people received income support in 1992 (Department of Social Security 1993: vi). An additional 500 adjudication officers based in the local offices of the Employment Service make similar decisions about entitlements to unemployment benefit, for which there were some 4.7 million claims in 1992 (Wikeley and Young 1992: 239; Department of Social Security 1993: vii). If appeals against benefit decisions are not upheld by an internal review, claimants may appeal to a social security appeals tribunal, consisting of a legally qualified chairperson and two other members, with the right of an appeal on a point of law to a Social Security Commissioner and, beyond that, to the Court of Appeal and the House of Lords.

For many people, the tribunals of the welfare state form 'the immediate point of legal contact': they have been described as 'poor people's courts' (Fulbrook et al. 1973: 14). It is generally agreed that tribunals have several advantages over ordinary courts of law, being quicker, cheaper and more informal. Given the type of cases involved, these advantages are particularly important. Individuals claiming social security benefit, in particular, require 'informal, cheap, and speedy adjudication' (Greenwood and Wilson 1989: 305).

There has been a long-running debate about the procedures of such bodies. Since the criticisms made in 1957 by the Franks Report concerning the lack of independence from departmental control and the procedural deficiencies of many tribunals, especially those involved with the adjudication of appeals involving social security benefits, successive governments have attempted to judicialize the procedures of these particular tribunals in an attempt to make them more 'open, fair and impartial'. In the words of Franks (1957: para. 64), 'Informality without rules of procedure may be positively inimical to right adjudication.' Thus social security appeal tribunals are now chaired by lawyers and characterized by more formal approaches towards points of law and the admissibility of evidence. Some observers maintain that this process should be supplemented by the extension of legal aid to tribunal proceedings (see, for example, the discussion in Justice – All Souls 1988).

But as social security tribunals have become more like the courts, many of the advantages which they are claimed to have over the courts have become less obvious (Greenwood and Wilson 1989: 307). Thus the involvement of lawyers in tribunal procedures is seen as a threat to the informality which is supposed to be one of the major benefits of this form of adjudicatory body (see, for example, Fulbrook et al. 1973: 11).

Despite some criticisms, the tribunals of the welfare state provide an independent method of resolving grievances, as well as ensuring that the agencies responsible for the delivery of social services and benefits are accountable. Social security appeals tribunals, in particular, are said to 'cast a long shadow' over the work carried out in the local offices of the Benefits Agency and the Employment Service (Wikeley and Young 1992: 260). Thus researchers have referred to a 'tribunal effect', the existence of tribunals having a clear impact on the quality of the initial decision-making and the review process in local agency offices (Wikeley and Young 1992: 257).

Despite the existence of social security appeals tribunals, grievances against decisions involving two of the most important social security benefits (claims for assistance from the controversial Social Fund and claims for housing benefit) are the responsibility of internal reviews and not independent tribunals. Thus applicants dissatisfied with the decision of a local Social Fund officer have the right of appeal to a system of internal review and, ultimately, to a Social Fund Inspector. In the case of housing benefit, there is a right of appeal to a two-tier review system, consisting of an internal review by housing benefit officers followed, if necessary, by a hearing conducted by a Housing Benefit Review Board consisting of local councillors. The operation of both these sets of arrangements has been the subject of much criticism. Thus the absence of an independent appeal against decisions made about payments and loans from the Social Fund has been described by the Council on Tribunals, the watchdog of the working of tribunals, as 'a highly retrograde step' (1985: para. 2.36), the Council pointing out that the discretionary nature of Social Fund decisions is no different in principle from the system in operation before the new arrangements were introduced (1986: para. 11). Another observer has described the exclusion of such appeals from a tribunal as 'a significant and sinister breach of the general principle that disputed claims to State benefits should be subjected to independent arbitration' (Elcock 1990: 36–7). In the case of housing benefit appeals, research has shown that there are wide variations in local authority practice and that in some cases the review process can become 'highly personalised and so informal as to be virtually invisible' (Eardley and Sainsbury 1993: 479).

Welfare delivery and maladministration: the role of ombudsmen

Complaints about the delivery of social services can also be investigated by the ombudsmen institutions which cover all three major types of welfare delivery agency. The British ombudsmen – although only pale shadows of their West European namesakes – are generally concerned with investigating whether decision-making procedures conform to the standard of reasonableness. This is what one commentator has referred to as 'procedural accountability' (Smith 1981: 1168).

Complaints alleging injustice caused to individuals as a result of maladministration in central government's social service departments and their agencies can be referred through an MP to the Parliamentary Commissioner for Administration (PCA). Although the concept of maladministration is not defined in the relevant legislation, it is generally agreed that it includes such bureaucratic lapses as bias, delay, incompetence and arbitrariness. Given the numbers of people in receipt of social security benefits, it is not surprising that the Commissioner's annual reports have revealed that the major central government department directly responsible for the delivery of welfare, the DSS (and its predecessor, the DHSS) has consistently been at the top of the complaints league table, with some 30 per cent of total referrals in 1993. But, although many complaints are made about the way the staff of the DSS handle individual cases, only about one in four are actually upheld (Parliamentary Commissioner for Administration 1994). The most common grounds of complaint found proven are relatively minor ones, including delay, mishandling of cases and incorrect advice about entitlement to benefit.

The impact of the PCA on the procedures of the DSS and the other government department directly responsible for the delivery of welfare, the DEmp, is difficult to assess. Former holders of the office have argued that the mere presence of the PCA has a 'tonic effect' upon government departments in improving the quality of administration, and that there has been evidence of 'a healthy regard' on the part of officials for the need to avoid the PCA's attentions (Compton 1970: 6; Clothier 1986: 207). Other commentators, however, maintain that the presence of the PCA encourages a play-safe attitude amongst civil servants.

At the local government level, there are a number of Local Commissioners for Administration, three for England, one for Wales and one for Scotland, popularly known as the local ombudsmen. Closely modelled on the PCA (although they can receive complaints directly from members of the public) the local ombudsmen are also confined to investigating injustice caused by maladministration. Thus, although the local ombudsmen may investigate the administrative procedures of a local authority's education service, they are not allowed to investigate complaints about the internal affairs of schools. The main subject of complaints received has been housing, which has consistently had over one-third of all annual complaints, with the personal social services and education a poor third and fourth in recent years. Recent examples of cases where maladministration causing injustice have been found include failure to deal properly with a couple's claim for housing benefit, unreasonable delay by a social services department in assessing the needs of a disabled couple, and failure to deal properly with a boy's exclusion from school (Commission for Local Administration in England 1994: Chapter 4).

The ombudsman responsible for the third major delivery agency of the welfare state – the Health Service Commissioner (HSC) – is also modelled on the PCA. The HSC can investigate allegations of injustice caused by maladministration by health authorities, NHS Trusts and other NHS bodies. In addition, he can also investigate alleged injustice or hardship as a result of a failure in a service provided by a health service body or failure to provide a service which it was the body's duty to provide. Examples of recent cases include delays in ambulances responding to emergency calls and lack of attention to patients. Unlike his central government counterpart, the HSC can receive complaints directly from members of the public, although the health authority concerned is expected to have been given the opportunity to investigate and respond to the complaint.

Despite his wider terms of reference, jurisdictional limitations have meant that the HSC can only deal with a small proportion of complaints referred to him: results reports were issued on only 14 per cent of the cases concluded during 1986–91 (Giddings 1993: 381). The major grievances were about failure in care and lack of or incorrect information. The major limitation to the HSC's jurisdiction is that he is not allowed to investigate any complaints which involve solely the exercise of clinical judgement, an important and controversial manifestation of the medical profession's success in blocking the introduction of any changes which would adversely affect their position. During the first two decades of the HSC scheme, by far the largest number of complaints rejected (some 19 per cent) involved clinical judgement (Giddings 1993: 392). Complaints concerning clinical judgement are dealt with by a separate process, involving a review by two independent hospital consultants (see Longley 1993: 69–70), although the Wilson Report on hospital complaints procedures in 1994 recommended that the Government should consider extending the role of the HSC to allow him to investigate complaints of this kind (Department of Health 1994).

The ombudsmen have been described as 'the most developed independent grievance-remedial devices' found in the field of British public administration (Birkinshaw 1985: 127–8). They also have the advantages, unlike administrative tribunals, of not requiring complainants to present their evidence in court-like proceedings. But, as a recent study of complaints procedures concludes, 'it is doubtful if their full potential is being tapped' (Lewis and Birkinshaw 1993: 139).

One obvious obstacle to the full realization of this potential is that none of the British ombudsmen have the power to initiate investigations, a limitation which is seen as restricting the investigation of cases involving those users of social services unable to complain in their own interests, such as the residents of local authority nursing homes and long-stay patients in NHS hospitals (Lewis and Birkinshaw 1993: 129). Moreover, the jurisdiction of the ombudsmen is restricted, particularly in the case of the HSC, who, as we have seen, is prevented from investigating complaints involving clinical judgement. Neither are any of the ombudsmen able to directly enforce their recommendations, although the absence of such powers appears to have been more of a problem with the local ombudsmen than with the others (Giddings 1993: 386, 390).

Another problem is that of under-utilization. The PCA is clearly underused (less than 1000 cases were referred to him in 1993) partly because of the lack of direct access and partly because of the lack of enthusiasm on the part of many MPs towards the office and its operations (Gregory and Pearson 1992). The HSC is also under-used, receiving only just over 1000 complaints each year. Significantly, since the introduction of direct access in 1988, there has been an increase in the number of complaints made to the local ombudsmen. But although the local ombudsmen have managed to publicize their activities more successfully, the PCA and the HSC clearly suffer from a lack of public visibility (Gregory and Pearson 1992: 485–6; Lewis and Birkinshaw 1993: 134). However, as Lewis and Birkinshaw (1993: 134) observe:

> as long as the British ombudsmen systems are so littered with exceptions to their jurisdiction, increased publicity is only likely to lead to frustration and disappointment by those who had hoped they had found a champion but had found someone fighting with one hand tied behind their back.

The development of ombudsmen at the national and local levels, together with the reforms in the procedures and composition of social security appeals tribunals, has been part of a series of important developments since the early 1960s, intended to strengthen the users of services in their dealings with the delivery agencies of the welfare state. For many, however, the arrangements for making complaints to, and securing redress against, welfare delivery agencies are still inadequate. As we have seen, many local authorities have failed to develop adequate complaints procedures for their social services, the tribunals of the welfare state have been criticized for their excessive judicialization, important areas of the social security system are not covered by tribunals, and the various ombudsmen have yet to achieve their potential.

There is no shortage of suggestions for improving the way that such redress machinery works: they include the provision of legal aid and advice for those appearing before social security appeals tribunals, direct access to the PCA, and the extension of the HSC's jurisdiction to include clinical judgement. As Deakin and Wright (1990: 213) point out, however, redress against the deliverers of public services only has meaning in relation to 'a framework of rights, standards of performance, and legitimate expectations'. According to this view, such a framework should be seen as 'an integral part' of a users' charter. As we shall see in Chapter 9, some of these ideas have been embodied in the Citizen's Charter introduced by John Major's Conservative Government in 1991.

User participation in welfare delivery

Closely linked to the whole question of 'accountability downwards' to the users of social services is the issue of user participation. In the early years of the post-war welfare state, there was little provision for user participation in the delivery of welfare. The public administration model which underpinned the organization of the delivery of the major social services was dominated by the providers of welfare, viz. the bureaucrats and professionals. According to one commentator, the founding fathers of the welfare state 'never felt called upon' to address the issue of user involvement. Not only was it assumed that the users of social services had little interest in the making of welfare policy, but it was also felt that they had little to contribute to the process (Richardson 1983: 2–3). In the words of Hadley and Hatch (1981: 15–16), 'The public was cast in the role of spectator and consumer, not co-partner'.

There was no place for 'shared management' with the users of social services. Welfare professionals, bureaucrats and politicians were seen as having the responsibility for ensuring that services met the needs of users.

One group of writers was later to remark that the 1950s and 1960s had been an era when it was considered 'inappropriate to ask local people what they wanted – the job of deciding what they needed was left to politicians and experts' (Lansley et al. 1989: 3). However, this view began to change in the late 1960s and the early 1970s, when user participation in the delivery of the services of the welfare state became fashionable. As Richardson (1983: 102–14) has shown, the interest in participation was partly the result of pressure from the users of services (such as council house tenants and parents of school children, who became not only more demanding, but also better organized) and partly the result of the needs of the providers of services, who began to seek contact with service users as the growth in the size and scale of delivery agencies widened the gap between the two sides. As a consequence of such factors, the 1970s and the 1980s witnessed the development of a number of initiatives involving user participation in the major social services delivered by both local government and the NHS.

User participation is now a feature of all three major social services provided by local government. Participatory mechanisms exist within the local education service. Following the recommendations of the Taylor Report 1977 on the management and government of schools, the Education Act 1980 laid down that at least two elected parents be appointed to the board of governors of every local education authority school, a requirement which was extended by the Education Act 1986, which gave parent governors equal representation with governors appointed by the local education authority. Despite these initiatives, the reaction of parents has been patchy, with no elections at all held in many schools in the first round of parent governor elections (see Gyford 1991: 68). Scepticism has also been expressed about the potential influence of parent governors. Research into state schools in Sheffield (where parent representation on school governing boards was introduced as long ago as the early 1970s) found that parent governors often had little knowledge of how the educational system worked and looked towards the head teacher and the clerk to the governing body for advice and guidance (Bacon 1978: 128). The study concluded that the system of parent governors simply gave 'an illusion of local participation in the decision-making processes' (Bacon 1978: 135).

Since the early 1980s, there has also been an increasing interest in the development of participatory initiatives in local authority housing. The Housing Act 1988 (which introduced a 'tenants charter' for local authority tenants) imposes a duty on local housing authorities in England and Wales to introduce a form of tenant participation in the management of council housing by requiring them to consult those tenants who are likely to be substantially affected by a matter of housing management. The details of implementation are left to the discretion of the local authority, but most local housing authorities have introduced arrangements for tenant participation, ranging from tenant representation on advisory committees or local authority housing committees to questionnaire surveys (Cairncross *et al.* 1994). A number of local authorities have gone much further. Thus some authorities, such as Hackney, have involved tenants in the management of council estates through estate management boards, while others, such as Islington, have established tenant management cooperatives (see Power 1988). But despite such developments, it appears that many local authorities have not taken their responsibilities under the legislation seriously enough. Thus, one study of housing management in English housing authorities in the late 1980s found that only one-fifth of tenants believed that they were consulted by local authorities on important issues, with only half of those who had been consulted believing that their views had been taken seriously (Maclennan *et al.* 1989).

Clapham (1990: 65) has concluded that the general picture appears to be of a local authority housing service in which tenants 'have little control, either individually or collectively, over the type or quality of service received'. Writing with two colleagues, he has suggested two strategies to resolve this problem. One approach involves the encouragement of greater tenant participation through such devices as tenant management cooperatives, while the other involves encouraging the 'diversification' of public housing through the introduction of a wider range of different landlords, such as housing associations, private landlords and cooperatives, the argument being that this would give tenants greater consumer choice (Clapham *et al.* 1990: 245–6). As we shall see in Chapter 6, the opportunity to choose alternative landlords was given to council tenants by the Housing Act 1988.

In the case of the third major local authority social service, the personal social services, user participation has been on the agenda ever since the Seebohm Committee reported in 1968. Seebohm (1968: paras 137 and 491) argued that the participation of individuals in the planning and delivery of the personal social services was vital if such services were to be sensitive to local needs. It accordingly recommended the involvement of users in both the provision and planning of the personal social services through, for example, representation on local authority social services committees or sub-committees (1968: para. 628). But, as Gyford (1991: 69) points out in his discussion of participation in local government, unlike local authority education and housing services, which both have clearly defined focal points (local schools and housing estates) around which to organize user participation, the personal social services (with their wider range of activities and client groups) do not possess such a clear focus.

Despite this limitation, there have been important developments in user participation in this particular area of local welfare delivery. Thus some local authorities co-opt representatives of voluntary groups onto social services committees, and a national survey of social services departments, carried out in the late 1980s, concluded that user participation was now more broadly established and beginning to become more routine (Beresford and Croft 1990: 18). As we shall see in Chapter 7, user involvement is an objective of the community care reforms introduced in the early 1990s. These reforms require not only that assessments of need by local authority social service departments take account of the wishes of the individuals concerned, and where possible include their active participation, but also that efforts should be made to offer individuals flexible services which will enable them to make choices (Department of Health 1989b: para. 3.2.6). Despite this requirement, however, reservations have been expressed that this development effectively leaves user participation to professional definitions and that it is 'an improbable strategy' for shifting the balance away from social work professionals and towards service users (Warner 1992: 226).

User participation in the NHS

What about user participation in the other major delivery agency of the welfare state, the NHS? For just over the first 25 years of the NHS, the users of its services were what Klein (1989: 77) has graphically referred to as 'the ghosts in the NHS machinery'. Although early plans for the NHS had included a strong emphasis on the desirability of public participation, there was not much evidence of this in the structure which finally emerged in 1948 (Pater 1981: 168).

The tripartite structure set up in 1948 did include members chosen after consultation with voluntary organizations and local authorities. Local authority representation was also built into the unified NHS structure established in 1974 and, although the numbers were reduced, was also included in the streamlined structure introduced in 1982. But this was not user participation in the sense of the users of services influencing the nature of the services being delivered: it was what has been described as community involvement – the representation of the local community through the members of elected local authorities and other concerned bodies (Brown 1975: 262–3). As Brown (1975: 261–2) has pointed out, the most important type of participation in the NHS has been the syndicalist type, in which those working in the NHS (especially the medical profession) have had an important say in the running of the service through their representation on health authorities. As another observer has put it, the views of users 'have always come a poor second' to the views of the professionals in the making of decisions about the delivery of health care (Hogg 1990: 174).

Important changes in the arrangements for the representation of user views within the NHS did take place with the re-organization of 1974, when a deliberate decision was taken to separate responsibility for the management of the service and the representation of the community. Thus the RHAs and AHAs established as part of the re-organized service were given managerial responsibilities, whilst responsibility for representation was given to Community Health Councils (CHCs), set up to represent the interests of the public in their particular community. Currently, each health district has a CHC to represent the interests in the health service of the local community to the management of the DHA. CHCs were introduced partly to compensate for the absence of any 'direct democracy' in the management of the NHS (Boaden *et al.* 1982: 120), and their members are nominated (one-half by local authorities, one-third by voluntary organizations and the remaining one-sixth by the RHA). Although they are advisory bodies, with no executive powers, CHCs were given certain statutory rights, including the right to be consulted about plans, the right to information from health authorities and the right to inspect NHS premises.

However, the impact of CHCs has been limited. Even before they were officially established they were described by an Opposition spokesperson as 'the strangest bunch of administrative eunuchs that any department had yet foisted upon the House, a kind of seraglio of the Secretary of State of utterly useless and emasculated bodies which have no powers' (House of Commons Debates: 1 July 1971, col. 599). Studies of CHCs have emphasized the limitations of these so-called watchdogs. Thus Hogg (1990: 170–1) points to the variations in the standard of the services provided by CHCs, some of which have encouraged the public to participate in their activities, whilst others have not. The effectiveness of CHCs is also undermined by their lack of resources (an average budget of £35 000 and two full-time staff) and the difficulty of deciding what role they should adopt, that of 'snivelling lapdogs' or that of 'rabid curs' (see Ham 1977: 103).

As a result of the NHS reforms of the early 1990s, the role of CHCs has actually been weakened: they have lost their right to to be consulted whenever the DHA intends to introduce a substantial change to local services. Using the 'ladder of citizen participation' constructed by the American academic, Sherry Arnstein (1971), which ranges from manipulation and therapy, through information, consultation and placation, to partnership, delegated power and citizen control, one commentator has concluded that the powers of CHCs are restricted to the lower rungs of the ladder (Allsop 1984: 196–7).

As we saw earlier, the mechanisms which attempt to provide service users with the opportunity to participate in the delivery of the three core social services provided by local authorities also appear to be located on the lower rungs of the ladder of participation. Clearly, some benefits have been achieved as a result of these kinds of initiatives, but as Boaden and his colleagues (1982: 179) concluded in their survey of such developments in the 1980s, 'little has been achieved by way of a fundamental shift in power'. Indeed, in the case of the NHS, participation has actually been weakened as a result of the reforms of the early 1990s. The representation of the community on health authorities via local authority nominees was removed altogether, with ideas now being drawn from 'the world of private sector business rather than from notions of participative democracy' (Allsop 1992: 159). As we will see in Chapter 9, since the late 1980s, there has been an emphasis on improving the position of the user – or 'customer' – of social services through the marketplace.

Part II

New directions in the delivery of welfare

6

The rolling back of the local welfare state

As we saw in our discussion in Chapter 3 of the government of welfare beyond Whitehall, local authorities have traditionally been the major delivery agencies of the welfare state, with responsibility for the direct provision of the key collective consumption services of education, housing and personal social services. In providing these 'from the cradle to the grave' services, local authorities (although enjoying a great deal of autonomy and answerable to local electorates) have operated within a framework of central government controls and influences.

Since the election of the Conservative Thatcher Government in 1979, developments have taken place which represent a major shift in the nature of the central–local relationship and which have had major consequences for the traditional role of local authorities in the welfare state. Radical changes have been introduced in the system of local government finance in an attempt to control the expenditure and income of local authorities. In addition, legislation has challenged the role of local authorities as front-line delivery agencies of social services, resulting in a 'rolling back' of the local welfare state.

An examination of the changing relationship between central government and local authorities since the election of the first Thatcher Government is crucial to an understanding of the role of local government in the delivery of welfare. Before examining these developments, however, we need to discuss the nature of the central–local relationship before 1979.

Central-local relations before 1979: partnership and consultation

In their discussion of the evolving relationship betwen central and local government in the post-war period, Hartas and Harrop (1991) analyse the relationship between the two sides in the years up to 1979 in terms of two periods: the period from 1945 to 1976, which was characterized by the expansion and consolidation of local authorities as delivery agencies of the welfare state, and the much shorter period from 1976 to the election of the Conservative Government in 1979, which was marked by an increasing concern with the level of local authority spending.

During the first period, covering the 30 years or so following the end of the Second World War, local government played a central role in the launching and consolidation of the modern welfare state, developing the key services of education, housing and what were to be later labelled the personal social services. The development of the local government welfare state was reflected in the increase in local authority spending, which rose steadily in the post-war years. Whereas local authority expenditure as a proportion of total public spending was only about one-quarter at the end of the 1940s, it had risen to nearly one-third by 1976, largely as a result of the growth in spending on the three key services of education, housing and the personal social services (Else and Marshall 1979: 15). Public spending on the education service, in particular, expanded markedly, tripling in constant prices between 1945 and 1965 (Kogan 1978: 26). By 1976, education consumed well over one-third of total local government current spending. Spending on education, housing and the personal social services accounted for nearly 62 per cent of local government current spending in 1976, compared with just over 24 per cent in 1945 (see Table 6.1). There was also a marked increase in the share of capital spending by the three services, particularly on housing.

The dramatic increase in local government spending during this period was fuelled by increases in the level of central government financial support, notably through the Rate Support Grant (RSG) after the mid-1960s, underpinned by the steady economic growth of the post-war years. By 1976, central

Table 6.1 Local government current and capital spending on social services in England and Wales 1945 and 1976 (as a percentage of total local government spending)

Sector	Current spending		Capital spending	
	1945	1976	1945	1976
Education	17.6%	37.6%	1.7%	9.9%
Housing	6.6%	17.7%	32.9%	64.9%
Personal Social Services	–	6.6%	–	1.6%

Source: 1945 figures adapted from figures in Jackman (1985) 151–2; 1976 figures from *Annual Abstract of Statistics 1979*.

government grants made up nearly 47 per cent of total local government revenue income in England and Wales compared with just over 30 per cent at the end of the war. In the words of one observer, not only did central government extend the territory of local authorities, but it also provided a 'large financial incentive for [them] to cultivate the new territory' (Glennerster 1992a: 74). As Glennerster (1992a: 75) has pointed out, national politicians during this period actually took much of the credit for the schools and council houses built by local authorities under their particular government.

The 1945–76 period was also characterized by a basic consensus between central and local government on the way in which local services were provided. The relationship between the two sides was one of 'partnership' and 'interdependence' (Loughlin 1985: 139). This was a period when both major political parties were 'content to give (when they occupied Westminster) and to receive (when they controlled town halls) local discretion over service provision' (Goodwin and Duncan 1989: 69). The degree of 'local discretion' over service provision during this period has been highlighted by academic studies of local government spending, which have revealed substantial variations in the patterns of spending between different local authorities on the three major social services (see, for example, Boaden 1971; Davies 1972).

'Partnership' has been used to describe the relationship between central government and local authorities in the field of education during this period. The two sides in this 'partnership' were clearly not equal, but as one commentator has argued, 'no other term would do as well'. The contribution of both the central government department responsible for education and the local education authorities was essential, with the two sides working together 'for the good of the service' (Regan 1977: 35). The government of education was dominated by what another writer has described as a 'consensual model', which took account of the two 'potentially conflicting legitimacies' of a central government with a national mandate and local authorities who were legitimated by local government elections (Kogan 1987: 47). In the case of the other major local authority social service (housing) the responsible central government department was described by the standard work on central–local relations, written in the mid-1960s, as having a *laissez-faire* attitude towards local housing authorities, leaving them to decide local needs and how far they should be met (Griffith 1966: 519). It went on to describe the (then) Ministry of Housing and Local Government as being 'historically associated with encouraging local authorities to be autonomous' (Griffith 1966: 519), a philosophy confirmed by a former Permanent Secretary of the Ministry who, writing in the late 1960s, asserted that local authorities probably enjoyed greater independence from central government in the field of housing than any other major service (Sharp 1969: 74).

National political leaders during this period were not interested in the detailed supervision of the activities of local authorities: what was regarded as 'real politics' took place at Westminster, with 'proper government' being seen as the concern of Whitehall. As a result, there was what has been termed a 'dual polity': a structure of central–local relations in which central government and local authorities 'operated, by and large, in two separate compartments'. As long as central government was able to control 'high' politics (such as the economy, defence and foreign policy) it was content to leave matters of 'low' politics to local authorities (Bulpitt 1983; Bulpitt 1989: 66–7).

There were, of course, occasions when there were clear, and publicly expressed, differences between the two sides concerning the local implementation of particular national social policies. One such dispute concerned the implementation of the Conservative Government's controversial Housing Finance Act 1972, with the Labour-controlled Clay Cross Urban District Council in north-east Derbyshire refusing to implement the provisions of the Act which required it to raise council house rents to the level of a 'fair rent'. The council's inaction ultimately resulted in the Government using the default powers given to it in the legislation to appoint a Housing Commissioner to take over responsibility for housing in Clay Cross, culminating in the surcharge and disqualification from holding public office of the councillors involved.

Another well-documented case of local authority recalcitrance during this period, this time involving a Conservative-controlled local authority, was the case of Tameside Metropolitan Borough in Greater Manchester, which decided in 1975 not to proceed with the outgoing Labour council's plans for the re-organization of its secondary schools on comprehensive lines. The Secretary of State for Education argued that the local education authority was acting unreasonably, and, exercising his powers under the Education Act 1944, issued a directive requiring Tameside to go ahead with the re-organization plans. After a protracted court case, the House of Lords rejected the Government's case, declaring that there was no evidence that the Tameside council was acting in a way which no reasonable council would do.

However, despite these and other conflicts, the normal style of central–local relations between 1945 and the mid-1970s was one of partnership. Dunleavy and Rhodes (1986: 125) have argued that central government's dependence upon local authorities for the delivery of such key services as education and housing meant that 'they trod carefully' around the issue of local government autonomy, relying more on partnership and consultation than on the full exercise of the instruments of control available to them. The partnership between central government and local education authorities was part of the post-war settlement. Thus when the Labour Government of the mid-1960s decided to press ahead with its controversial policy of introducing comprehensive education in secondary schools, it deliberately decided to rely on a policy instrument which emphasized local authority cooperation. It issued a departmental circular 'requesting' local education authorities to submit re-organization plans for their areas on comprehensive lines, rather than choosing the 'big stick' of legislation, which would have compelled those authorities to go comprehensive (Kogan 1971: 191; Dunleavy and Rhodes 1983: 123).

The local government spending which helped to fuel the post-war expansion of the welfare state reached its peak in 1976, when it accounted for nearly one-third of public expenditure. The period of expansion came to an end with the economic recession of the mid-1970s, brought about by the quadrupling of oil prices and double figure inflation. In 1976, the Labour Government was obliged to negotiate a loan from the International Monetary Fund, a condition of which was sharp cuts in public expenditure. An era of public expenditure growth was replaced by one of public expenditure restraint. In the oft-quoted words of Anthony Crosland, the then Cabinet Minister responsible for local government, 'the party' was over (see, for example, Crosland 1982: 295; Whitehead 1985: 150). A new phase of central–local relations had begun.

The central–local relationship during the period 1976–79 was dominated by the Labour Government's attempts to achieve reductions in local authority spending as part of its wider attempt to reduce public expenditure, through cuts in central government grant and the setting of annual targets for local authority spending. Apart from the controls on borrowing, however, the financial instruments used by central government were 'ones of influence rather than control' (Elcock et al. 1989: 28): the mechanisms of central government intervention were based on 'consultation and persuasion rather than coercion' (Alexander 1982b: 104). Furthermore, the Labour Government of the late 1970s was only concerned with the total of local government expenditure and not with the spending of individual local authorities. Labour's approach involved the 'incorporation' of the local authority associations (who represented the individual local authorities in negotiations with central government) into the policymaking process, with the Government trying to persuade them of the harsh realities of the economic situation (Rhodes 1992a: 53). The key forum for this particular approach was the Consultative Council on Local Government Finance, which brought together the Treasury and representatives of the local authority associations to discuss local government expenditure, and was what one observer has described as an institutionalized means of reaching 'gentlemen's agreements' on local government spending (Glennerster 1992a: 76). Such agreements were generally successful, with the eventual out-turn of local government spending in each of the years 1976–79 being within 2 per cent of the targets set by central government.

Reviewing the nature of the central–local relationship in the post-war years up to 1979, John (1991: 59) concludes that it was a model of central–local relations where (although the centre had a wide range of controls available to it) central government 'tended to be concerned with setting the broad lines of policy, its implementation being left in local hands'. Although responsible for the implementation of centrally determined policies, local authorities had a certain amount of discretion in the way they did this. This relationship was to undergo a dramatic change with the election of the Conservative Thatcher Government in 1979.

Central–local relations since 1979: trying to put the cap on spending by the local welfare state

The partnership between central government and local authorities from 1945 to 1979 was part of a wider consensus which underpinned British politics during the post-war period. As long as the assumptions underpinning the post-war welfare state remained unquestioned, issues about the central–local relationship were of 'peripheral importance' (Loughlin 1986: 3). But 1979 saw the election of a Conservative Government opposed to the traditional consensus of the post-war years. It was committed to the reduction of public expenditure, a policy which was seen as central to its goal of cutting public borrowing. As Travers (1986: 80) has pointed out, given that the new Government had promised in its election campaign to increase defence spending and protect spending on social security and the NHS, its commitment to reducing public spending was, in effect, a commitment to cut spending on those services which were mainly delivered by local government. The Thatcher Government's commitment to rolling back the state and encouraging the values of independence and self-reliance also clearly had implications for the welfare state role of local authorities. As a result, local government was elevated from the level of 'low' politics to become a subject of relatively 'high' politics.

A major theme which ran through the developments of the 1980s was the search by successive Conservative Governments for more effective control over local government spending, as opposed to the attempts to influence local government spending associated with the more consensus based approach before 1979 (see, for example, Rhodes 1992a: 51). In addition to its commitment to reduce local authority spending as part of its wider goal of reducing public expenditure, the Government's concern with local government spending reflected more specific right-wing criticisms of local authorities, Ministers claiming that local government was 'wasteful, profligate, irresponsible, unaccountable, luxurious and out of control' (Newton and Karran 1985: 116).

Since central government had no direct means of controlling local government spending (having to rely upon the influences of exhortation and cuts in central government grant; Travers 1986: 81) successive Conservative Governments since 1979 have attempted to remedy this omission by introducing a series of measures designed to strengthen central government controls over local government spending. As we shall see, the Conservative Government came to see central government grants (which had been such an important factor in the expansion of local government services in the late 1960s and early 1970s) as a form of control.

Attempts to control the level of local government spending began with the reform of the complicated system of RSG, once described by one local government Minister as 'Byzantine in its compexity' and 'probably fully comprehended by those who have a taste for scholastic theology' (House of Commons Debates, 16 January 1985: col. 413). The old system of RSG, in which the distribution of central government grant was determined by the past spending patterns of local authorities, was replaced by a system of block grant. Under the new system, the distribution of grant was determined by the Government, a local authority's grant being reduced if its spending rose above the level that the Government considered was required to meet a standard level service.

Despite the introduction of this new system, local government spending continued to rise in real terms, many local authorities circumventing cuts in grant by raising extra revenue through the local property tax, the rates. When further measures (the introduction of a complicated system of targets, with penalties in the form of loss of grant if they were exceeded, and the abolition of the power to levy supplementary rates) failed to curtail local spending, the Conservative Government turned its attention to restricting the sources of local government revenue. In 1985, the introduction of 'rate capping', with the Government being given the power to fix an upper limit to the rates levied by high-spending local authorities, removed the means to maintain service levels through increases in local taxation. But despite this plethora of legislation, the Government still found themselves, in the words of Stoker (1988: 170), 'constrained by their lack of direct control over local government'. Many local authorities evaded the new controls by the use of such devices as creative accounting to offset their loss of income.

The next stage in what has been described as the 'knee-capping' of local government (Newton and Karran 1985: 114) was the abolition of the rating system and its replacement in 1990 by the community charge (popularly known as the 'poll tax') a flat-rate charge payable by all adults over the age of 18 years. Like the rates it replaced, the community charge could be 'capped' by central government. In addition, RSG was simplified and renamed Revenue Support Grant, which was to be allocated on the basis of central government's assessment of the necessary level of spending, while non-domestic rates were set and collected centrally and then redistributed to local authorities.

A major strand in this new reform package was the perceived need to strengthen local accountability, which was (as we shall see later) to become a central theme in the developments which followed the Conservative's 1987 General Election victory. The Government argued that if local electors were aware of the costs of local authority services, they would then penalize high-spending councils at local elections. But for its critics, the real task of the community charge was to contain local government spending, the view of one of the local authority associations being that the measures revealed 'only too clearly that the Government's long-term aim is to use the poll tax to force councils into providing the barest minimal services for use only by those who can't afford to buy them in the market place' (Association of Metropolitan Authorities 1987).

Observers have described the legislation which introduced the controversial community charge as one of a succession of Acts of Parliament in the late 1980s which marked 'the most decisive break in British social policy' since the Labour Government of the early post-war years (Glennerster et al. 1991: 389). (We shall discuss the other legislation later.) For those on the New Right, this new form of local government taxation was seen as an important element in what has been described as a system of local government conforming to 'the Neo-Conservative dream', in which there was no reason why local government services should be provided by the public sector at all. According to this vision of local government, most of the major social services provided by local authorities could be hived off to the private sector or voluntary organizations. The community charge was seen as an important element in such a system, as it was viewed as a way of discouraging local government spending and thus encouraging local authorities to privatize services and to surrender functions (Glennerster *et al.* 1991: 390–1, 408).

The Conservative Government, now headed by John Major, decided to abandon the controversial community charge soon after Margaret Thatcher's resignation as Prime Minister in 1990. The charge was replaced by a council tax in 1993. Labelled the 'son of poll tax' by Glennerster (1992a: 86), the new tax is based on property values, but, like its predecessor, takes into account the number of adults in each household. One result of the new system is that local government has an even narrower tax base than before (central government now controls some 85 per cent of local authority income, including non-domestic rates) and the capping powers of central government have been strengthened. This combination of controls has been seen as giving central government 'almost unlimited powers' to dictate both the level of spending of local authorities and the level of local taxation (see Midwinter and Monaghan 1993: 132).

The changing role of local education authorities

The first two terms of the Thatcher Government, 1979–87, focused on attempts to control the spending of the local government welfare state. But following the Conservative's third successive victory in the 1987 General Election, the Government's programme for local government entered a much more radical phase. As Rhodes (1992b: 213) has observed, the Conservative's 'narrow fixation' on local government spending was replaced by a market-oriented strategy intended to return control of local authority services to their users. Described by some observers as 'revolutionary' (see, for example, Audit Commission 1988a: 1) and by others as inaugurating a 'new era for social policy' (Glennerster *et al.* 1991), the post-1987 programme involved fundamental changes in the arrangements for the delivery of all three social services traditionally provided by local authorities.

A significant part of this new approach to the delivery of welfare was a piece of legislation intended to transform the local government education system. Described as creating 'the most radical recasting of the government of education' since the Education Act 1944 (Ranson 1992a: 10), the Education Reform Act 1988 introduced a series of changes which have substantially diminished the traditional role of local education authorities. As a result of the Act, local education authorities were obliged to share their powers with three other groups – upwards with the Secretary of State for Education, downwards with individual schools, colleges and their governors, and outwards with parents and other groups in the community (Audit Commission 1989: 2–3).

The 1988 Act was the culmination of a long period of debate about local authority education. As we saw in Chapter 1, the local education service had been seen by critics on the New Right as having been 'captured' by the 'producers'. Typical were the views of the Hillgate Group, who argued: 'Like every monopolized industry, the educational system has begun to ignore the demands of the consumers – parents and children – and to respond instead to the requirements of the producers – LEAs and teachers' (Hillgate Group 1986: 3). This view of the delivery of local education was echoed in 1987 by the Secretary of State for Education, Kenneth Baker, who believed that 'education was too serious a business to leave to the professional educationalists' (see Jenkins 1987: 268). The panacea for the perceived ills of the local education system was seen as increased consumer accountability. As Ranson (1990: 189, 195) put it, parents were to be 'brought centre stage in the establishment of an education market place'.

The notion of market accountability is at the heart of the 1988 Act, described by one observer as a piece of legislation intended to produce a consumer-oriented education system 'driven by the twin engines of choice and competition' (Wilcox 1989: 31). Thus the Act permitted schools to opt out of local authority control, following a ballot of parents, and be financed directly by the DFE as grant maintained schools. It also permitted the establishment of City Technology Colleges (CTCs), specializing in science and technology and funded directly by central government and private industry. Parental choice and the promotion of competition for pupils were also to be increased by the introduction of open enrolment, which removed the right of local education authorities to set limits on the number of pupils enrolling at particular schools.

In addition to increasing parental choice, the 1988 Act also pushed power downwards to schools, giving them the freedom to manage their own budgets, which were delegated to boards of governors through the new system of 'local management of schools' (LMS). The powers of the Secretary of State were also strengthened, notably over the establishment of the national curriculum. The Act also removed local education authority responsibility for higher education, giving the (then) polytechnics and colleges of education self-governing cor-porate status with direct funding from the Polytechnics and Colleges Funding Council (later replaced by the Higher Education Funding Councils).

Although the 1988 Act was seen as consigning the local education auth-ority to 'a distinctly subordinate role' in the implementation of educational policy (Whitty 1990: 315), it still left it with potentially an important role to play in strategic planning and quality assurance (Ranson 1992a: 32). In the event, the functions of local education authorities have been further dimin-ished. Following the Further and Higher Education Act 1992, local education authorities lost their responsibility for further education colleges, tertiary col-leges and sixth-form colleges, which were given independent status as corporations financed directly by the Further Education Funding Council. What has been seen by some as the 'final nail in the local education authority's coffin as a provider of local education services' (Wilson *et al.* 1994: 90), however, was the Education Act 1993. In an attempt to increase the number of grant maintained schools (less than 300 of the 25 000 local authority schools had opted out by the end of 1992) the 1993 Act streamlined the procedures for grant maintained status. Opting-out was also encouraged by the introduction of the Technology Colleges scheme (restricted to grant maintained and voluntary aided schools), involving additional government funding for schools which emphasize science, technology and mathematics and which develop a close relationship with business sponsors. The 1993 Act also requires the governing bodies of all local education authority schools to consider a ballot on grant maintained status each year. It also introduced additional limitations to prevent local education authorities from influencing the outcome of ballots.

Local government control of the education service was also reduced by the creation of a new quasi-governmental body, the Funding Agency for Schools (FAS), which has taken over responsibility for the funding of grant maintained schools, as well as the monitoring of their expenditure and wider planning responsibilities. Once 10 per cent of school pupils in a local education authority area are in grant maintained schools, the authority has to share its duty for providing sufficient school places with the FAS. The local education authority ceases to have responsibility for securing sufficient places once this figure reaches 75 per cent, when the duty passes to the FAS. A similar funding authority has been introduced for Wales.

The 1993 Act's abolition of the requirement for local education authorities to establish education committees was a further indication of the Government's intention to dismantle local government control of education. Symbolically, the 1993 Act removed the reference in the Education Act 1944 to national policy for providing an educational service being secured by local authorities under the control and direction of the Minister, thereby removing the local education authority from its central position in the delivery of local education (Ranson and Travers 1994: 227). To quote one observer, local education authorities are 'to be diminished to a service agency role' (Ranson 1992b: 140).

The decline of local authority housing

The themes of choice and competition which have been such an important feature of the development of the Conservative Government's education reforms since 1987 can also be found in its approach to local authority housing. A number of radical changes have taken place which affect the traditional role of local housing authorities as providers of social housing.

As we shall discuss in greater detail in Chapter 7, the centrepiece of the Government's housing policy in the early 1980s was the 'right to buy', with the Housing Act 1980 providing certain council house tenants with the statutory right to purchase their properties at substantial discounts of the market value. As with the education reforms of the late 1980s, for the New Right, the 1980 Act represented an escape from the bureaucracy and paternalism of local government, council house sales being compared by the Conservative Party to the 'freeing' of 'feudal tenants' who were 'subjugated to the patronage and paternalism of local political barons' (Bassett 1980: 291). The introduction of the 'right to buy' signalled an important change in the relationship between central government and local authorities. As Forrest and Murie (1991: 200) have put it, the policy eroded what had been 'one of the most significant and visible' of local government activities, and was seen as not only a threat to locally determined housing policies, but also as an undermining of local democracy. About 1.2 million council houses were sold under the 'right to buy' between 1980 and 1990, equivalent to some 20 per cent of the 1979 local authority housing stock.

The Conservative Government's attempts to break up the near monopoly position of local authorities in the field of social housing were continued with the Housing Act 1988. The Minister for Housing stated in 1987: 'The next great push after the right to buy should be to get rid of the State as a big landlord and bring housing back to the community' (Waldegrave 1987). This 'great push' was to involve the run down of local authorities as major providers of housing and the development of housing associations, who would become what one commentator has called 'the new main engine' of social housing (Spencer 1989: 95). This approach reflected increasing criticism of the role of local housing authorities. There was a growing feeling (not restricted to those on the right of the political spectrum) that there were problems with both the scale and management of council housing. In 1986 the Audit Commission referred to a 'crisis' in local authority housing (Audit Commission 1986b). One academic study depicted local housing departments as 'unwieldy, bureaucratic structures remote from tenants' (Power 1987: 1), a description echoed in 1987 by the Secretary of State for the Environment, who referred to insensitive allocation procedures and management arrangements which were often cumbersome, remote and inflexible (House of Commons Debates, 30 November 1987: col. 620). Another housing Minister later argued that the 'basic conditions for customer satisfaction' simply did not exist in the local authority housing service: 'People became council tenants not on the whole by choice but because there is practically nowhere else to go. Escape is only possible if their financial circumstances change' (Trippier 1989). As one observer later concluded, all this criticism amounted to 'an assault on the confidence and credibility of local authorities as housing providers' (Malpass 1992: 15).

It is the intention of the Conservative Government to encourage local housing authorities to move away from their traditional role as direct providers of housing and to see their role as being essentially a strategic one, identifying housing needs and demands (Department of the Environment 1987: para. 5.1). In future, local authorities are expected to see themselves as enablers who will ensure that people in their area are adequately housed. As part of this process, the 1988 Act introduced the so-called 'tenants' choice', under which council tenants could ballot on whether they wish to be transferred from local authority control to an alternative landlord (who has to be approved by the Housing Corporation) in the housing association or private sector. Tenants were also given the right to own and run their own estates as tenant cooperatives. The Conservative Government clearly sees housing associations as the main vehicle for social housing in the 1990s, either as builders of new rented housing or as alternative landlords for dissatisfied council tenants through 'tenants' choice'.

Another mechanism introduced by the 1988 legislation to 'rescue' council tenants from incompetent local housing authorities was that of Housing Action Trusts (HATs) (Karn 1993: 75). Central government gave itself powers to set up HATs, modelled on the urban development corporations set up to regenerate certain inner city areas, to take over selected local authority estates and to renovate the housing stock before handing it over to private landlords.

Although (as we shall see in Chapter 7) 'tenants' choice' and HATs have not had the impact hoped for by the Government, the importance of developments in local authority housing since the late 1980s cannot be ignored. As Malpass and Murie (1990: 131–2) put it, the Government's preference for housing associations as providers of social housing and the promotion of an 'enabling' role for local authorities 'marks a final phase in the breakdown of central government's use of local authorities as the major instruments of housing policy'. In the opinion of another observer, eventually the local housing authority could be reduced to the role of 'a residuary welfare housing agency', being left to deal with the most difficult problems that other housing providers fail to resolve (Spencer 1989: 96).

Community care: the contract culture

In his analysis of post-1987 developments in local government, Stoker has argued that the reforms in education and housing are characterized by an 'ideological coherence' (Stoker 1988: 245). The emphasis on competition and consumer choice reflects the thinking of public choice theorists, who (as we saw in Chapter 1) have been highly critical of public bureaucracies and have emphasized the need to achieve greater consumer choice by the breaking up of existing public bureaucracies. The dismantling of local authority monopoly control of state schools and council estates, and the creation of 'exit' options for the consumers of these services, is intended to create greater choice. Whether this will actually be available to all the consumers and potential consumers of these services is another matter.

The theme that local authorities should no longer perform the role of direct providers of services has also been applied to the third major local authority social service, the personal social services. The personal social services have long been characterized by a 'mixed economy of welfare' (in which substantial contributions to the delivery of welfare have been made by the voluntary and private sectors) and the Conservative Government since 1979 has emphasized the desirability of local authority social services departments making the fullest possible use of the non-statutory sectors in the delivery of social care.

Following increasing criticisms about the delivery of community care policies, including concern about the fragmentation of responsibilities between local authorities and health authorities (see Chapter 4), the Griffiths Report of 1988 made a number of proposals for radical change. Griffiths recommended that local authorities should no longer be monopolistic providers of community care services, but should ensure that services are provided within the appropriate budgets by the public or private sector, according to where they can be most economically and efficiently provided (Griffiths 1988a: vii). As one group of commentators was to put it some years later, Griffiths was 'looking back to the traditional emphasis on stimulating community resources' and looking 'forward to the new world of purchasing and provision in which the private sector would be encouraged to compete alongside statutory and not-for-profit agencies' (Wistow et al. 1992: 27). This latter emphasis upon the purchasing role of local authorities was central to the Government's response to Griffiths (Department of Health 1989b: para. 3.1.3), which said that local authority social services departments would be responsible for securing the delivery of services 'not simply by acting as direct providers but by developing their purchasing and contracting role to become "enabling authorities"'.

Accordingly, as a result of the National Health Service and Community Care Act 1990, since April 1993 local authorities have been expected to see themselves as purchasers rather than providers of community care services. Local authority social services departments have the duty to assess the community care needs of any individual they believe requires such care and to decide what services that individual needs. Local authorities can then either provide the services themselves through 'self-managed' units, invite tenders from private and voluntary bodies, stimulate the establishment of not-for-profit agencies or encourage new voluntary sector activity (Department of Health 1991a: para. 2.1.4).

The community care reforms, together with those which have been introduced in housing and education, have questioned the traditional assumption that local authorities should both finance and provide services. The result has been the separation of the purchaser and provider roles and the development of what have been labelled 'quasi-markets' (see Chapter 7).

Losing a welfare empire, finding a role: from providing to enabling

It has been argued that the Conservative Government's post-1987 programme for local government goes beyond the changes of the 1979–87 period because of 'the breadth and common themes of the restructuring it proposes', including a commitment to competition, an increased emphasis on consumer choice, the separation of the responsibility for a service from its actual provision, and an emphasis on new forms of accountability (Stewart and Stoker 1989: 2–4). All of these themes have underpinned changes in the delivery of welfare since the late 1980s.

One concept which helps to draw together all these developments is that of 'enabling'. Indeed, it has been suggested that if the Conservative Government has a vision for local government in the 1990s, then it is that of the 'enabling authority' (Leach 1992: 5), while other observers have described the enabling role as 'the new orthodoxy' (Hollis et al. 1992: 28). The concept of enabling was first made fashionable in the late 1980s by the (then) Secretary of State for the Environment, Nicholas Ridley, who argued that local authorities should be concerned with 'enabling not providing'. In Ridley's opinion, the role of local authorities should be reduced from that of universal, front-line providers of such major services as housing and personal social services to that of minimalist, enabling authorities. According to this view of local government, there should be a much more pluralistic system of local service provision, with a variety of public, private and voluntary agencies working alongside local authorities. Although local authorities would no longer be the universal providers of services, they should continue to have a key role in ensuring that there was adequate provision to meet needs (Ridley 1988a: 16–17, 25).

The concept of the enabling authority is at the centre of the Conservative Government's thinking in its review of local government in the early 1990s (see Chapter 3). Thus it has stated that the role of local authorities in the provision of services should be to assess the needs of their area, plan the provision of services and ensure their delivery (Department of the Environment 1991b: para. 4). The Government's dissatisfaction with the historical role of local authorities as the direct providers of services was also emphasized in its Citizen's Charter (Prime Minister 1991: 34), which argued that the Government believed that it was now time for a new approach to the delivery of local services. What it described as 'the real task' for local authorities lay in concentrating on 'strategic responsibilities', i.e. setting priorities, determining the standards of service and finding the best ways of meeting them. This is the role envisaged for local authorities in the Government's housing reforms of the late 1980s, with the 1987 White Paper on housing (which preceded the Housing Act 1988) maintaining that, rather than acting as local landlords, local authorities should 'increasingly see themselves as enablers who ensure that everyone in their area is adequately housed; but not necessarily by them' (Department of the Environment 1987: para. 1.16). The approach was later elaborated in a departmental circular in 1989:

> Local authorities are ceasing to be the main providers of subsidized housing for rent; but they will remain responsible for ensuring, as far as resources permit, the needs for new housing in their areas are met, by the private sector alone where possible, with public sector subsidy where necessary. This will require some of them to take a broader view of their

responsibilities than they have in the past, and to develop their information sources and monitoring arrangements accordingly.

(Department of the Environment 1989: 1–2)

According to this approach, local authorities should facilitate the efforts
of housebuilders, housing associations and private landlords to deal with local
housing needs. Various ways in which local authorities can undertake this new
enabling role were identified by the Cabinet Minister responsible for the 1988
legislation and included: the use of planning powers; assessing housing needs
and conditions; offering improvement grants; the provision of assistance to
schemes for private renting; sponsoring housing association schemes; cooperat-
ing with housing associations over their allocation of tenancies; and working
with housing associations to make sure that housing is available for vulnerable
groups (Ridley 1988b).

The Government also envisaged an enabling role for local education
authorities following the Education Reform Act 1988, with local authorities
becoming promoters of education policies rather than providers of education
services (John 1990: 34, 37). In its discussion of the 1988 Act, the Audit
Commission argued that although local education authorities might have lost
their 'empires', they still had an important role to play (1989: 2). Despite their
loss of powers to grant maintained schools in some areas of the country, they
still retained important responsibilities in the areas of finance and resources, the
curriculum, planning and provision, quality assurance, information and training. Other observers have argued that the development of new relationships
with individual grant maintained schools, further education colleges and TECs
can be seen as a shift to an enabling role in which local education authorities
take on the kind of functions highlighted by the Audit Commission (Hollis *et
al.* 1992: 85–8).

As we saw in the last section, the post-Griffiths developments in community care were also intended to give local authorities more of an enabling,
and less of a providing, role. Local authority social services departments were to
become responsible for assessing local care needs, purchasing that care from
either the social services department itself or the private or voluntary sectors,
and monitoring performance.

Thus the enabling concept is a feature of developments in all three local
authority social services. To paraphrase the Audit Commission (1989), local
authorities may have lost a welfare empire, but have they found a new role to
perform (that of enabling) in the aftermath of these changes?

The answer to this question is a mixed one. The development of the
enabling concept in the fields of housing and education is seen by some
observers as problematic. Thus, although it has been suggested that local housing authorities could become 'leaders not obstructors of change' (Glennerster *et
al.* 1991: 403), the enabling function in housing has been described as 'ill-
defined' (Cole 1993: 150). The shift from the traditional delivery role to one of
enabling seems to be proving difficult for some local housing authorities and

other authorities are uncertain about what the enabling concept actually means (Hollis *et al.* 1992: 64). The Government has also been criticized for giving local authorities neither the extra powers nor the resources to carry out the enabling role envisaged in social housing. In the words of Clapham (1989: 9), 'there is little to encourage or persuade them to do so. It is difficult to escape the conclusion that the Government regards this role as a voluntary one'. It has also been suggested that the changes introduced by the Education Act 1993 mean the end of any enabling role being played by local authority education authorities (Jones and Stewart 1992, 17).

It is in the third major local authority social service, the personal social services, that the enabling role seems to be clearest, with the local social services department acting as the lead authority in its relations with other organizations (see, for example, John 1991: 71). But the community care reforms are a model of enabling which has been described as 'market development', with an emphasis on contracts and the creation of markets rather than a model of enabling which mobilizes community-based resources and allows local authorities to shape those resources (Wistow *et al.* 1992: 39).

Given the different ways in which the enabling concept has been used in the delivery of local services, one observer (John 1990: 64) has concluded that the concept is:

> more a rationale for reducing the powers and functions of local author-
> ities and handing them to other bodies than a new philosophy of service
> provision. The policy comes more from the idea of creating markets in
> local government than from the idea of an 'enabling' council.

We turn to a discussion of the role of markets in the delivery of welfare in Chapter 7.

7

The privatization of welfare delivery

One major, and controversial, policy response to the problems perceived to be associated with traditional approaches to the provision of services by the delivery agencies of the welfare state, has been privatization. The privatization of welfare delivery has been one of the major strategies employed by the Conservative Government since 1979 in its attempts to restructure the arrangements for the delivery of social services.

Associated with the views of the New Right, privatization is a policy which, in the words of Hambleton and Hoggett (1988: 14), sets out to challenge the very idea of collective and non-market provision for social need. As we shall see, the privatization of welfare delivery is a strategy which covers a number of different approaches, ranging from the selling of the assets of welfare delivery agencies to the application of market principles and practices to their operations.

Privatization is a concept beset with definitional uncertainties. As Donnison (1984: 45) has observed, it is a word which should be 'heavily escorted by inverted commas as a reminder that its meaning is at best uncertain and often tendentious'. For Donnison (1984: 45), 'privatization' is:

> a word invented by politicians and disseminated by political journalists. It is designed not to clarify analysis but as a symbol, intended by advocates and opponents of the processes it describes to dramatise a conflict and mobilise support for their own side.

The confusion about the meaning of, and the use to which politicians have put, the concept of privatization is well illustrated by the debate during the 1992 General Election campaign over the setting up of self-governing hospitals (the so-called 'opting out' of the NHS) as part of the Conservative Government's NHS reforms (see Chapter 8). Opponents of this initiative charged the Government with plotting the dismemberment of the NHS, with Labour Party critics describing the measures as 'privatization' (see, for example, the 1992 Labour Party Manifesto, Labour Party 1992: 15), and with preparing NHS hospitals for sale to the private sector (see *The Times*, 28 January 1989). Not surprisingly, given the continuing high levels of public support for the principles of a comprehensive, universal and tax-funded NHS, Conservative Government Ministers were quick to defend the establishment of self-governing hospitals on the grounds that such hospitals, while being given a degree of independence, remained, and would remain, an integral part of the NHS (see, for example, the comments of William Waldegrave, the then Secretary of State for Health, on LWT's *Walden Interview*, 20 October 1991).

We consider these problems of definition below. Having provided a brief overview of the subject, we then examine in more detail some of the main forms that the privatization of welfare delivery has taken since 1979.

Approaches to the privatization of welfare delivery

One definition of privatization is that suggested by Young (1986: 236), who defines it as:

> a set of policies which aim to limit the role of the public sector, and increase the role of the private sector, while improving the performance of the remaining public sector.

A similar approach is taken by Ascher (1987: 4), who views privatization as an umbrella term used to describe 'a multitude of government initiatives designed to increase the role of the private sector'.

Privatization takes a number of forms. Young (1986) identifies seven distinct forms of the process, including the selling of public sector assets and the contracting out of services to the private sector. The privatization of welfare delivery has included both these forms, as well as the encouragement of welfare provision by the private sector as an alternative to public sector provision, and the application of market principles to the operations of delivery agencies. Also, as we shall see on p. 118, a major strand of the Government's policy on the privatization of welfare delivery has involved developing the role of the voluntary sector. Thus privatization 'involves much wider and deeper changes than is usually appreciated' (Young 1986: 238).

The privatization of welfare delivery is not new. Local authorities and health authorities have long contracted out services to the private sector, while local authority social services departments have also made use of voluntary organizations in the delivery of certain services. However, although the idea may not be new, the context of the concept of privatization in welfare delivery has changed dramatically since the election of the first Thatcher Government in 1979.

Selling the welfare state: the case of council house sales

One form of privatization has involved the sale of the assets of welfare delivery agencies to the private sector. Although sales since the early 1980s have included the disposal of local authority residential homes, the major example of this particular kind of privatization has been the sale of council houses, a policy described by Forrest and Murie (1991: 1) as 'the most important element in the privatisation programme of the Thatcher governments' in social, political and economic terms.

Privatization was a dominant theme in the Conservative Government's approach to council housing during the 1980s. Indeed, as Malpass and Murie (1990: 22) observe, the Government's whole housing strategy during this particular decade was based on the assumption that council housing was 'both unnecessary and unsuccessful', and that it was possible to develop a housing system which is almost entirely located in the private sector. Central to this strategy has been the sale of council housing to sitting tenants through the 'right to buy' policy.

In 1979, council housing made up just over 31 per cent of the total housing stock in Britain, far in excess of the 14 per cent accounted for by the privately rented and housing association sectors. It is possible to identify two waves of policymaking on council housing since the election of the first Thatcher Government in 1979 (Hills and Mullings 1991: 140–2). The first wave was represented by the Housing Act 1980, which gave local authority tenants the statutory right to buy their homes at attractive discounts of the market value – up to a maximum of 50 per cent (later increased to a maximum of 60 per cent on houses and a maximum of 70 per cent on flats) – together with a guaranteed mortgage from the local authority. The scheme was extended even further in 1993 with the introduction of a 'rent to mortgage' scheme, allowing tenants to purchase their homes for the same cost as their council rent. The 'right to buy' policy has been extremely popular (the programme has been described by one writer as 'the sale of the century'; Stoker 1988: 176) with some 1.2 million properties being sold between 1980 and 1990.

But by the late 1980s it became clear that this particular approach to the privatization of local authority housing was in decline, with council house sales in England and Wales having peaked at just over 200 000 properties in 1982. The residualization of council housing once better-off tenants had purchased their homes reduced the number of potential purchasers, and the Government had to develop other initiatives in its attempt to demunicipalize local authority housing. The Government's solution was contained in a second wave of policymaking, the major component of which was the Housing Act 1988, which extended the privatization policy to involve the sale of local authority houses not only to sitting tenants through the 'right to buy', but also to alternative landlords. The 1988 Act gave approved private landlords and housing associations the right to purchase blocks of council housing or even whole council estates, provided that such sales were preceded by successful ballots of the tenants concerned, a policy described by the Government as 'tenants' choice'. The initiative for the transfer of ownership through 'tenants' choice' could come from either the tenants themselves or prospective alternative land-lords, irrespective of whether or not the local authority wished to participate in such transfers. In the event, very few transfers of housing stock have taken place as a result of 'tenant's choice'. Neither alternative landlords nor local authority tenants have demonstrated much interest in this particular type of transfer of ownership, although it has been suggested that the initiative might have more effect once the property market recovers from the recession of the early 1990s (Malpass and Means 1993: 187–8).

The Housing Act 1988 also gave the Government powers to introduce Housing Action Trusts (HATs), which, following a ballot of the tenants in-volved, would take over large, run-down council estates and transfer them to private or voluntary sector landlords after necessary repairs and improvements had been carried out. Eighteen local authority estates were originally desig-nated by the DoE for HAT status, but, following a marked lack of support from tenants, none of the schemes were actually established. According to one observer of this initiative, a combination of the confrontational way in which the new policy was presented by the Government, the fear of privatization and the loss of democratic accountability made HATs unacceptable to both local authorities and tenants' associations (Karn 1993: 76). Subsequently, the original concept of HATs was 'redesigned' and, by the summer of 1994, six local authorities (Hull, Waltham Forest, Liverpool, Birmingham, Tower Hamlets and Brent) had set up 'voluntary' HATs on estates in their areas. The terms of these new model HATs are very different from those originally laid down, the tenants involved having the right to choose to return to local authority control after their estates have been improved (Baker 1993: 41).

Despite the limited impact of 'tenants' choice' and the HAT initiative, they have had important consequences for the organization of housing delivery by local authorities. According to one observer, the threat of potential compe-tition has 'galvanized' many local housing authorities into developing more efficient and responsive services (Bramley 1993: 159). As a result, housing management in many local authorities has been 'reformed from within' (Cole and Furbey 1994: 217), key features of such reforms being the decentralization of the housing service and the development of more customer-oriented approaches (see Chapter 9).

A far greater contribution to the privatization of local authority housing than either of the two policy instruments introduced by the Housing Act 1988 has been the large-scale voluntary transfer of housing by many local authorities. Large-scale voluntary transfers were originally undertaken as a means of coun-tering the perceived threat of 'tenants' choice', and have subsequently been stimulated by Government restrictions on local housing authorities (Mullins *et al.* 1993: 171). A large number of local authorities have transferred (after a successful ballot of tenants) all, or nearly all, their housing stock to housing associations. Most of these associations were specifically formed by the local authorities concerned and are known as 'local community housing associations'. The high point of voluntary transfers came in 1992, when the London Borough of Bromley transferred 12 000 homes to the newly formed Broomleigh Housing Association. By the end of the first phase of transfers in the summer of 1993, a total of some 120 000 properties had been transferred by 23 local authorities. Following Treasury concern about the increased housing benefit costs involved, the DoE introduced a rationing system in 1993, under which only a certain number of properties can be transferred each year. In the event, the costs to the Treasury were lower than anticipated, and permission was granted for some 40 000 other dwellings to be transferred in the 1993–94 programme (Audit Commission 1993). Large-scale voluntary transfers represent a significant contribution to the privatization of local authority housing: indeed, it has been suggested that the development of local community housing associations might mean the death of local authority housing 'by a self-administered suicide pill' rather than through the attempts to demunicipalize council housing associated with the 'right to buy' policy, 'tenants' choice' and HATs (Mullins *et al.* 1993: 182–3).

Contracting out welfare provision

Another important manifestation of the privatization of welfare delivery, especially in the NHS, is contracting out: the purchase of services, which would otherwise have been provided by in-house staff, from private contractors (Ascher 1987: 7–8). This form of privatization has operated for many years in the delivery of social services. Thus some NHS hospitals have long contracted out their cleaning and catering services, whilst many local authority personal social services (such as meals on wheels) have long been supplied by voluntary organizations. In 1978–79, over 11 per cent of local government spending on the personal social services was contracted out, the bulk of it on residential care (Judge 1982: 399). Contracting out has grown in importance since the early 1980s and is not only closely linked with the Conservative Government's search for efficiency in the public sector (see Chapter 8), but also with another central principle of Conservative policy, i.e. encouraging the expansion of the private sector (Key 1988: 65).

Contracting out has been an important feature of attempts to improve the efficiency and cost-effectiveness of the NHS. Early attempts by the first Thatcher Government to persuade health authorities to introduce this form of privatization in the hospital ancillary services were unsuccessful, and the Government resorted to compulsory competitive tendering (CCT). In 1983 a DHSS circular instructed health authorities to put the three hospital ancillary services of cleaning, laundry and catering (the so-called 'hotel services') out to competitive tender. In the event, however, CCT has had only limited success in transferring these services to the private sector, as the majority of contracts have been won by in-house tenders. Thus, by the end of 1991, only 14 per cent of contracts in the three ancillary services had been awarded to private companies (H.M. Treasury 1991: 15).

The financial savings produced by competitive tendering in the NHS are difficult to quantify. Writing in 1988, Key (1988: 79) concluded that there were indications that the ultimate savings varied not only between different health authorities, but also between different services, estimating that the total savings might amount to no more than 10 per cent of NHS domestic spending. More recent official figures, however, state that savings have been substantial: the cost of cleaning and other domestic services fell by 29 per cent in real terms between 1984–85 and 1989–90 (H.M. Treasury 1991: 14).

Contracting out has not progressed nearly as fast in the social services delivered by local authorities. While the Local Government Act 1988 did introduce CCT for certain 'defined areas' of local government, the areas included are mainly technical and ancillary services outside the mainstream social services. The list does, however, include catering for schools and the personal social services, as well as the cleaning of buildings, and local authority education departments are usually the main clients for both these types of services (Council of Europe 1993: 68). Despite the limitations of the 1988 Act, some local authorities, including what Stoker (1991: 42) has labelled the 'urban ideologues', have taken much more radical initiatives in the contracting out of social services. Thus the London Borough of Wandsworth, for example, has contracted out residential care for its old people.

In the early 1990s, the Conservative Government stated that local authorities 'should be looking to contract out work to whoever can deliver services most efficiently and effectively' (Department of the Environment 1991b: para. 4), an approach clearly linked with the enabling concept discussed in Chapter 6. The Local Government Act 1988 does give central government the power to add to the list of services subject to CCT, and the process of implementing CCT in the important area of housing management is to be phased in by local housing authorities from April 1996. As part of the Government's market-testing plans (see Chapter 8), the NHS has been asked to further exploit the opportunities for tendering support services (H.M. Treasury 1991: 17). Having seen the benefits of applying competitive tendering to the hospital 'hotel services', managers in many health authorities have already put other support services, including transport, out to tender (H.M. Treasury 1991: 15).

Whilst competitive tendering has undoubtedly led to efficiency savings within both the NHS and local government, it has been argued that its main significance has been to facilitate a new style of management in these key delivery agencies of the welfare state, encouraging the introduction of market mechanisms and disciplines (see, for example, Walsh 1989: 48–9; Flynn 1992: 162). As we saw earlier, similar conclusions have been made about the impact of attempts to privatize council housing on the management of local authority housing departments.

Efficiency savings and management improvements are, of course, only one side of the coin when attempting to evaluate the impact of this form of privatization. Critics of contracting out argue that it has major implications for the quality of services, and there have been many alleged cases of poor service delivery by outside contractors. It has been claimed, for example, that standards of ancillary services in hospitals have fallen as a result of contracting out, with private contractors failing to perform to the standards specified in contracts (see, for example, McGregor 1990). Almost 5 per cent of contractors have had their contracts terminated, one example involving Bromley DHA, which cancelled a contract with a private cleaning company following allegations of falling standards of hygiene (Baggott 1994: 150, 152). At the local government level, the London Borough of Wandsworth discharged the private contractor responsible for running old people's homes in its borough after discovering that the meal portions provided had been severely reduced in order to protect profit margins (Elcock 1993: 167). But, despite such cases, research has shown that few local authorities feel that overall standards have worsened (Walsh and Davis 1993: para. 15.3).

Observers have also pointed to the fact that contracting out has consequences for accountability, as it changes the pattern of control over welfare delivery. Under contracting out, the direct control which has traditionally been exercised over staff and levels of service within delivery agencies is replaced by a form of indirect control (Wood 1988: 127). Such a change has important implications for the redress of grievances in the services concerned, with complaints about service quality no longer being handled directly, but having to be referred to the contractors for their comments.

Despite these kinds of misgivings, however, advocates of privatization have argued that the process of contracting out in both the NHS and local government has not gone far enough. Thus the Adam Smith Institute has argued that the number of local authority services open to CCT should be increased to include such services as the provision of residential homes and day centres (see Mather 1989: 222), while the then general director of another right-wing pressure group, the Institute of Economic Affairs, has argued that contracting out need not be confined to support services, pointing out that many personal social services are already delivered by voluntary organizations acting on behalf of local authorities (Mather 1989: 223). As we saw in Chapter 6, as a result of the Government's community care reforms, local authority social services departments are expected to invite tenders from private and voluntary bodies.

Encouraging the private provision of welfare

Another form of privatization is government encouragement of the provision of welfare by the private sector. One part of the private sector which has been particularly encouraged since the Conservative Government came into office in 1979 is the private health sector. Part of the compromise between the Labour Government and the medical profession which underpinned the creation of the NHS in 1948 was that private practice and pay beds in NHS hospitals were allowed to exist alongside the public sector. The potential for private medicine has been increased by a number of initiatives since 1979. Higgins (1988: 84–9) has identified four such developments:

- the introduction of legislation in 1980 designed to reduce the restrictions on private medicine imposed by the previous Labour Government;
- the use of tax concessions to encourage the growth of private health insurance;
- changes in contracts enabling all NHS consultants to engage in private practice;
- government encouragement of greater collaboration between the NHS and the private health sector.

The effect of these developments has been to 'set in train a cumulative process which [has] altered the traditional balance between public and private medicine' (Higgins 1988: 84). The private health care sector underwent tremendous changes in the 1980s: the percentage of the UK population covered by private health insurance more than trebled between 1979 and 1989. There was also a rapid growth of private hospitals, the private sector's share of hospital-based health care in the UK doubling between 1984 and 1990 (Baggott 1994: 153, 156).

The Government's encouragement of the role of the private sector in the delivery of welfare has also included the arrangements for pensions and residential care for the elderly. Thus the social security reforms of 1986 provided generous incentives for those individuals taking out occupational pensions with private companies. This particular aspect of privatization has been described by Bradshaw (1992: 96) as 'a roaring success', it being estimated that there will eventually be six million private pensions in force, eight times the Government's original estimate. The 1980s also saw the expansion of the provision of private residential care, the number of private residential homes in Britain increasing by an average of just over 18 per cent each year between 1979 and 1986, a phenomenon described by one observer as constituting 'one of the growth industries' of the 1980s (Johnson 1990: 165). By 1990 the private sector had 45 per cent of the share of the places in residential homes compared with just under 14 per cent in 1970 (Baggott 1994: 223). In the meantime, the local authority share of the places in residential homes had declined from some 63 per cent to 42 per cent, the result, according to one commentator, of a combination of stick and carrot (Walker 1989: 207–8). The stick had involved reducing the financial resources available for personal social services to local authorities, whilst the carrot had involved the then DHSS agreeing to pay the full cost of care in private residential and nursing homes for those receiving supplementary benefit (later replaced by income support).

Another example of a policy designed to promote the role of the private sector in the area of welfare delivery since the early 1980s has been the increased public funding of private education. The Education Act 1902 which (as we saw in Chapter 3) introduced local authority control of education in England and Wales, launched a scheme whereby independent schools received a direct grant from central government in return for providing a number of

places (up to 25 per cent) for children nominated by local education authorities, an arrangement which had been abolished by the Labour Government in
1976. Under the Assisted Places Scheme introduced by the first Thatcher
Government in 1981, selected independent schools were allowed to offer
places to children at reduced fees related to the income of parents, the difference in the fee income being re-imbursed by central government. By 1994
the scheme offered nearly 34 000 places.

The marketization of welfare delivery: the introduction of quasi-markets

As Le Grand (1991: 1258) notes, the contracting out of ancillary services by
health authorities in the early 1980s, the payment of the cost of care for elderly
people in residential homes, and the introduction of the assisted places scheme
for independent schools were all early examples of attempts to move the state
away from its traditional role as both funder and provider of social services. The
introduction of what have become known as 'quasi-markets' into the delivery
of social services has continued with even more radical developments in the
core social services of housing, education, personal social services and the
NHS. In the words of Le Grand (1991: 1257):

> In each case, the intention is for the state to stop being both the funder
> *and* the provider of services. Instead it is to become primarily a funder,
> purchasing services from a variety of private, voluntary and public pro-
> viders, all operating in competition with one another.

What has been described as 'the big bang' occurred in the late 1980s (Le
Grand 1991: 1258). The 'tenants' choice' provisions of the Housing Act 1988
introduced a degree of competition within social housing by giving council
tenants the opportunity to opt out of local authority control and choose
alternative landlords, either from the private sector or from the housing association sector. The Education Reform Act of the same year allowed schools to
'opt out' of local education authority control and become grant maintained
schools. As well as being in competition with each other for pupils, grant
maintained schools are also in competition with the schools which remain
under the control of local education authorities. Market mechanisms were also
introduced within the local education authority sector with the introduction of
'open enrolment', under which local education authority schools are obliged to
admit pupils up to their standard numbers. The introduction of this provision
meant that local education authorities could not protect the less popular
schools in their authorities by restricting the entry to popular schools.

The introduction of competition is also a feature of the community care
reforms of the early 1990s. Thus local authority social services departments are
required to appoint care managers, with budgets, who are responsible for
constructing packages of care for individual clients, after considering bids from
competing service providers in the public, private and voluntary sectors.

Recent reforms in the organization of health-care delivery also involve the introduction of quasi-markets. Since April 1991, DHAs, fund-holding GPs (now those with more than 7000 patients) and private insurers have been able to purchase health care on behalf of their patients from DHA-managed hospitals, self-governing hospitals and hospitals in the private sector, who would be in competition for patients. We will discuss this particular package of reforms in more detail in Chapter 8.

All these developments are examples of what Le Grand (1991: 1259–60) terms 'quasi-markets'. They are 'markets' because the traditional monopolistic providers of the welfare state are replaced by competing providers. However, they are 'quasi' markets because they are different from ordinary markets: the competing suppliers of services (e.g. housing associations and grant maintained schools) are not necessarily privately owned nor concerned with the maximization of profits; and in areas such as community care and health care the consumers are represented in the market, not by themselves, but by agents (e.g. a care manager in a local authority social services department or a fund-holding GP). Such developments are also 'quasi' markets because the purchasing power of consumers under these new arrangements is not expressed in terms of cash, but in the form of an ear-marked sum which can only be used for the purchase of a particular service (e.g. the budgets of fund-holding GPs).

The introduction of quasi-markets into the delivery of welfare is defended on the grounds that such arrangements will promote not only a more economical use of resources, but also an expansion of consumer choice, as the users of social services will have alternative sources of supply. Despite such claims, however, many observers have expressed scepticism. Thus, Le Grand (1991: 1263–5) concludes that, far from reducing the cost of services, quasi-markets may actually lead to overall cost increases. Thus, it has been estimated that the annual costs of monitoring the new internal market system in the NHS could be as high as £500 million. There will also need to be a very large investment in the development of the infrastructure needed to operate the new system for delivering community care. As has been pointed out, improvements in efficiency resulting from quasi-markets will need to be balanced against the costs of setting up these new systems (Hudson 1992: 133, 137).

Doubts have also been raised about the impact of quasi-markets on consumer choice. Critics argue that the consumers of health care are not really empowered. Thus, in reality, consumers have little say over the kind of care they receive in the NHS: the purchasing agencies act as the patient's agent (see Ranade 1994: 71; Harrison and Pollitt 1994: 127). It has also been suggested that a quasi-market in the field of health care will result in worse access to services for certain groups (e.g. the poor and less educated) and that individuals most in need of a service (such as the chronically sick) might be excluded from access to that service on the grounds of their high cost (Le Grand 1990: 358). The securing of choice and equity is also seen as 'problematic' in the new arrangements for the delivery of community care, as the users of such services will have no 'market power' to reveal their preferences. As with the case of health-care reforms, there is also the danger of 'adverse selection' of the users of community care, with private residential homes possibly being reluctant to provide accommodation for difficult cases (Hudson 1992: 137).

In the light of such misgivings, one commentator has observed that 'it is difficult to avoid the conclusion that the benefits of a quasi-market in both health and social care have tended to be *asserted* rather than *demonstrated*' (Hudson 1992: 141). Certainly, there has been much debate about the benefits of the introduction of a quasi-market in health care since the new system was set up in 1991. The NHS Management Executive's review of the early stages of the NHS reforms indicated that more patients were being treated and waiting lists were falling as a result of the new system (NHS Management Executive 1991). Critics of the new arrangements, however, have argued that the NHS is disintegrating, pointing to the hospital trusts that are facing severe financial difficulties, the cancelling by some hospitals of non-urgent operations half-way through the financial year, and the allegations that a two-tier NHS is emerging as hospitals give preference to patients referred by fund-holding GPs. Under the new internal market system, critics argue, it is money – not medical need – which is increasingly determining hospital treatment priorities (see, for, example, *The Guardian*, 21 September 1993; Mason 1993).

Privatization and the voluntary sector

The privatization of welfare delivery does not simply mean the selling of public assets, the contracting out of social services to the private sector, the encouragement of private sector provision or the introduction of quasi-markets. The concept is also used to include the development of the role of the voluntary sector as a vehicle for the provision of welfare. As Sugden (1984: 70) has pointed out, voluntary organizations are 'private' in the sense that they are outside the public sector. Indeed, he suggests that the voluntary sector can be seen as 'the counterpart of the private market in the realm of public goods. Like the market system, the voluntary sector is adapted to supply diverse goods in response to individuals' wants' (Sugden 1984: 88).

The voluntary sector has played an important role in the delivery of welfare in Britain for many years: indeed, it was a major provider of welfare for much of the nineteenth and early twentieth centuries. With the establishment of the post-war welfare state, however, the voluntary sector came to be seen as marginal to state provision. As we saw in Chapter 1, the welfare state which was developed and consolidated in the post-war years was deliberately based upon large-scale state social services, organized on the basis of bureaucratic structures and staffed by professionally qualified personnel. The voluntary sector was seen as either unnecessary or as a threat to the adequacy of public provision (Webb and Wistow 1982: 59). But, despite the downgrading of the voluntary sector in the post-war period, there continued to be a 'mixed economy of welfare' consisting of the public, private and voluntary sectors (together with the informal sector of care provided by families and friends).

Voluntary organizations continued to play an important role in the provision of welfare, and in some fields (such as care for the elderly and the handicapped) it made a substantial contribution (see, for example, Hatch 1980).

Voluntary organizations do not match a single stereotype. How could they, given that there are thousands of them, of all shapes and sizes, ranging from large national bodies such as Barnado's and Help the Aged to locally based organizations like local community housing associations and small local self-help groups, all with different organizational structures, funding arrangements and types of activity? The world of the voluntary sector is bewildering, as is the variety of bodies and activities within it. As one writer in this area has commented, the voluntary sector has a 'chameleon-like character': 'the many different bits of the sector between them, can sing almost any tune provided the score is clearly written and the fee is adequate' (Hatch 1986: 390).

But what score should the voluntary sector play with regard to the delivery of welfare? In the late 1970s, the Wolfenden Committee (1978: 26), reporting on the future of voluntary organizations, argued that the voluntary sector complemented, supplemented, extended and influenced the informal and statutory sectors of welfare provision. Wolfenden stressed the importance of a pluralistic system of welfare delivery, in which the voluntary sector would play a greater role in delivering welfare alongside the delivery agencies of the welfare state. This was a theme which was taken up by writers in what has become known as the 'welfare pluralist tradition'. Thus, Hadley and Hatch (1981) referred to the 'failure' of the state in social welfare and emphasized the importance of voluntary organizations in contributing to greater diversity and participation in welfare provision. Another writer in this tradition has argued for a 'de-monopolising strategy', involving a greater role for voluntary action (Gladstone 1979: 100).

Other observers, notably on the New Right, have argued a very different case for extending the role of the voluntary sector. For these critics of the public face of welfare, the voluntary sector is not so much an opportunity for increasing diversity and participation in welfare provision, as a means of providing a substitute for public provision (Harris 1986: 11). In 1980, one Conservative Minister actually spoke of the statutory sector as a 'long stop' for the special needs going beyond the scope of the voluntary sector (Patrick Jenkin, quoted in Webb and Wistow 1982: 73).

The early 1980s witnessed what has been described as 'a crescendo of political rhetoric' in support of the voluntary sector, particularly in relation to the personal social services (Brenton 1985b: 177). The Conservative Government elected in 1979 had campaigned on a manifesto which argued that central government should encourage the voluntary sector, the reasons for this being spelt out by the newly appointed Secretary of State for Social Services, Patrick Jenkin (quoted in Brenton 1985a: 147) later that year:

As the Government sets about the tasks for which it was elected – cutting income tax, cutting public spending and curbing the burgeoning bureau-

cracies of the public sector – we shall be looking to the voluntary movement to take up more of the running.

Since 1979, Conservative Government Ministers have praised the value of the
voluntary sector's contribution to welfare provision. Thus in 1984, Jenkin's
successor as Secretary of State, Norman Fowler, referred to a 'wider conception' of social services, declaring that society must look away from the state and
tap 'a great reservoir of voluntary and private effort'. As one commentator later
observed, the advantages of such an approach were clearly seen to lay in the
opportunity to cut public expenditure and diminish the role of the state, as well
as according with the Conservative Government's values of self-help and individual responsibility (McCarthy 1989: 43).

Similar sentiments were expressed in the 1983 Conservative Party manifesto, which welcomed what it described as the 'vital contribution' made
by voluntary organizations to the social services, and pledged to continue to
give such organizations strong support (Conservative Party 1983). Government funding of the voluntary sector increased considerably during the
1980s, amounting to over £4 billion by 1987, an increase in real terms of
over 90 per cent since 1979 (Taylor 1992: 163). The Thatcher Government
also introduced additional tax concessions to encourage financial donations to
charities. Writing in 1985, Brenton (1985a: 213) commented that the Conservative Government's enthusiasm for the voluntary sector was 'a refraction
of the market ideology'. The personal social services were particularly important, as the use of the voluntary sector in this area offered 'the possibility
of privatising this part of the welfare state in a non-market form' (Brenton
1985a: 143).

Further significant developments followed the Conservative Party's victory in the 1987 General Election, with the voluntary sector moving from a
position where it complements state provision towards one where it is expected to provide a substitute for such provision (Taylor 1992: 156). As we saw
in Chapter 6, one manifestation of this movement has been the housing legislation introduced in 1988, which gave local authority tenants the right to choose
their own landlords, a policy designed to encourage the expansion of a particular part of the voluntary sector (housing associations) as alternatives to local
authorities as the major providers of social housing.

But an even more important development since the late 1980s which has
implications for the voluntary sector has been the introduction of quasi-
markets in the personal social services. As we have already seen, the community care reforms of the early 1990s separated the roles of local authorities as
purchasers and providers of community care and introduced arrangements in
which voluntary organizations and private firms bid for contracts. Under these
new arrangements, local authorities are not only expected to make the maximum use possible of the voluntary and private sectors in the provision of
community care, but also to stimulate the development of new voluntary
sector activity.

Thus recent developments envisage a greater role for the voluntary sector in the delivery of welfare, particularly in the field of housing and the personal social services. But how desirable is the expansion of the voluntary sector in areas which have traditionally been provided directly by the delivery agencies of the welfare state? As Johnson (1987: 122) has noted, the voluntary sector has several features which give rise to serious misgivings. Not only is it characterized by an uneven coverage of services, but it has also been criticized for its weak accountability and lack of internal democracy. Housing associations, which are controlled by voluntary unpaid management committees, have been the subject of particular criticism, with suggestions that such groups not only run the danger of becoming self-perpetuating oligarchies, but also becoming merely rubber stamps for the decisions of their full-time managers (Hills 1987: 34). In Johnson's view, these kinds of defects are 'major failings' which can only be tolerated so long as the voluntary sector plays a relatively marginal role in the delivery of welfare (Johnson 1987: 122).

Anxieties have also been expressed that the development of contracts – as in community care – for the purchase of services may compromise the independence of voluntary organizations. There is the danger that as such organizations diversify into areas which will attract contract funding they will be diverted from more innovative and consumer responsiveness functions (Taylor 1992: 156–7). Similar concerns have been expressed by voluntary organizations themselves (see, for example, Common and Flynn 1992: 32).

Others argue that dependence on funding on terms decided by government may distort the objectives of voluntary organizations. Waine (1992: 85) cites the example of housing associations, who, as a result of changes in the funding criteria made by the Housing Act 1988, have been required to either borrow money or charge higher rents in order to meet their development costs, thereby being obliged to operate in a much more commercial environment. Similar conclusions have been reached by a leading figure in the housing association sector, who uses the term 'reprivatization' to describe the way in which housing associations have been pushed towards the private sector since the 1988 Act, as well as suggesting that such organizations have become subject to more central government control (Randolph 1993: 39–40).

Thus while the 1980s and early 1990s have seen the creation of conditions for the expansion of the role of the voluntary sector in the delivery of welfare, as Waine (1992: 86) points out, this period can also be seen as a time when voluntary organizations 'increasingly became agents of the State'.

8

The search for efficiency and value for money

The contracting out of certain services and the attempts to introduce market mechanisms into the delivery of welfare are part of a wider series of developments since 1979 designed to improve the management and efficiency of the delivery agencies of the welfare state. Such developments have been part of what has been described as 'a set of beliefs and practices, at the core of which burns the seldom-tested assumption that better management will prove an effective solvent for a wide range of economic and social ills' (Pollitt 1993: 1).

Concern with management and efficiency had, of course, been a theme in the debate about the delivery agencies of the welfare state long before the 1980s. As we saw in Chapter 4, developments in the management of local authority services in the late 1960s and early 1970s centred around the issues of improved coordination and the introduction of corporate management. In the NHS, the restructuring which took place in 1974 emphasized better management as being the key to successful re-organization. However, the turning point in the debate about efficiency came in 1979 with the election of the first Thatcher Government, concerned to reduce both the cost and scale of the state. According to a former member of Margaret Thatcher's Efficiency Unit during this period, a major reason for this concern was that the theory of the welfare state had not included any emphasis on efficiency or value for money (Priestley 1986: 115).

As Pollitt (1993: 49) has pointed out, managerialism was a key element in the policies of the New Right towards the public sector, 'better management' providing a banner under which various initiatives could be introduced, including the injection of private sector disciplines, cost cutting, the reduction of professional autonomy, and the setting up of a quasi-competitive framework to 'flush out the "natural" inefficiencies of bureaucracy'. The 1980s was also, of course, a period dominated by the idea that the public sector had a lot to learn from the management systems and techniques employed in the private sector. Typical were the views of Michael Heseltine (1980: 68), the then Secretary of State for the Environment, with responsibility for local government, who argued in 1980 that 'the management ethos' should run throughout central government, local authorities and the NHS, as well as the private sector. This was a theme which was to be central to the Thatcher Government's emphasis upon greater efficiency and better value for money in the delivery of social and other public services.

According to Mather (1989: 213) the Thatcherite commitment to better value for money was:

> a straightforward concept, based on the underlying premise that monopoly services provided free at the point of consumption and untested by competitive forces are unlikely to be efficient in the medium and long-term; that they are likely to perpetuate restrictive practices and producer-led service delivery; and that they entangle the interests of those specifying the services . . . with those providing them.

The result was that the gospel of the 1980s became what has been described as 'managerialism couched in the language of the health farm'. Public sector organizations such as local authorities and the NHS were seen as being fat and needed to be slimmer (Gray and Jenkins 1982: 47). The principles behind this new approach were the search for efficiency, effectiveness and value for money (Gray and Jenkins 1986: 171). This commitment has led to a series of important initiatives in all of the organizations responsible for the delivery of welfare: central government's social service departments, particularly the DSS (formerly DHSS), and the other delivery agencies of local government and the NHS.

At the heart of the debate about the management of the delivery agencies of the welfare state since 1979 has been the emphasis on the achievement of the so-called 'three Es' – the values of economy, efficiency and effectiveness. The three concepts have been defined by the Audit Commission (1983: para. 36):

> *Economy* may be defined as the terms under which the authority acquires human and material resources. An economical operation acquires those resources in the appropriate quality and quantity at the lowest cost.
>
> *Efficiency* may be defined as the relationship between goods and services produced and the resources used to produce them. An efficient operation produces the maximum output for a given set of resource outputs; or, it has minimum inputs for any given quantity and quality of service provided.
>
> *Effectiveness* may be defined as how well a programme or activity is achieving its established goals or other intended benefits.

Effectiveness is the most difficult of the three concepts to measure, not only because of the problems involved in assessing the achievement of the goals of welfare delivery agencies, but also because the measurement of effectiveness invariably involves political issues (Radford 1991: 929). There have also been criticisms that Government-inspired managerial initiatives since 1979 have used effectiveness and efficiency as substitutes for economy, the three concepts in practice often being reduced to economy or cost cutting (Greenwood and Wilson 1989: 12–13).

Central government social service departments and the search for efficiency

Initiatives to improve the efficiency of central government social service departments have been part of a broader programme of reform in central government. Not surprisingly, in view of the amount of government expenditure involved and the range of services provided, the department responsible for the delivery of the massive social security programme (what used to be the DHSS, now the DSS) has been at the forefront of this programme. In addition to large cuts in civil service staffing (which in the 1980s fell particularly heavily on the DHSS and the two other social service departments of the DoE and DES; see Drewry and Butcher 1991: 200), social service departments have been affected by a series of other initiatives designed to improve the efficiency of government departments since the early 1980s.

One important initiative was the programme of detailed scrutinies of government departments designed to improve efficiency and eliminate waste, and undertaken by Sir Derek Rayner, the then managing director of Marks & Spencer, who was appointed as head of the Prime Minister's Efficiency Unit following the 1979 General Election. The Rayner scrutinies investigated a broad range of mainstream functions in the DHSS and uncovered a number of areas of waste and inefficiency, including the arrangements for the payment of social security benefits (see Warner 1984), the payment of benefit to unemployed people, and the arrangements for checking national insurance contributions. In the mid-1980s, the DHSS estimated that the Rayner scrutiny recommendations accepted for implementation would ultimately result in annual savings of over £53 million (National Audit Office 1986: 16). Improvements in the operational efficiency and administrative costs of the social security benefits system were also expected to result as a consequence of the massive computerization programme (the Operational Strategy) first announced in 1982 (Department of Health and Social Security 1982). More on the impact of the Operational Strategy will be given in Chapter 9.

The search for efficiency in the operations of central government in the early 1980s also required departments to improve their financial management. 1982 saw the launching of the Financial Management Initiative (FMI), involving moves towards the devolution of budgetary authority within departments, with middle and junior managers being held accountable for the management of the costs under their control and for the results achieved. The response of the DHSS was to establish a system of management based upon the principles of the FMI throughout its regional organization and central offices, based on cost centres with devolved budgetary responsibility. Speaking about the consequences of the introduction of the FMI at Newcastle Central Office (which included the operations now delivered by the Contributions Agency) one DHSS senior civil servant stated that managers at all levels had become more cost-conscious and able to work in 'a much more systematic fashion' (Thorpe-Tracey 1987: 335). The other government department responsible for the delivery of social security benefits (the DEmp) also devolved budgetary responsibility to line managers.

The most dramatic change in the organization of the arrangements for the delivery of social security benefits has been the establishment of executive agencies like the Benefits Agency as a result of the Next Steps programme, a reform package associated with the Ibbs Report of 1988 (Efficiency Unit 1988), and reflecting the devolved budgeting principles of the FMI. Concerned by what it saw as an insufficient focus within central government departments on the delivery of services, Ibbs recommended that there should be a quite different way of delivering services, involving the hiving off of the service delivery functions of departments from their policymaking core. The Next Steps programme involves the eventual transfer of most of the service delivery functions of departments to semi-autonomous executive agencies. The managers of these agencies are given certain managerial freedoms, but operate within the terms of framework documents set by the parent departments, which set out policy, the agency's budget and specific targets.

The day-to-day delivery of social security benefits by both the DSS and the DEmp is now the responsibility of executive agencies. Since 1990, the Employment Service agency has been responsible for the administration of the payment of unemployment benefits and the running of the job centre network. The massive social security benefits delivery operations of the DSS were transformed into the Benefits Agency in 1991 to become the flagship of the whole Next Steps programme. The launching of the Benefits Agency followed on from the creation of the DSS's Information Technology Services Agency the previous year and the Resettlement Agency in 1989. The subsequent establishment of the Contributions Agency, the Child Support Agency (CSA) and the War Pensions Agency brought the total number of DSS agencies in 1994 to six, employing some 97 per cent of the Department's staff.

The establishment of agencies is transforming the structure and culture of the arrangements for the delivery of social security benefits. The delegation of important managerial freedoms to the chief executives of the Benefits Agency and the Employment Service, together with the setting of financial and quality targets, has led not only to greater efficiency and value for money, but also to greater customer responsiveness (see Chapter 9). Thus the Benefits Agency achieved or exceeded 19 of its 26 key performance targets in 1993–94, and (with the exception of the CSA) the other DSS agencies met the overwhelming majority of their performance targets (Chancellor of the Duchy of Lancaster 1994: 100–7). However, although figures show that the DSS agencies have met, and in many cases exceeded, their performance targets, this does not necessarily mean that there have been improvements in the efficiency and effectiveness of these organizations. As one student of the agency initiative points out, there is the possibility that performance targets are being set too low in order to make agencies a 'public relations success' (Greer 1994: 124).

Indeed, there has been some concern about the efficiency of some aspects of the delivery of social security benefits by the new agencies. The controversial CSA, only set up in 1993, has been the subject of intense media interest, being heavily criticized for long delays in deciding maintenance orders, slowness in responding to enquiries and for making too many errors in assessments. Concerns about the way the CSA worked were acknowledged by the Cabinet Minister responsible, with the Agency being given a 60 per cent increase in its budget and management consultants being brought in to inject business efficiency into its operations (*The Times*, 6 July 1994). Neither has the Benefits Agency, the flagship of the whole agency initiative, escaped criticism, being reprimanded by both the Parliamentary Commissioner for Administration and the House of Commons Social Security Committee over the chaotic introduction of the new disability living allowance in 1992. Worse was to follow in 1993, with the National Audit Office estimating that the Benefits Agency had made errors of £716 million in income support payments and accounts in 1992–93, and the Chief Adjudication Officer criticizing the Agency's standards of accuracy in social security payments (*The Guardian*, 26 November 1993).

Critics of the agency initiative have also maintained that there has been insufficient attention paid to the implications for accountability, especially with regard to the sensitive area of social security benefits payments. Particular concern has been expressed about the possible undermining of ministerial responsibility as a consequence of questions from MPs being referred directly to the chief executives of the Benefits Agency and other agencies (see Chapter 5). However, the troubled history of the CSA shows that in sensitive areas like child maintenance payments, an arm's length relationship cannot be maintained between the responsible Minister and the agency's chief executive.

The latest stage in the Government's attempts to improve efficiency and value for money in its delivery of social (and other) services has been the introduction in 1992 of the market-testing programme, whereby government departments and executive agencies are required to test the cost of providing services in-house against the cost of purchasing them from a private contractor, an extension of the CCT initiatives introduced in the NHS and local government in the 1980s (see Chapter 7). The market-testing programme is seen by government as part of the increasing movement of public services to a culture in which relationships are 'contractual rather than bureaucratic' (H.M. Treasury 1991: 2). Although the early rounds of testing, like that in local government and the NHS, have been confined to ancillary and support services (examples include the DSS's accommodation and audit services, and office services in the DoH), it is intended that the initiative should proceed to areas 'closer to the heart of government'.

Market testing clearly raises important issues. Thus a Benefit Agency feasibility study has warned that the contracting out of the Agency's social security fraud division, being considered as a candidate for contracting out under the market-testing programme, could lead to blackmail and abuse of the system by unscrupulous employees of private firms (*The Guardian*, 21 June 1993). Some observers see the market-testing programme as a stepping stone to the eventual privatization of services currently delivered by government departments and their executive agencies. Indeed, in 1992 the Minister in charge of the Government's privatization programme announced that the Government was applying the 'back to basics' test to the Government's activities, emphasizing the need to consider the privatization of civil service functions (see Treasury and Civil Service Committee 1993: para. 11). The crucial question is how far the contracting process will proceed once the obvious support services have been market tested (Stott 1994: 46). How far will this particular initiative bite into the heartlands of service delivery in such areas as social security? As one commentator has observed, it may be that private insurance companies (or even management teams of Benefits Agency staff) will eventually be able to tender for the delivery of parts of the social security system to the public (Hill 1994: 251).

The search for efficiency in local government

The concern with efficiency, cost-consciousness and value for money associated with developments in central government departments has also been a feature of parallel developments in the field of local government. Attempts to improve the efficiency of local authorities are, of course, not new. Inefficiency and financial waste were identified as important consequences of local authority departmentalism by the Maud Committee in 1967 (Maud 1967: para. 108). As Elcock and his colleagues (Elcock *et al.* 1989: 139, 146) remind us, the introduction of corporate management in the 1970s – stimulated by the Bains Report of 1972 – was seen partly as a means of improving value for money in local authorities, being linked to the idea that failures of coordination between local authority departments led to 'sub-optimal expenditure'.

The attacks on inefficiency in local government by the Conservative Government since 1979, and its attempts to encourage a more business-like approach to the affairs of local authority services like education, housing and the personal social services, have manifested themselves in a number of ways. The 1980s saw the introduction of a series of measures designed to tighten central government's control over local authority spending, notably the new system of distributing central government funding through block grant introduced in 1980, the system of spending targets for individual local authorities, rate capping, and the introduction of the controversial community charge, itself replaced by the council charge in 1993. One result of these initiatives was to put pressure on individual local authorities to make financial economies and to encourage the more efficient use of resources.

Since 1979, the Conservative Government has also attempted to introduce market disciplines into the operations of local authorities by requiring them to apply competitive tendering to a range of services previously provided 'in-house'. Although, as we saw in Chapter 7, CCT has not yet bitten deeply into the delivery of local authority social services, the development of the concept is a significant marker for the future. The reforms in community care which separate the assessment of need from the commissioning of care by local authority social services departments are also part of the 'new managerialism' which now characterizes the local government welfare state, and have been seen as setting in motion a process of change which will 'turn organisations upside-down' (Audit Commission 1992a: para. 45).

Initiatives aimed at increasing efficiency have also been introduced into the education and housing services. Thus the introduction, following the Education Reform Act 1988, of LMS, which devolved responsibility for at least 75 per cent of a school's budget to school governing bodies, is an attempt to increase management efficiency through the clear identification of responsibility for the delivery of educational services (McVicar 1993: 197). In the case of housing, since 1990, local housing authorities in England and Wales have been working within a new financial regime which 'ring-fences' the housing revenue account so as to prevent contributions from the local authority's general fund. The aim of this new regime is to ensure that the cost of housing services not met by subsidy will be covered by rents, the previous system having been criticized as providing a 'cover for inefficiency' in the management of local authority housing (Malpass and Murie 1990: 186–7; Forrest 1993: 46).

Probably the most important attempt to improve efficiency in local government, however, has been the creation of the Audit Commission in 1983, established as a result of the Local Government Finance Act of the previous year. In the words of one commentator: 'While central government applied the resources brake, the Audit Commission stepped on the managerial accelerator' (Kelly 1991: 179). The Audit Commission has had a major impact on the management of the local authority departments responsible for the delivery of social services.

The Audit Commission is responsible for the external auditing of local authority accounts (and since October 1990 the accounts of health authorities), either by the Commission itself or by private accountancy firms appointed by it, a task which had previously been carried out by the DoE's District Audit Service, a body which had its origins in the mid-nineteenth century. The original concept of local authority audit focused on the narrow concern with legality and regularity, ensuring that proper accounting practices had been observed and that spending had been in accordance with the law. Although the 1982 legislation retains the concept of legality, it also requires individual auditors and the Audit Commission to promote value for money in local authorities. Thus individual auditors are responsible for ensuring that local authorities have made proper arrangements for securing economy, efficiency and effectiveness (the 'three Es') in their use of resources. The Commission is required to undertake studies leading to recommendations for improving the 'three Es' in the delivery of local authority services. Thus, one consequence of the Audit Commission's work has been a move away from the traditional concern with legality and regularity towards what has been described as a management consultancy-style approach (Radford 1991: 930).

Value for money in local authorities is therefore directly linked with the 'three Es'. Each year, the Audit Commission produces a statistical profile for each local authority which looks at each of the services provided by that authority and tells it how its levels of service compare with similar authorities. Each year, the Commission also undertakes special studies of three or four individual services or areas of expenditure across a number of local authorities in an attempt to identify 'best practice'. These special studies have included reports on the effective delivery of services for the elderly, housing the homeless, and the management of secondary schools (Audit Commission 1985; 1986b, c). Following the publication of such studies, the Commission produces a detailed guide for auditors to use in determining how individual local authorities measure up against best practice.

The Audit Commission, therefore, acts as an important body in promoting management change in local authorities and in identifying possible savings in the cost of local social services. In the words of one study of local government budgeting (Elcock *et al.* 1989: 164), the Commission has been 'the external muscle behind VFM [value for money] in local government'. There is little doubt that it has identified substantial savings in the cost of the social services delivered by local authorities. Thus it claims to have identified annual savings of £80–100 million in the costs of the administration of council housing (Audit Commission 1986b: 4), while its report on the care of the elderly claimed that many local authorities might be able to provide 15–20 per cent higher service levels of residential care for elderly people at no extra cost (Audit Commission 1985: 3).

The Audit Commission's emphasis upon the potential for such savings and its use of league tables is seen by Stoker (1991: 242) as an attempt to provide a 'countervailing force' to what public choice theorists see as the budget maximizing tendencies of local authority bureaucrats. Doubts, however, have been expressed about the methodology employed by the Commission (see McSweeney 1988), and it has been suggested that its reports on council housing are based on little practical experience of the organization and delivery of local authority housing (Malpass and Murie 1990: 160).

Critics have also argued that there is an 'effectiveness gap', the Audit Commission having placed too much emphasis on the two 'Es' of economy and efficiency, at the expense of the third 'E' of effectiveness. Certainly, in its early years, the Commission did concentrate on encouraging efficiency, though since 1987 there has been a shift of emphasis towards the promotion of effectiveness (Henkel 1992: 75–6). One manifestation of this change has been the introduction of the idea of 'service effectiveness': thus the key questions for local authorities identified in the Commission's 1988 action guide included: 'Is the service getting to the right customers, in the right way, with the right services, in keeping with its stated policies?' (Audit Commission 1988b: 5).

Whilst recognizing that it is often difficult to measure performance in terms of service quality and effectiveness, the Audit Commission does understand the need to evaluate the outcomes of local services by, for example, the use of surveys to test the views of the users of social services, especially in the areas of local authority housing and some of the personal social services, particularly those for the elderly. The Commission's growing concern with the users of services, increasingly described in the 1990s as customers, is highlighted by its statement that one of the key factors which characterize a well-managed local authority is that it 'understands its customers' (Audit Commission 1988a: para. 25). We will discuss the increasing customer orientation of local authorities in Chapter 9.

Towards a more efficient National Health Service

Management has been on the agenda of the NHS since it was first established, but it is a concern which has been characterized by changing ideas. Thus, from the creation of the NHS in 1948 to the early 1980s, health service managers were what Harrison (1988: 30) has described as 'diplomats', concerned with minimizing conflicts within the service and facilitating the work of the medical profession, rather than with attempting to bring about major change in the organization and delivery of health care.

Management as 'diplomacy' was reflected in the tradition of consensus management which was a major feature of the NHS during its first three-and-a-half decades. There was shared managerial responsibility between senior medical and nursing staff and health administrators. A key feature of the re-organization of the NHS in 1974 was the institutionalization of this concept: in the words of Strong and Robinson (1990: 18), the NHS was to be managed 'not by a boss, but by a group of equals'. The idea of a chief executive responsible for the management of the new health authorities was specifically rejected, the DHSS stating that professionals were 'most suitably managed by members of their own professions' (Department of Health and Social Security 1972a: 57). Instead, the management structure of health authorities was based on a multi-disciplinary management team, which brought together senior medical, nursing, administrative and financial staff. The management style was one of consensus, with the members of the management team taking decisions as 'a consensus-forming group', each of them having a veto over any particular decision (Department of Health and Social Security 1972b: para. 2.42). Consensus management undoubtedly had its strengths, including the wider dimension that it brought to decision making and the commitment of management team members to the implementation of particular decisions. But the system also had its disadvantages, notably the fact that it often led to delays in the decision-making process as well as encouraging management team members to avoid difficult decisions (see, for example, Merrison 1979: paras 20.13–20.15).

Up to the early 1980s, central government showed little interest in placing the medical profession in the NHS under managerial control (Harrison 1988: 22). As a result, the profession was able to exercise a large degree of discretion in the allocation and management of resources within the service. Since the election in 1979 of the first Thatcher Government, however, with its commitment to improving the efficiency and cost–effectiveness of the public sector, the NHS has been dominated by what has been described as a 'managerialist agenda' (Wistow 1992a: 103). The Conservative Government inspired a series of initiatives in which the manager was viewed as 'scapegoat' rather than as 'diplomat' (Harrison 1988: 56). Drawing upon practices in the private sector, these initiatives have been designed to encourage efficiency and the better use of resources by health authorities. As Robinson (1988: 9) has observed, the NHS has served, in many ways, as a 'testing ground' for the injection of an 'enterprise culture' into the public sector.

The starting point for these initiatives was 1982, a year identified by Davidson (1987: 43) as when 'management and managerial preoccupations took over the NHS'. Area health authorities were abolished in 1982 as part of the 'slimming down' of the NHS, and annual accountability reviews of RHAs by the DHSS were introduced, a process which was later extended downwards to include reviews of DHAs by the appropriate RHAs and reviews of individual units by DHAs. In the same year, drawing upon the experience of the efficiency scrutinies pioneered in central government departments, the DHSS also adopted the concept of Rayner-type scrutinies. These scrutinies have involved in-depth studies of particular areas of the NHS where savings are thought to be possible, including such areas as residential accommodation, ambulance service control systems and catering costs.

Cost-improvement programmes requiring DHAs to save money by operating more efficiently were introduced in 1984. Two years later, following a number of experiments in management budgeting, the Resource Management Initiative (RMI) was launched in order to develop systems which will provide senior medical and nursing staff with information enabling them to make better informed decisions about resource allocation (see Packwood et al. 1990). Other measures introduced during this period, designed to improve efficiency, included compulsory competitive tendering (see Chapter 7) and performance indicators (see below). All of these initiatives were based on the assumption that they would lead to improvements in efficiency within the NHS (Harrison et al. 1990: 86).

The high point of Government-inspired initiatives to improve efficiency in the delivery of health care during this period, however, was the Griffiths Report of 1983. Concerned by what it saw as a lack of management in the NHS, the Conservative Government appointed a team of businessmen, led by Roy Griffiths (deputy chairman and managing director of Sainsbury's, the retail supermarket company), to give advice on 'the effective use and management of manpower and related resources' in the NHS. The inquiry's report was highly critical of consensus management, arguing that 'if Florence Nightingale were carrying her lamp through the corridors of the NHS today she would almost certainly be searching for the people in charge' (Griffiths 1983: 12). The report's diagnosis was that the NHS lacked general management support, with the result that there was 'no driving force seeking and accepting direct and personal responsibility for developing management plans, securing their implementation and monitoring actual achievement' (Griffiths 1983: 12).

Although recognizing that the NHS was not concerned with the profit motive, Griffiths argued that there were clear similarities between NHS management and business management, and, in particular, the level of services, the quality of products, meeting budgets, cost improvement, productivity, and motivating and rewarding staff. The inquiry said that it was surprised to find that there was no real continuous evaluation of performance in the NHS: precise management objectives were rarely set; there was little measurement of health output; clinical evaluation of particular practices was not common; and economic evaluation of these practices was very rare (Griffiths 1983: 10).

Griffiths' recommended cure for these perceived ills of NHS management was the appointment of general managers at the regional, district and unit levels of the service. General managers would be the best persons for the job regardless of discipline, with responsibility for the planning, implementation and control of performance at their particular level of the service. Griffiths also recommended the streamlining of the central management of the NHS through the establishment of Supervisory and Management Boards (see Chapter 3). As Day and Klein (1983: 1813) put it, the management of the NHS was to change from a system that was based on 'the mobilisation of consent' to one based on 'the management of conflict', from a system that had 'conceded the right of groups to veto changes' to one that 'gave the managers the right to override objections'.

The Griffiths Report was accepted by the Government in 1984, and two years later most regions, districts and units had appointed general managers on short-term contracts. The introduction of this 'new managerialism' was followed by the incorporation of such private-sector practices as cost improvement programmes and management budgeting (see above), the introduction of individual performance review and performance-related pay for general managers, and the development of improved performance indicators enabling health authorities to compare their performances (Moon and Kendall 1993: 180; Pollitt 1993: 64).

The Griffiths Report, and the developments which followed it, was a radical change in the organization and culture of health-care delivery. In the words of one observer, the NHS was transformed from a classic example of 'an *administered* public-sector bureaucracy into one that increasingly is exhibiting the qualities that reflect positive, purposeful *management*' (Best 1987: 4). The Griffiths Report pushed management to the heart of the NHS: 'Where once there had been administration, now there was management from the top to the bottom of the service' (Strong and Robinson 1990: 27).

For critics of this 'new managerialism' (Townsend *et al.* 1988: 25), Griffiths represented 'the triumph of a set of beliefs about what was important and how things should be done':

> It thrust management and management preoccupations to the very centre of NHS thinking, pushing aside, or at least subordinating, the arguably less clearly formulated collection of ideas about service and the public good which had hitherto provided the dominant ethos.

The management revolution in the NHS during the 1980s has been the subject of much criticism, particularly the concern that the culture of private-sector management is inappropriate for a public-sector organization which has traditionally had a consensus style of management. Anxieties have also been expressed that the search for efficiency in the NHS constitutes a threat to the traditional values of the service. Thus for some critics, the developments of the 1980s constituted a change of direction from a concern with the overall quality of the service being delivered to 'a preoccupation with how resources can best (most productively) be used' (Townsend *et al.* 1988: 26). It was argued that the focus of attention had turned from questions of need to questions of efficiency. In the view of Townsend and his colleagues (1988: 26):

> in substituting efficiency for need, the health service is turning in on itself and away from the social context within which it is operating.

On the other hand, other observers argued that the search for efficiency in the NHS in the 1980s did not go far enough, and that more radical initiatives were required. As one assessment of general management concluded, the Griffiths Report was only a beginning (Strong and Robinson 1990: 182). Despite its radicalism (Strong and Robinson 1990: 164):

> Griffiths . . . was only a partial break with the past . . . the service was still trapped, for general managers at least, within a national straitjacket. Local initiative was frustrated by ministers, by civil servants, by supervisory management tiers and by powerful professional bodies.

The real attempt to break with the past came in 1991 with the introduction of the NHS internal market. This was an idea very similar to one suggested a few years earlier by Alain Enthoven (1985), who argued that an approach to health-care delivery in which market forces operated within the NHS would improve efficiency in the use of resources. The internal market was the centrepiece of the package of NHS reforms contained in the 1989 White Paper Working for Patients (DoH 1989a) and given legislative effect a year later by the National Health Service and Community Care Act. As we saw in Chapter 7, this involves the separation of the purchaser and provider roles of DHAs, who (along with fundholding GPs) purchase health-care services from their own hospitals, hospitals in other districts, the new self-governing hospitals run by the NHS trusts, or the private sector. The theory behind the internal market has been concisely put by Perrin (1992: 266–7):

well-managed providers will have incentive to improve efficiency and performance quality in order to attract more 'sales' of services to purchasers, thus increasing their share of funding but also consequently exerting pressure on less successful competitors to, in turn, improve their own efficiency and quality so as to avoid cut-backs or possible redundancies or closures.

Thus a key objective of the NHS reforms is to improve value for money in the delivery of health care by introducing systems and incentives designed to achieve greater efficiency (King's Fund Institute 1989: 5). The reform package includes other measures designed to strengthen management and the control of spending, such as the extension of the RMI, the introduction of medical audit, and the inclusion of a management element in the criteria for consultants' merit awards (see Department of Health 1989a). According to Wistow (1992b: 71), this was a set of reforms which seemed to represent a government committed to the achievement of 'a substantial transfer of power and influence from medicine to management'.

The implementation of the reforms has been the subject of much debate. Although the introduction of an internal market for health care was introduced more slowly than originally planned, with DHAs being encouraged to use block contracts which reflected the current patterns of service (the 'steady-state' approach; Baggott 1994: 188), the experience of the first few years of the market system led to it being described as 'a maelstrom'. Critics argued that the restructuring of the health service in areas such as London could not be reconciled with a market system (see, for example, *The Guardian*, 21 September 1993), and the new system's shortcomings were officially recognized at the end of 1993, when the Government announced that it was intervening to prevent the Camden and Islington DHA from purchasing patient care in a way that would threaten the viability of a major central London hospital (*The Guardian*, 16 December 1993). Writing in the summer of 1994, one leading commentator on the NHS referred to the continuing uncertainty about the way in which the reforms were evolving, arguing that there was no overall plan guiding their implementation. As a result, some of the most important questions about the NHS reforms remained unanswered, including the crucial one concerning the balance between competition and management (Ham 1994: 351–2).

Performance indicators and welfare delivery

A key element in attempts to improve efficiency and encourage value for money in all three major delivery agencies of the welfare state has been the development of performance indicators, a concept described by one Conservative Minister in the mid-1980s as having a vital part to play in ensuring that public money is being spent as efficiently as possible (Pollitt 1985: 4). Yet another technique which has been transplanted from the private sector, performance indicators in the public sector draw heavily on the private-sector concept of management accounting (Greenwood and Wilson 1989: 10–11).

The central government department responsible for the social security system has used performance indicators for many years. Indicators designed to compare the performance of local social security offices through the regular monitoring of such aspects as work done and the accuracy of payments, were introduced in the then DHSS as long ago as the mid-1970s (Garrett 1980: 124). New performance targets for the Department were introduced in 1988. At about the same time, the Department also introduced a nationwide Quality Assessment Package, measuring such quality of services indicators as caller waiting times, the quality of interviews, and the quality of correspondence within local social security offices (see Carter et al. 1992: 96–100). As we saw earlier, the setting of annual performance targets is central to the operations of the DSS agencies, although the emphasis of such targets is on quantitative efficiency indicators such as clearance times for the handling of benefit queries, efficiency savings and benefit assessment accuracy. There are few effectiveness indicators, especially regarding quality and customer satisfaction (Greer 1994: 74; Carter and Greer 1993: 412).

Performance indicators have also become an important factor in the work of local government. Many local authorities introduced performance indicators during the 1980s, a leader in the field being the London Borough of Bexley, which introduced targets for each of its services, together with comparisons of performance in previous years (Bexley 1984). The National Consumer Council (1986) helped to develop performance indicators for local authorities for housing and services for the under-fives. Local housing authorities are required by the Local Government and Housing Act 1989 to publish the results of their peformance in the form of a list of specified indicators. Evidence shows that performance indicators in local authorities, like those used in social security agencies, have concentrated on economy and efficiency rather than on issues of effectiveness and quality (Burningham 1992: 89).

Further developments in the measurement of local authority performance have taken place as a result of the Citizen's Charter (see Chapter 9), which emphasized the importance of providing the public with comparative information on how public services perform, partly as a way of pressurizing delivery agencies to emulate others. One important manifestation of this approach has been the requirement since 1993–94 for local authorities to measure their performance in individual services against indicators drawn up by the Audit Commission and to publish details in a local newspaper. After comparing the levels of performance in different authorities, the Commission will publish a national report. Indicators for the three local authority social services in the first year of this exercise included the success of housing authorities in collecting rent, the numbers of under-fives receiving education, and the number of people cared for in residential homes (Audit Commission 1992b). Another spin-off from the Citizen's Charter has been the publication since 1992 of annual statistics for examination results and attendance rates for secondary schools.

Performance indicators have also become an important feature of management in the NHS, enabling comparisons to be made between different health authorities and assisting Ministers and RHAs in their attempts to assess the performance of DHAs in the efficient use of resources. Developed in response to parliamentary criticism of the then DHSS's failure to ensure effective financial control over health authorities (see Public Accounts Committee 1981), the first set of NHS indicators was introduced in 1983 and consisted mainly of the repackaging of existing statistics, such as the average length of stay in bed by hospital speciality. As Carter and his colleagues (1992: 107) have graphically observed, statistics that had been available in the NHS for decades 'suddenly emerged re-born and re-christened as performance indicators'. Following criticisms that too many of the indicators referred to costs and not health-care outcomes, subsequent sets of indicators have become more sophisticated. They have, nevertheless, still been criticized for being too concerned with efficiency rather than effectiveness, thereby reinforcing a cost-containment approach to management (Long 1992: 64). The tables providing information on the performance of NHS hospitals and trusts first published by the DoH in 1994 (comprising 23 indicators, of which 16 relate to waiting times for surgery) have also been criticized as telling patients nothing about the quality of care delivered.

Although the use of performance indicators has become an increasingly important feature in the operations of all the delivery agencies of the welfare state, both their design and use have been seen as 'highly problematic' (Carter 1989: 136). Indicators have concentrated primarily on the criteria of efficiency and economy rather than broader questions of effectiveness and quality. Not surprisingly, it has been suggested that this emphasis might be a reflection of the concern of the Conservative Government since 1979 with cutting public expenditure and attacking inefficiency (Pollitt 1986: 159). On the other hand, Carter and his colleagues (1992: 39) have suggested that the subordination of effectiveness to the other two 'Es' may be a reflection of the technical problems involved in establishing a causal relationship between the outputs and outcomes of welfare policies.

There has been particular debate about the Government's comparative tables on school examination performance and the performance of NHS hospitals and trusts. Concern has been expressed that what appear in the tables to be low-performing schools are, in fact, performing very well in terms of apparently unpromising academic material, and it has been suggested that value-added tables measuring how much individual schools add to the performance of their original intakes would be a much better indication of performance (see, for example, *The Guardian*, 17 November 1993). Doubts have also been expressed about the value of hospital tables which compare different-sized hospitals with different kinds of case loads and located in different areas. The hospital tables have also been criticized for only covering administrative matters (waiting times, operations cancelled and day-case surgery) with no attempt to include clinical indicators.

As Carter (1989: 133) points out, the use of performance indicators in the social services is also complicated by the problem of determining who actually 'owns' performance. Performance is often constrained by the interdependence of different units or activities within a delivery agency. He cites the NHS as an example of such interdependence, involving as it does the involvement of a number of different staff – radiologists, anaesthetists, surgeons, nurses, social workers, etc. – whose individual contributions to the care of a patient may be difficult to disentangle. It is also difficult to unravel the effects of outside influences on performance. Thus critics of school league tables argue that they fail to take account of the impact of social class on the performance of school children (Carter *et al.* 1992: 32).

An important difference between performance indicators used in the public and private sectors is that the latter are often much more consumer sensitive and attempt to measure consumer satisfaction (Carter *et al.* 1992: 174). The lack of similar indicators in the public sector has been the subject of much criticism (see, for example, National Consumers Council 1986: xix; Pollitt 1988). However, as we shall discuss in Chapter 9, the delivery agencies of the welfare state are increasingly making use of user surveys and other mechanisms to evaluate the performance of services.

From welfare administration to welfare management

Thus there have been a series of developments since the early 1980s designed to ensure that the various delivery agencies of the welfare state adopt a more business-like approach to their operations. The guiding principles behind these developments have been the search for efficiency and value for money. Such initiatives have introduced 'a world where bureaucrats . . . are redefined as *accountable managers*, public sector operations sub-divided into *businesses*, and the public seen as the *customer*' (Gray and Jenkins 1986: 171).

Critics have argued that attempts to introduce managerialism into the delivery agencies of the welfare state are incompatible with the values of the public administration model which has traditionally underpinned the organization of the delivery of welfare. Discussing recent developments in central government departments, Greenwood and Wilson (1989: 141) argue that the attitudes and practices of the private sector 'cannot *easily* be transplanted' into the public sector. In particular, concerns about accountability and equity – two of the traditional features of the public administration model of welfare delivery – are seen as obstacles to the wholesale introduction of such techniques. Thus the decentralization of responsibility to line managers may conflict with traditional notions of accountability (Greenwood and Wilson 1989: 139), while the search for value for money may lead to the downgrading of the imperative of equity of treatment (Gray and Jenkins 1985: 157).

As we have seen, the search for efficiency has also been criticized for its narrow concern with cost cutting and inputs, the first two 'Es' of economy and efficiency. The 1990s, however, have been characterized by a greater concern with the third 'E' of effectiveness and there has been a greater emphasis on customer responsiveness and issues of quality within the delivery agencies of the welfare state, what has been referred to as 'managerialism with a human face' (Pollitt 1991: 3). We turn to these developments in Chapter 9.

9

The customer orientation

In addition to the challenges posed to traditional methods of welfare delivery by such developments as privatization, in its various manifestations, and the search for efficiency and value for money, the 1980s and the 1990s have been characterized by a growing concern with the encouragement of greater consumer responsiveness. The delivery agencies of the welfare state have been expected to become more sensitive to the demands of their service users or customers, as they are increasingly described by government. There has been a growing recognition that the delivery of welfare involves much more than value for money, and one commentator has even extended the 'three Es' of economy, efficiency and effectiveness associated with the managerialist approach discussed in Chapter 8 to include the fourth 'E' of 'excellence' (Gunn 1988: 21).

Central to this growing concern with 'excellence' has been the recognition that the consumers of service – the customers – should be at the heart of the arrangements for delivering welfare. Like most of the initiatives associated with the managerialist approach discussed earlier, the concept of consumerism and customer care is an idea which has its origins in the literature of private-sector management. The importance of being close to the customer is particularly associated with the ideas of two influential North American writers on organizations, Tom Peters and Robert Waterman, the authors of the best-selling book *In Search of Excellence* (1982). Written when the authors were both partners in a leading management consultancy firm, McKinsey & Company, the book developed a set of basic principles shared by what Peters and Waterman describe as America's 'best run' companies. One of these principles was being 'close to the customer'. Peters and Waterman concluded that 'excellent' companies were dominated by an organizational culture which focused on customers, learning their preferences and catering to them. Customers were not regarded as a nuisance or ignored, but were regularly listened to, with companies often getting some of their best product ideas from them. 'Excellent' companies had what amounted to an 'obsession' with customer service (see, for example Chapter 6 of Peters and Waterman 1982).

Closeness to the customer is part of what Connelly (1992: 30) has described as the weak version of consumerism. It is a view of consumerism which is:

> an orientation towards the consumers of goods/services rooted in a sense of public service with its concomitant moral obligations towards the public. It is simply the desire to make things better for the consumer by taking the consumer's point of view and attempting to improve service in the light of that standpoint.

A second, and stronger, version of consumerism is rooted in the notion of customer sovereignty. In this sense of the concept, consumerism leads to the situation in which an organization 'provides the goods and services that customers want in the quantity, quality and manner in which they want them' (Connelly 1992: 30). It is a concept derived from the private sector, where if customers cannot obtain high-quality goods and services from a particular supplier, then they will go elsewhere for them. Although Connelly (1992: 31) argues that consumerism in this strong sense of the concept cannot apply to the NHS and the other social services, as we saw in Chapter 7, market mechanisms were introduced into welfare delivery in the late 1980s and early 1990s through such initiatives as the contracting out of services, the introduction of open enrolment in schools, and the creation of quasi-markets in the NHS and community care.

Consumerism in the weaker sense of the concept – closeness to the consumers of services – is an approach which has increasingly been taken on board by welfare delivery agencies in Britain, especially local authorities. Thus a report published by the Association of County Councils (ACC) in the early 1990s argued that improving closeness to the customer is one of the main challenges facing local government. The customer-oriented council is one which puts the needs, wants and priorities of the public 'at the centre of everything it does' (Webster 1991: 7). The customer orientation in local government has also been emphasized by the Audit Commission, the watchdog of local government efficiency and value for money, which has stressed the importance of local authorities 'understanding customers', rather than simply assuming what the needs of those customers ought to be (Audit Commission 1988a: para. 25).

Beyond the local government welfare state, other welfare delivery agencies, such as health authorities and the central government executive agencies concerned with the delivery of social security benefits, have also recognized that customer care should be at the heart of the delivery of services. Thus the architect of general management reforms in the NHS, Sir Roy Griffiths (1988b: 196), maintained that the consumer dimension must 'be seen as part of a total management and organizational philosophy', while the giant Benefits Agency has identified 'customer service' as one of the core values paramount to its business. The customer orientation is also manifested in the Citizen's Charter programme developed by the Conservative Government in the early 1990s, with its emphasis on greater sensitivity to consumer needs.

In the words of one writer on recent developments in this field, consumerism in the arrangements for delivering social services has become 'an officially-approved fashion' (Pollitt 1987: 43). The remainder of this chapter will critically examine some of the ways in which the customer orientation has manifested itself in the organization and workings of the delivery agencies of the welfare state.

Consumerism in local government: the public service orientation

An important approach which transfers Peters' and Waterman's concept of being 'close to the customer' to the public sector in Britain, an 'anglicised version' of their philosophy (Cole and Furbey 1994: 227), is the 'public service orientation'. A term originally devised by Michael Clarke and John Stewart (1985), the public service orientation is an approach which is associated primarily with local authorities, although, as we shall discuss later, elements of its philosophy can also be found in initiatives being undertaken by health authorities.

The emphasis of the public service orientation is on 'service *for* the public' and not 'service *to* the public' as the major organizational value of local authorities (Stewart and Clarke 1987: 167). It argues for greater responsiveness to the public as customers of local services, arguing that local authorities should look at their services from the viewpoint of the public, rather than simply from the viewpoint of the local authority. The public service orientation argues that local authorities should get closer to the customer by seeking views and opinions on services, maximizing customer choice, and providing customers of services with standard of service statements, as well as making services more accessible. Thus, the public service orientation stresses delivery agencies which are outward looking and proactive, rather than inward looking and reactive (Elcock 1991: 104).

The values of the public service orientation have been echoed by the chairman of the ACC, who has argued that the customer orientation is one of the keys to the success of local authorities in the 1990s. It is seen as something which must be a central theme for the future and not something which is just bolted on to other local authority activities (Webster 1991: 3). The concept of the customer orientation and customer care has gained increasing prominence in local government: typical is the London Borough of Wandsworth's managers' handbook, which stresses that the development of customer responsiveness should be 'a priority for all managers' (Wandsworth 1991: B4).

Since the early 1980s, local authorities have undertaken a range of initiatives in an attempt to become more consumer responsive in the delivery of welfare (Fenwick 1989; Fenwick and Harrop 1990; Webster 1991). These initiatives have included: discovering more about customers' views; providing the public with more information about services; improving access to services; using performance indicators; increasing public participation and accountability; and developing a customer culture. Performance indicators and issues of public participation and accountability were discussed in Chapters 5 and 8. This section therefore concentrates on the other types of initiative designed to improve consumer responsiveness. (The discussion draws upon a range of sources: see, for example, Webster 1991; Labour Party 1991.)

Finding out what the public need and want from local authority services is 'at the heart' of getting closer to the public (Webster 1991: 16). Thus local authorities, a notable example being Kent County Council, have undertaken surveys in an attempt to obtain information about what the public needs and wants from education and the personal social services. Surveys have also been used by local authorities to assess customer satisfaction with local services. Examples include a survey of neighbourhood team areas by the Social Services Department of Humberside County Council, and the views of handicapped people on the services provided by Kent County Council's Social Services Department. Other local authorities have actively sought complaints and comments from the public as a means of discovering what customers think about services. Norfolk Social Services Department, for example, has provided prepaid cards for clients who wished to complain about services.

Making more information available about services is another important element of the customer orientation. Thus some social services departments, including Kent and Cumbria, have provided information packs on the services that they provide, while Humberside has produced a handbook and code of practice on the care of elderly people in its residential homes.

As we saw in Chapter 1, one criticism which has been made of local authorities has been the lack of attention given to providing access to services. The barriers to access have included geographical inaccessibility, inconvenient opening hours, language restrictions and unwelcoming reception areas. As will be discussed below, many local authorities have re-organized their delivery of the key welfare services of housing and social services on the basis of decentralized offices, in an attempt to ensure that services are geographically accessible to consumers. Other attempts to improve access for the public include experiments with different opening hours to reflect customer demand. For example, Berkshire Social Services Department introduced a late opening evening on the same day as the town's shops. The translation of social services departments' leaflets and other information about services into ethnic minority languages is a feature in many local authorities. Many social services departments have also improved reception areas in attempts to create more welcoming atmospheres for the consumers of their services. Local authorities are also increasingly recognizing that training has an important part to play in getting front-line staff to be more customer sensitive.

Thus the culture of many local authorities has changed dramatically since the early 1980s: local authorities have begun to place the customer at the centre of their arrangements for welfare delivery. One local authority which is at the forefront of such initiatives is Kent County Council, where the primary principle of education management is being 'closer to the customer', an approach which involves 'changing the focus of attention to the sharp end of the organisation where the relationship with our various customers takes place' (quoted in Ranson 1992a: 156).

Another important manifestation of the customer orientation in the delivery of welfare by local authorities is the increasing use of users' charters and customer contracts giving local residents specific guarantees of certain standards of service, an approach which has subsequently been taken up at the national level by all three major political parties and manifested in the Conservative Government's Citizen's Charter (see below). Such charters were pioneered by the City of York, whose Labour-controlled council introduced a citizen's charter in 1989. York's charter includes a tenants' charter, which allows council tenants to choose how much they can afford to pay in rent for such price-listed improvements as new kitchens, central heating and interior decoration, as well as providing contracts for housing repairs. Wrekin District Council promises residents applying for housing benefit a reply within 14 days of application, while Newcastle-upon-Tyne City Council pays its council tenants compensation if housing repairs are not completed within a promised time limit or are not carried out to the required standard.

Going local: the decentralization of welfare delivery

An important element of the customer orientation within local authorities is the attempt to make local services more accessible to the public. One aspect of this approach has involved the transfer of managerial responsibility for service delivery to decentralized offices. As a result of developments since the 1980s, locally-based offices are now almost the norm in local authority housing and social services departments (Lowndes 1992: 53), and it is expected that decentralization will continue to be a major trend in local government throughout the 1990s (Hambleton 1992: 10).

The decentralization of local services like housing and the personal social services is not a completely new phenomenon. Decentralization initiatives can be traced back to the area management experiments undertaken in such authorities as Stockport and Newcastle-upon-Tyne in the mid-1970s (see, for example, Harrop et al. 1978), but the real starting point for recent developments is the metropolitan district of Walsall, which set up a network of thirty-two neighbourhood housing offices in the early 1980s (see Fudge 1984). Although closely associated with what have been described as New Urban Left local authorities (Hackney, Islington, Manchester, Birmingham and others) and their criticisms of paternalistic and unresponsive local authority bureaucracies (Gyford 1985), the decentralization of services has been introduced by local authorities of all political complexions, including the formerly Liberal Democrat-controlled London borough of Tower Hamlets and the Conservative-controlled East Sussex. As one commentator argues, decentralization has been seen as a new 'managerial paradigm', which is accompanied not only by increased customer responsiveness, but also by increased efficiency (Lowndes 1992: 53).

Individual local authorities have approached the decentralization of housing and the personal social services in a number of different ways. Many schemes involve what Elcock (1988: 44) describes as 'departmental decentralization', where a single local authority department decentralizes its delivery of services to local offices. Housing has been at the forefront of such initiatives, with London boroughs like Hackney and Lambeth decentralizing housing management, partly as a response to the challenges directed at the local authority housing service by the Thatcher Government during the 1980s. County councils like East Sussex and Humberside have decentralized the personal social services through 'patch' systems in which small teams of social workers and other social care staff are responsible for particular neighbourhoods (see, for example, Elcock 1986b). By contrast, other local authorities have developed decentralization across departmental boundaries, what has been termed 'corporate decentralization' (Elcock 1988: 44). A notable example of this latter form of decentralization is the London Borough of Islington, where, since the mid-1980s, housing services, personal social services, environmental health services, welfare rights and community work have all been decentralized to 24 neighbourhood offices serving average populations of 6500 (Burns et al. 1994: 112–14).

An even more radical form of decentralization has been introduced in another inner London borough, Tower Hamlets, which has combined administrative decentralization with political decentralization. Since 1986, Tower Hamlets has been divided into seven neighbourhoods, each of which has a Neighbourhood Committee, consisting of councillors from wards in those neighbourhoods, which is given an annual budget and responsibility for the delivery of the council's services in their area. Managerial responsibility in each neighbourhood is in the hands of a team of six neighbourhood managers, headed by a chief executive who reports to the Neighbourhood Committee, who are each responsible for particular functions, including housing and the personal social services (Lowndes and Stoker 1992).

One advantage of decentralization is that, because they are smaller and closer to local residents, neighbourhood and area offices are more accessible to local people. Corporate decentralization is also seen as enabling local people to be able to identify more with a single multi-service neighbourhood office than with a range of individual service offices. Decentralization is also said to generate a greater responsiveness to the needs of local areas by the deliverers of services, who are able to acquire information about the needs and priorities of the people in their particular neighbourhood. The staff of neighbourhood offices can also build up contacts with local community associations and voluntary organizations

(Lowndes 1992: 54–5; see also Elcock 1986b: 46; Elcock 1988: 47). The close-ness of the deliverers of local social services to the customers of their services may also lessen the risk of the 'accountability outwards' of welfare professionals to professional colleagues becoming too dominant compared with their 'account-ability downwards' to users (Elcock 1986b: 36).

Despite such advantages, the decentralization of local services like hous-ing and the personal social services has met with a certain amount of resistance. Decentralization challenges the principles of bureaucratic structure and profes-sionalism which have traditionally underpinned the organizational arrange-ments for delivering local authority services, and which have underpinned the public administration model of welfare delivery (see Stewart 1987: 50). It involves an increase in the powers of the front-line staff of local social services and housing departments, the so-called 'street-level bureaucrats', responsible for the actual delivery of services at the area or neighbourhood level, thereby weakening the roles of senior staff at the centre. In addition to resistance from senior managers, there has also been opposition from local authority trade unions, concerned about the implications of service decentralization for the employment conditions of their members. Inevitably, decentralization also involves considerable capital and staffing costs (Stoker 1988: 205–6).

The decentralization of local services has been criticized as being essen-tially a managerialist exercise. Thus it has been suggested that the decentraliza-tion of the personal social services in East Sussex was a means of resolving the problem of controlling field units in the county's social services department (see Chandler 1991: 128). A study of the decentralization of housing services has concluded that local councillors have supported an approach to decentraliz-ation which has been stronger on such qualities as convenience and accessibility than on council tenant control or empowerment (Cole 1993: 164). As Ham-bleton and his colleagues (1989: 42) have concluded, whilst some local author-ities may have moved managerial power downwards within the local authority organization, only a few have attempted to move power from the organization to the local community. Decentralization has been predominantly a con-sumerist approach to the problems of delivering welfare at the local authority level, rather than a collectivist approach which focuses upon such issues as the empowerment of council tenants through control by user groups and other approaches (see also Hambleton and Hoggett 1988).

Consumerism in the National Health Service: rhetoric and reality

The importance of 'getting closer to the customer' has also been a key theme in the restructuring of the NHS since the mid-1980s. As we saw in Chapter 1, the NHS has been criticized for being 'producer orientated' rather than 'consumer orientated'. The subject of consumerism was placed firmly at centre stage by the Griffiths inquiry into NHS management in 1983. Echoing Peters and Waterman, Griffiths stressed the importance of customer opinion in the management of the NHS. Griffiths was critical of the NHS's failure to look after what it described as its customers, stating that (Griffiths 1983: 10):

> Businessmen have a keen sense of how well they are looking after their customers. Whether the NHS is meeting the needs of the patient, and the community, and can prove that it is doing so, is open to question.

Griffiths (1988b: 196) later argued that consumerism must be centre stage in the NHS:

> it is central to the approach of management, in planning and delivering services for the population as a whole, to ascertain how well the service is being delivered at local level by obtaining the experience and perceptions of patients and the community: these can be derived from Community Health Councils and by other methods, including market research and from the experience of general practice and the community health services.

Consumerism had, of course, not been completely neglected in the NHS before the Griffiths Report. Community Health Councils (CHCs) were set up in the mid-1970s with the specific task of representing the interests of the local community to those responsible for the management of local health services, whilst a Health Service Commissioner was appointed to supplement the procedures available for the redress of grievances within the NHS. However, neither of these two developments was the result of a deliberate decision to give greater priority to the interests of the NHS's consumers: they were both *ad hoc* reactions to particular problems within the service (Harrison 1988: 28). Also, both initiatives have been criticized for their limited impact.

Following the Griffiths critique, there has been an increased awareness by NHS managers of the importance of consumerism. A number of techniques have been introduced in an attempt to improve the responsiveness of the NHS to its users. Health authorities have attempted to discover what the public thinks of hospital services through the use of patient satisfaction surveys and questionnaires, often in conjunction with CHCs. Other initiatives have included the development of improved patient literature and information, such as the newspapers circulated by some DHAs, and the establishment of staff development programmes for dealing with the public. In addition, all RHAs have a designated member of staff with responsibility for either quality assurance or customer relations (Carr-Hill *et al.* 1989: 5). On a broader level, some health authorities have published 'mission statements' focusing on the consumer.

Despite such developments, however, these initiatives have been criticized for being part of what has been described as the 'customer relations movement'. Echoing the concerns expressed about consumerism in local government, critics have argued that consumerism in the NHS is about customer relations, rather than about empowering the consumer. Consumerism in the NHS has been described as a 'supermarket model' of health care, denying patients the right to be consulted about what should be 'on the shelves' and failing to encourage them to seek redress if the goods are faulty (Scrivens 1988: 184). According to Winkler (1987: 1), consumerism in the NHS is a 'harmless version' of consumerism, an approach which 'requires little serious change, but much public visibility. It is about the appearance, not substance, of change'. Other critics argue that while consumerism may well lead to better communication and feedback, it does not contribute very much to solving the problems of scarce resources and staff shortages which may help account for the poor quality of many social services, 'a smiling doctor or nurse is not contributing much to effectiveness when telling a patient that he or she has to wait months for an operation' (Harrow and Willcocks 1990: 295).

Consumerism in central government

The growing attention given to the customer orientation has also been taken on board by the two central government departments directly responsible for the delivery of welfare, the DSS and the DEmp. The bigger spender of these departments, the DSS and its predecessor, the DHSS, has not scored well on the criterion of 'closeness to the customer', having long been the subject of complaints regarding the quality of its service delivery (see Chapter 1). The importance of the customer orientation was forced to the top of the Department's agenda in 1988 following critical reports on the quality of service it delivered to members of the public from both the House of Commons Public Accounts Committee and the body which provides its supporting professional assistance and information, the National Audit Office. The report by the National Audit Office (1988) on the quality of service at the DHSS's nationwide system of local offices revealed that there was a significant amount of dissatisfaction with the services provided, notably over high levels of inaccurate payments, delays in processing claims, long waiting times, and the poor accommodation and facilities provided for both staff and claimants. Such concerns were reinforced by the Public Accounts Committee (1988), which concluded that there were a number of local offices providing a poor standard of service.

Criticisms about the quality of the delivery of social security benefits were repeated in a report by a group of DHSS civil servants, who were given the task of examining the organization and location of social security work and advising on a new structure for the Department's local office network. The new structure was expected to maximize the opportunities to improve the quality of services delivered to the public. Known as the Moodie Report, after its principal author, and published in 1988, the group's findings concluded that the service provided for the DHSS's customers varied enormously 'from the quite outstanding to the quite appalling' (Moodie et al. 1988: para. 6). Like the Public Accounts Committee and the National Audit Office before it, the group highlighted examples of poor-quality service, including the time taken to process claims, waiting times in local offices and accuracy in the making of payments. Two of the group's main conclusions were that the social security system's regional organization should be restructured with the customer in mind and that the system had to project a consistent and recognizable image which transmitted 'positive messages' to its customers (Moodie *et al.* 1988: 2). As the group's report put it: 'Social security is in the business of service. Its product is good quality service' (Moodie *et al.* 1988: para. 2).

Thus the Moodie Report put the customer at centre stage. Speaking of the social security system, it said (Moodie *et al.* 1988: para. 3):

> Few organisations can have greater claims to be a consumer organisation. Social security is a service which at some point or another, in some form or another, touches the whole population in ways which are uniquely personal and intimate.

One immediate manifestation of this new customer orientation emerged the following year in the form of a set of 'principles of good service' that the staff of what was now the DSS had to adopt (including efficiency, responsiveness to the public's needs and fairness) and which emphasized that the new department aimed 'to provide a good service to the public – a professional service that is fair, impartial, prompt, courteous and accurate, and which recognises each one of our customers as an individual' (Department of Social Security 1989). The commitment to improving the quality of service to its customers had been further reflected in the introduction of a Quality Assessment Package (QAP) in the late 1980s (see also Chapter 8), which involved the monitoring of the quality of the service provided to the public (National Audit Office 1988: para. 2.3; see also Carter *et al.* 1992: 99–101).

Improving the quality of service delivery to the public has also been one of the objectives of the massive computerization of the social security system, known as the Operational Strategy (OS) and completed in the early 1990s. One of the objectives of the OS is to improve the quality of service delivery by treating individual claimants as 'whole people' rather than according to the particular benefit being claimed (Margetts 1991: 327–8). Unfortunately, the project, which is the largest civil computerization programme ever installed in Europe, has been beset with problems and critics claim that not all of the hoped for benefits have been achieved. Margetts (1991: 341) concludes that the OS has been characterized by top–down design and implementation, and that although social security claimants might have been renamed 'customers', their needs have remained a low priority.

Despite these developments, the most significant manifestation of the recognition of the customer orientation in the DSS, and the other central government department responsible for the delivery of social security benefits, the DEmp, has been the creation of executive agencies as a result of the Next Steps programme launched in 1988 (see Chapter 2). A major aim of the Next Steps initiative is to deliver services in a way which is more responsive to the needs of customers. As one senior DSS official told the House of Commons select committee investigating the whole Next Steps initiative, the Benefits Agency stood to be judged by 'the extent to which there is an observable and, indeed, a measurable difference in the quality of service we give'. In his opinion, if the Benefits Agency did not improve service, 'we shall have wasted our time' (Treasury and Civil Service Committee 1989: para. 48).

Both the Benefits Agency and the Employment Service have developed a clear customer orientation. The main way in which service to the customers of the two agencies is measured is by the setting of service delivery targets. For instance, in 1994–95, the Benefits Agency was set the target of clearing 71 per cent of income support claims within 5 days and clearing 60 per cent of family credit claims within 13 days. The Benefits Agency has also published local targets and standards for each of its districts. In the same year, the Employment Service was set the target of placing 1 700 000 unemployed people into jobs and ensuring that the accuracy of the total value of unemployment benefit paid was at least 97 per cent. Like the Benefits Agency, it also has local standards for the level of service to clients. Given that, unlike customers in the private sector, the customers of these two agencies cannot 'shop around for the best deal', the use of such performance targets is clearly important in helping to provide incentives for improved service to the public (Treasury and Civil Service Committee 1990: para. 54).

As part of its attempts to develop an efficient and customer related delivery service, the Benefits Agency also undertakes a national, independently conducted customer survey every year. The Employment Service also carries out national and local customer satisfaction surveys, testing views on the quality of service being provided. As we shall discuss in the next section, both the Benefits Agency and the Employment Service, along with other key delivery agencies of the welfare state, have published customer charters setting out the standards of service which the users of their services are entitled to expect.

The way in which the Benefits Agency delivers its services is also being transformed by the introduction of the 'one-stop' programme, the first phase of which was officially launched in late 1993. The ultimate aim of this programme is to eventually provide a service which will enable customers to have their claims and problems dealt with in one place, by one member of staff and at one time, thereby cutting down on duplication and providing a more personal service.

Despite the establishment of the Benefits Agency and the Employment Service and their emphasis on customer care and service, some observers are sceptical about these initiatives. Thus the civil service unions argue that although executive agencies have been given greater managerial freedoms to enable them to provide better levels of service, they also need adequate resources in order to develop service quality (Treasury and Civil Service Committee 1989: para. 51). Similar criticisms about lack of resources have been made about the Conservative Government's Citizen's Charter initiative, to which we now turn.

The Citizen's Charter: focusing on the customer

As we saw earlier in this chapter, the late 1980s and early 1990s witnessed the publication by several pioneering local authorities of charters informing the users of local services about the standards which their councils hoped to achieve in those services and explaining the arrangements for redress if these promises were not met. The early 1990s also saw the publication of proposals for national charters by the Labour Party (1991) and the Liberal Democrats (1991).

Following his appointment as Prime Minister in late 1990, John Major announced that the Conservative Government was developing 'the most comprehensive quality initiative ever launched', which would offer nothing less than 'a revolution in the way public services are delivered' (*The Guardian*, 11 May 1991). The initiative was officially launched as a White Paper entitled the Citizen's Charter in July 1991 (Prime Minister 1991). The stated purpose of the Citizen's Charter is to improve the quality of public services and to make them more responsive to their users (Prime Minister 1991: 2).

The underlying aim of the Charter was described by the then Treasury Minister responsible for its implementation as being 'to encourage those who work in public services to think about what they do in relation to how it affects the customer, the user of services'. He indicated that one of the most important principles underlying the Charter was the orientation of public services towards their users, in contrast to the preoccupations of the conventional bureaucratic structure, in which people 'tend to think about their own role in relation to others within the organisation rather than in relation to those outside'. The important relationship was seen as that which exists between the organization and the user of its services (Select Committee on the Parliamentary Commissioner for Administration 1992: question 3).

Echoing this description of the philosophy behind the Charter, the Deputy Director of the Government's Citizen's Charter Unit later stated that the Charter is about 'the outward face of the organisation: the relationship between public services and their users' (Goldsworthy 1993: 140). According to her, the Charter 'puts itself in the shoes of the recipient of services,' asking such questions as: 'What can I as an individual expect from this organisation?' 'Does this represent my full and fair entitlement?' 'Have I received what I was told to expect?' 'What is the organisation going to do for me if it fails to deliver the standards that I as an individual have been told I can expect?' Thus the aim of the Citizen's Charter is to raise the standard of public services and to make them more responsive to their users. It attempts to make the idea of the 'customer' 'a reality' (Goldsworthy 1993: 141).

In attempting to emphasize the customer orientation, the Citizen's Charter, like other developments in the arrangements for the delivery of welfare introduced since 1979, is based upon the assumption that the public sector can learn from the private sector (see, for example, Connolly *et al.* 1994: 27). The Government itself has stated (Prime Minister 1992: 1):

> Through these Charters the citizen can increasingly put pressure upon those responsible for providing services to deliver them to a high standard, rather as commercial competition puts consumer pressure on the performance of private sector organisations.

The Citizen's Charter has four main themes:

- to improve the quality of public services;
- to provide choice, wherever possible, between competing providers;
- to tell citizens what service standards are and how to act where service is unacceptable; and
- to give full value for money within a tax bill the nation can afford.

The Charter's principles apply to all the public services, including the wide range of social services delivered by the Benefits Agency, the Employment Service, local authorities and the NHS.

Described by the Conservative Government as the beginning of a long-term programme, 'a programme for a decade', the Citizen's Charter is only a starting point, being seen as 'a toolkit of initiatives and ideas to raise standards in the way most appropriate to each service' (Prime Minister 1991: 4; Select Committee on the Parliamentary Commissioner for Administration 1992: question 1). The means by which the Charter is to be implemented cover a range of different initiatives and ideas (Prime Minister 1991: 5), including: more privatization; increased competition; further contracting out; greater emphasis on performance-related pay; the publication of local and national performance standards; comprehensive publication of information on the standards achieved; more effective complaints procedures; tougher and more independent inspectorates; and better redress for the citizen when things go wrong. The Charter has been seen as John Major's 'big idea', the Prime Minister's attempt to put his own stamp on the reform of the public sector, or what one commentator has described as 'a vehicle for symbolically differentiating him from his predecessor' (Doern 1993: 20). As we have seen in previous chapters, however, some of the initiatives involved in the implementation of the Charter's principles, especially privatization, contracting out and performance indicators, are not new. They are clearly extensions of initiatives introduced by Margaret Thatcher in the 1980s.

Although part of a wider consumerist movement to bring such services as social security benefits, the NHS and the various social services delivered by local authorities closer to the customer, the Citizen's Charter also included initiatives which fit in with the stronger version of consumerism discussed in the early part of the chapter. Thus part of the solution to what are seen as the problems of consumer choice is seen as lying in the introduction of increased competition and choice, and the development of contracting out through the Government's plans for market-testing. The Cabinet Minister originally responsible for ensuring that the public services were implementing the Charter principles has stated that the introduction of competition into public provision 'cannot . . . properly be done without one key organisational reform, namely the separation of purchaser from provider' (Waldegrave 1993: 17).

Hence, as we have seen in previous chapters, the new arrangements for welfare delivery include the introduction of market-type conditions through such mechanisms as quasi-markets in the NHS and community care. This

Table 9.1   Social services charters 1994

Benefits Agency Customer Charter (1992 and 1993)

Charter for Higher Education (1993)

Charter for Further Education (1993)

Child Support Agency Charter (1993)

Council Tenant's Charter (1992)

Job Seeker's Charter (1991 and 1994)

Parent's Charter (1991 and 1994)

Patient's Charter (1991)

---

particular approach emphasizes the importance of the consumer, in that markets are expected to offer consumer choice, a key principle of the Citizen's Charter. However, as we saw in our earlier discussion of these developments, these changes do not really empower the consumer at all. Under these new arrangements, patients and users of community care are represented by fund-holding GPs and care managers in decisions about the choice of hospital or residential home.

The publication of the Citizen's Charter was the prelude to the publication of a number of specific charters in a range of public services, including those for parents of school-age children, students in further and higher education, NHS patients, council house tenants, job seekers and those receiving social security benefits (see Table 9.1). Three of these charters have already been updated, and in August 1994 the Government announced that local authority social services departments would be required to introduce local community care charters setting out standards (*The Times*, 4 August 1994). In the NHS, all of the FHSAs have published local charters.

One of the 'principles of public service' emphasized by the Citizen's Charter is the setting, monitoring and publication of service standards, so that the users of services know what to expect from those services. Thus the Job Seeker's Charter specifies that Job Centres will display service targets and results for the number of people it helps back to work, the time a job seeker has to wait to be seen in a local office, the time taken to answer the telephone, and the arrangements for paying the correct benefits on time. Quality standards and maximum waiting times are also included in the Patient's Charter. In addition to national charter standards, all local health authorities have set their own service standards and many have published local health charters, including such indicators as maximum waiting times for first outpatient appointments. As a result of the Council Tenant's Charter, all local housing authorities have to publish annual reports on standards of service and performance achieved.

Another major theme highlighted by the Citizen's Charter is information – about how services are run, how much they cost, how well they perform and who is in charge. Thus the Patient's Charter gives NHS patients the right to be given detailed information on local health services. The Job Seeker's Charter sets out the services which the Employment Service offers to its clients in helping to get them a job and to prepare them for the world of work. The importance of information is also emphasized by the Parent's Charter, which sets out the rights of parents with regard to choosing a school, the kind of education parents can expect, and the procedures to follow if things go wrong.

The Citizen's Charter also emphasizes the importance of choice and consultation with the users of services. Thus, as we have already seen, the Employment Service regularly surveys the views of its customers on the service they receive, and has also piloted local customer satisfaction surveys, with plans to undertake these on an annual basis.

As befits a document which emphasizes the interests of the consumers, and not the providers, of services, a central theme of the Charter is the promise of better machinery for the redress of grievances. Although originally envisaging a system of local lay adjudicators to handle minor claims for redress, the Government decided that the first step in the implementation of this particular aspect of the Charter initiative should be to ensure that the internal complaints mechanisms of the various public services should be brought into line with the principles of the Charter. Thus the Patient's Charter gives NHS patients the right to have any complaint about NHS services investigated, and to receive a full report and a prompt written reply from the chief executive of the relevant health authority or the general manager of the hospital concerned. As we saw in Chapter 5, there has been much criticism of the procedures for dealing with NHS complaints, and proposals for reform were made by a government inquiry in 1994 (Department of Health 1994). Following proposals in the Parent's Charter, local education authorities are required to include independent lay members on panels which hear parents' appeals if they do not receive a place for their child at a particular school. The Benefits Agency's Customer Charter informs people that compensation may be paid if a customer suffers financial loss as the result of a mistake by the Agency.

Despite the introduction of improvements in the machinery for redressing grievances, the Citizen's Charter emphasized that it would still be open to individual 'customers' of services to use the various ombudsmen systems discussed in Chapter 5 as external backups to the internal complaints procedures. Indeed, the Charter promised to introduce legislation to make the local ombudsmen's recommendations legally enforceable if some local authorities continued to ignore these recommendations in cases in which maladministration had been found, whilst the Patient's Charter sees the Health Service Commissioner as playing an important part in the development of effective complaints mechanisms in the NHS.

If the aims of the Citizen's Charter are achieved, one can look forward to the elimination of many of the complaints referred to the ombudsmen. On the other hand, it may well be that the higher level of expectations about standards of service delivery which will be generated by the Charter and the charters published for individual social services will actually lead to an increase in the number of complaints referred (see, for example, Parliamentary Commissioner for Administration 1992: para. 36).

Thus the Citizen's Charter is an official recognition of the importance of quality and consumerism in the public services: what has been described as 'an original and radical approach' to public-sector reform (Farnham 1992: 79). But as Drewry (1993: 251) observes, the Charter's invocation of 'citizenship' is 'highly misleading'. The Charter is about promoting the responsiveness of public services and not about enhancing people's rights as citizens. In the words of two observers (Stewart and Walsh 1992: 507):

> The emphasis is upon individual rights to choice and to quality, with little reference to citizens' duties. Accountability is seen as market based . . . The public is seen as having acquired rights to services through the payment of taxes rather than community membership.

Or as another commentator observes (Farnham 1992: 80), the Citizen's Charter appears to have a view of citizenship which is:

> stunted and uni-dimensional. It is rooted in the assumption that the citizen is primarily an economic person, a consumer and a tax payer who is concerned largely with economic and market rights rather than with any non-economic rights.

The contemporary concept of citizenship has conventionally been associated with the writings of the British sociologist, T.H. Marshall. Marshall (1963: 87) defined citizenship as 'a status bestowed on those who are full members of a community', and identified three rights with which it was associated – civil rights, political rights and social rights. Civil rights consist of the rights necessary for individual freedom, such as liberty of the person, freedom of speech, freedom of religion and equality before the law. Political rights involve the right to take part in the exercise of political power through either voting in elections or serving as an elected member of Parliament or a local authority. These civil and political rights were supplemented by the social rights introduced by the welfare state in the post-war period, such as rights to health care, education and a basic income (1963: 74).

According to Barron and Scott (1992: 533–4), the Citizen's Charter 'appears to contain little that Marshall might have acknowledged to be an enhancement of citizenship'. As they point out, the Charter suggests no new initiatives for the protection of civil liberties, says nothing on political rights and promises no new entitlements to social welfare. What they refer to as 'the novelty' of the Charter lies more in its language and ideology than in the policies which it sets out. The conception of the citizen as 'entitlement based on need' is reconceived as the conception of 'a paying customer, who as such is entitled to receive the level of quality which could be guaranteed were the provider constrained by the pressure of competition in the marketplace' (Barron and Scott 1992: 535, 543).

The Citizen's Charter is essentially a consumer's charter, and, as we shall discuss below, is the subject of the same kind of criticisms which have been made of other attempts to enhance consumerism in the delivery agencies of the welfare state. Its critics have accused it of adopting a 'simplistic approach' to the public services, concentrating on the 'repackaging' of existing services, and ignoring the more complicated considerations that are essential for the development of quality services in the public sector (Local Government Information Unit 1991: 4). The Charter has also been criticized for involving no extra resources for the development of those services. Thus the Patient's Charter, for example, points out that the 'rights' which it outlines 'are not legal rights but major and specific standards which the Government looks to the NHS to achieve, as circumstances and resources allow' (Department of Health 1991b). As the Citizen's Charter (Prime Minister 1991: 6) itself emphasizes, the Charter programme is about 'finding better ways of converting the money that can be afforded into even better services'. This particular feature of the Charter programme has aroused much criticism, an assistant manager in the Benefits Agency being quoted as saying that 'most of us see it as quite a cynical exercise to paper over the cracks in the service' (Willmore 1992), while another critic has argued that it will be no consolation to people who go to a local authority housing department 'to be told politely, quickly, efficiently and courteously that there are no houses available and it is unlikely that there will be any available to meet their demands' (House of Commons Debates 15 November 1991: col. 1365).

Consumerism or citizenship?

The 1980s and the 1990s have seen a growing concern with consumer responsiveness in the operations of the delivery agencies of the welfare state. Critics, however, argue that these kinds of developments are not sufficient. As one commentator has put it: 'Consumerism is fine as far as it goes, but it does not go far enough to affect a radical shift in the distribution of power' (Potter 1988: 157).

Thus, for observers like Rhodes (1987), the public service orientation within local government needs to be set in a wider context than service delivery. As we have seen, a major criticism of consumerist approaches in local government is that they are essentially managerialist. While such approaches enable the consumers of services to have a greater say in informing the deliverers of services about their needs, they do not normally involve consumers in meeting those needs. Thus consumerism in local government tends to see the public as customers rather than as citizens. Critics argue that reforms to the delivery of welfare services need to go beyond the consumerist approach. As Rhodes (1987: 66) observes, the consumers of public services are also citizens, defined by the Greeks as those who shared in decision and office. Thus the arrangements for the delivery of services need to recognize this duality of roles through, for example, a greater concern for citizens' rights of participation and representation.

Similar criticisms have been made of attempts to increase the responsiveness of local services through decentralizing the delivery of such services as housing and the personal social services, it being argued that decentralization has been mainly a modification to traditional ways of delivering services rather than a radical change in the workings of local authorities (Stewart 1987: 51). Whilst there have clearly been important gains, improved public access and more responsive local services, the decentralization of welfare delivery has not led to any fundamental change in the distribution of managerial – let alone political – power. Decentralization has been essentially concerned with the reform of the administrative arrangements for the delivery of local authority services. Critics of these initiatives emphasize the importance of the democratization of services, as well as the localization, of services (see, for example, Hambleton and Hoggett 1988). Such an approach includes the devolution of power to local communities through such mechanisms as user group participation and forms of local decision-making which involve both elements of local representative democracy and community groups.

The argument that the concept of the citizen has been defined too narrowly has also been a criticism of the more recent development of user charters for the major social services. Thus, in the Conservative Government's Citizen's Charter, elected local authorities, traditionally the major delivery agencies of the welfare state, are seen solely as agencies for the efficient and responsive delivery of services. Despite the fact that local government has traditionally been justified, in part, on the basis of its contribution to local democracy and accountability, local authorities are viewed as organizations that arrange for the delivery of services. There is no recognition of the role of local authorities as the representatives of local communities, nor of the importance of local democracy as a means of 'resolving conflicting aspirations for services' (Local Government Information Unit 1991: 4).

10

Conclusion: the changing face of welfare delivery

For most of the post-war period, the welfare state in Britain was dominated by what we described in Chapter 1 as the public administration model of welfare delivery. The five core social services which formed the basis of the classic welfare state which emerged in the late 1940s were delivered by a combination of national and local governmental organizations – the central government departments concerned with the payment of social security benefits, local authorities, and the NHS – who, for the most part, were responsible for both the funding and provision of social services. On the periphery of the public face of welfare, a number of quasi-governmental bodies, such as the Housing Corporation, carried out a range of important managerial and promotional functions.

Looking at the – still evolving – organizational arrangements for the delivery of welfare in the 1990s, there have been substantial changes. Although he was referring specifically to the introduction of quasi-markets, Le Grand's (1991: 1257) observation that the full implementation of the reforms of the late 1980s and early 1990s would result in the welfare state in the 1990s being 'a very different animal from the welfare state of the previous 45 years' applies equally to the other changes which are currently taking place in the delivery of welfare. At the national level, both of the Government Departments responsible for the delivery of social security benefits, the DSS and the DEmp, have been transformed, with semi-autonomous executive agencies, headed by chief executives on short-term contracts, now directly responsible for the day-to-day delivery of benefits. At the local level, elected local authorities, for long the major front-line delivery agencies of the welfare state, have moved towards an enabling role with a large number of quasi-governmental, voluntary and private-sector bodies now having increasing responsibility for the delivery of welfare in the fields of education, housing and the personal social services. The organization and management of the NHS has also undergone radical reform, with the introduction of the purchaser–provider split, and the creation of self-governing trusts, as part of the internal market system.

Borrowing the terminology used by Richards (1992) in her discussion of recent developments in the governance of public services, it is clear that the assumptions and practices of the traditional public administration model have been challenged, and that we have seen the emergence of an efficiency paradigm associated with private-sector management practices and market-type mechanisms. Even more recently, there has been the emergence of a new paradigm emphasizing the position of the consumer, associated with the Major Government's Citizen's Charter and other developments.

Reassessing the public administration model

In Chapter 1 we identified five key features of the traditional public administration model – its bureaucratic structure, the dominant role played by welfare professionals, the value of public accountability, the concern with equity and the notion of self-sufficiency – which characterized the organization of the delivery of welfare for most of the post-war period. The remaining sections of this concluding chapter will briefly reflect on the status of these traditional characteristics in the light of the emergence of newer approaches to the delivery of welfare.

Bureaucracy and welfare delivery

Bureaucratic structure, with its emphasis on hierarchy and uniformity, has been a key feature of the traditional organization of welfare delivery since 1945. But, as we saw in Chapter 1, welfare bureaucracies have been the subject of increasing attack from all sides of the political spectrum, ranging from complaints about inefficiency and waste in the use of precious resources to concerns about the failure of delivery agencies to be close enough to their customers in the delivery of those services.

A major consequence of such concerns has been the search for alternative forms of organizing the delivery of welfare. Thus, influenced by the proponents of the public choice school, with its preference for the dismantling of large centralized bureaucracies into smaller competing bodies, the 1980s and 1990s have seen attempts to break up traditional public bureaucratic structures like local authority housing empires through such policy initiatives as the 'right to buy', the opting out of many local education authority schools to the newly created grant maintained sector, and the transformation of the majority of NHS hospitals and other health-care units into self-governing trusts.

What Hoggett (1991: 247) refers to as 'the demise of bureaucratic control' and its replacement by post-bureaucratic forms of welfare delivery has also included a movement away from the traditional 'top–down' hierarchies associated with bureaucratic arrangements for delivering welfare. One manifestation of this particular trend has been the devolution of managerial freedoms to smaller operational units within the organizations responsible for welfare delivery. We have noted a number of developments in this area: local management has been introduced in schools; financial responsibility within the NHS has been devolved to hospital doctors through the Resource Management Initiative; fund-holding GPs have been established within the NHS; increased responsibility has been delegated to care managers in local authority social services departments; managerial and financial responsibilities have been devolved to chief executives in the newly created Benefits Agency and other executive agencies.

In some areas of the welfare state, notably community care and the NHS, we are seeing the abandonment of what has been referred to as 'control by hierarchy' and its replacement by 'control by contract' (Hoggett 1991: 250). One advantage of the use of contract as a means of delivering welfare is that by separating the purchaser and provider roles, it moves away from the traditional organization in which those responsible for a service have tended to identify with those providing it, rather than with those using it (Stewart 1993: 8). By setting out specific service targets, contracts are also a means of focusing attention on the quality of service delivery (see, for example, Longley 1993: 43). However, the contract culture has limitations, notably the dilution of public accountability, as members of the public will not always be certain who is accountable for particular services.

The movement away from welfare delivery by hierarchical structures has also included the development of the phenomenon of spatial decentralization within local authorities, the traditional bureaucratic approach to the delivery of local government welfare being challenged by the decentralization of the delivery of housing and the personal social services to neighbourhood and area offices. However, as we saw in Chapter 9, most local authorities have been cautious about the amount of freedom granted to decentralized offices, the values of bureaucratic forms of organization still being emphasized by senior managers.

Professionals and the delivery of welfare

The dominant role played by professionals in the delivery of welfare has also been challenged by the new paradigms of efficiency and consumerism. In this context, we have noted a number of developments since the early 1980s. Perhaps the most significant of these has been the threat to the position of the medical profession, as manifested by the increased emphasis upon the role of managers in the NHS and by the replacement of consensus management with general management, what has been referred to as the 'shifting of the frontier' between doctors and NHS managers. The role of general management within the NHS has been reinforced by the internal market reforms, with general managers being given a major role in the new contracting process and hospital consultants being made directly accountable to managers, as well as being given responsibility for clinical budgeting. On the other hand, one must be careful not to exaggerate the implications of such changes for the medical profession: the contracting process is effectively dependent on medical advice (see Moon and Kendall 1993: 186).

The position of welfare professionals has also been affected by the increasing concern with consumerism and customers. The introduction of the Citizen's Charter, together with the mini-charters published for the various social services, means that the environment in which welfare professionals, and other welfare delivery personnel, are working has changed. Detailed service standards and procedures whereby the consumers of social services can exert pressure on providers to improve the quality of services are now important features of the delivery of welfare. Performance indicators monitor the progress and compare the performance of different delivery agencies. League tables enable the users of services to compare the performance of competing delivery agencies.

The movement away from the professional mode of welfare delivery towards a more managerial mode has also involved what one commentator has referred to as 'creating managers out of professionals' (Hoggett 1991: 254), requiring them to be more interested in the costs of services provided and the management of scarce resources. Thus the introduction of local management of schools, the devolution of financial control to hospital doctors and fund-holding GPs and the devolution of responsibilities to care managers in local authority social services departments have resulted in welfare professionals such as head teachers and their senior staff, doctors and social workers being required to manage the day-to-day operations of their particular operational units, including the handling of budgets and dealing with contractors.

Despite attempts to redefine the role of welfare professionals, however, the long-running debate about their power in the delivery of welfare seems unlikely to have disappeared. The new delivery of welfare may be characterized by the language of consumer choice, but the creation of quasi-markets in the areas of community care and the NHS give welfare professionals the power to decide between the various services which are available. As Taylor-Gooby and Lawson (1993: 138) observe, the relationships between those involved in managing quasi-markets and the consumers that they are supposed to serve may well rekindle the debate about professional power.

Accountability and the public

The notion of accountability has been a recurring theme in the debate about the delivery of welfare. The weaknesses in traditional approaches to accountability have been the subject of concern for many years, with the accountability of elected representatives (whether they be central government Ministers or local government councillors) having long been recognized as an inadequate mechanism for securing the public accountability of delivery agencies and their personnel.

As we saw in Chapter 5, the 1960s and 1970s witnessed attempts to increase 'accountability downwards' to the users of services through the introduction of new complaints mechanisms such as the various ombudsmen institutions. The same period saw moves towards the development of user participation in the social services. Such mechanisms have been seen as ways of giving users 'voice' in the delivery of welfare (Bartlett and Le Grand 1993: 18). But it is the concern with the newer concept of consumer accountability which has been such a significant feature of changes in the arrangements for the delivery of welfare in the late 1980s and early 1990s. Recent initiatives have employed the concept of 'exit' (Hirschman 1970), whereby those consumers who are dissatisfied with the quality of public service provision can choose to leave those services. Thus, in the field of social housing council tenants have been given the opportunity to 'exit' from local housing authorities through the 'right to buy' or by transferring to alternative landlords. In the field of education, the Education Reform Act 1988 increases parental choice through open enrolment and allows parents to ballot for state schools to opt out of local education authority control.

Developments since the late 1980s have also seen the proliferation of non-elected bodies with responsibility for the delivery of large parts of the various social services formerly directly provided by elected local authorities and by health authorities which, although not elected, used to include local authority representation. What has been described as the 'new magistracy' (Stewart 1992: 7) can be found on the governing bodies of grant-maintained schools, CTCs and further education corporations. The boards of the new NHS Trusts and the small number of Housing Action Trusts are also made up of appointed members. The creation of such bodies has given rise to a debate about a so-called 'accountability crisis'. These new arrangements for welfare delivery have also resulted in confusion about the location of responsibility. Thus, it has been argued that confusion is 'written into' the new structure of education, responsibility for the delivery of education being divided between the governing boards of grant-maintained schools, the governing boards of schools which have remained in the local authority sector, local education authorities, the Funding Agency for Schools and the Secretary of State for Education (Stewart 1992: 6–7).

Equity and welfare delivery

A key theme in the restructuring of the delivery of welfare has been the introduction of quasi-markets, a phenomena which has major implications, not least for the traditional imperative of equity, which we identified in Chapter 1 as a key component of the public administration model of welfare delivery. Advocates of quasi-markets argue that the introduction of such mechanisms enhances consumer choice, a claim which has been the subject of much dispute. For example, as we saw in Chapter 7, under the new arrangements for community care and the NHS, choices about care are not made by the users of services, but by purchasers acting on their behalf – care managers, DHAs and fund-holding GPs.

Furthermore, not all potential users of social services have the same capacity for making choices. As has been pointed out, people in lower socio-economic groups may have lower expectations about services and less information about alternatives than those in more affluent groups of society (Bailey 1993: 21). The providers of particular services may also restrict the choices available to certain groups of potential users. As we saw in Chapter 7, it has been suggested that the new arrangements contained in the quasi-markets in health care and community care could tempt the providers of those services to engage in what has been described as 'adverse selection', with those people in most need of a service being excluded from its provision on the grounds of their costliness. Clearly these developments threaten the whole idea of social services underpinned by the notion of equity, as does the emergence within the new NHS since 1991 of what some observers view as a two-tier system of health care, with fund-holding GPs being able to secure preferential treatment for their patients.

Self-sufficiency

The introduction of the purchaser-provider split in services such as the NHS and community care has also challenged the other major assumption which supported the organization of the welfare state for most of the post-war period, the concept of self-sufficiency. The idea that the delivery agencies responsible for the core services of the welfare state also normally provided those services has been undermined by a number of developments. Local authority social services departments are increasingly engaged in relationships with private- and voluntary-sector organizations through contracts for the provision of community care. The notion of self-sufficiency is also challenged by the development of the enabling role in housing, education and the personal social services (Stewart and Walsh 1992: 509), seen by some as presaging the end of local government. Yet, while some see these developments as a threat to the traditional self-sufficiency of local authorities as front-line delivery agents of the welfare state, others see them as a possible opportunity, opening up a broader enabling role than the one envisaged by the Conservative Government and allowing local authorities to meet the needs of people in their areas (see, for example, Stewart 1989: 177; see also Clarke and Stewart 1988). Within the other major delivery agency of the welfare state, the NHS, the formerly self-sufficient DHAs now operate as purchasers of health care, buying services from a range of health-care providers, who include not only DHAs and NHS trusts, but also hospitals in the private sector.

Developments such as these are seen by some as empowering consumers. But unlike the private sector, where customers usually have a choice of competing firms, most users of the social services are not in a position where they can shop around and take their 'custom' elsewhere. Also, although more responsive social services, more sensitive staff and clearer standards are all essential components of better managed welfare delivery, as we saw in the last chapter, consumerism and the customer orientation by themselves are insufficient in the absence of adequate resources.

Despite such reservations, the initiatives of recent years have combined to create a system of welfare delivery in the 1990s which is very different to the system which emerged in the late 1940s, was consolidated in the 1950s and 1960s, and which still operated in the 1970s and early 1980s. A system dominated by central government departments, local authorities and the NHS, and based upon the practices and values of public administration – the public face of welfare – is being replaced by a new set of practices and values, based upon a new language of welfare delivery which emphasizes efficiency and value for money, competition and markets, consumerism and customer care.

Such changes are the product of a deliberate attempt to restructure the arrangements for the delivery of welfare. The issues that they raise are part of a continuing debate about the governance of the welfare state. It is a debate which will doubtless continue throughout the 1990s.

Further reading

Chapter 1   Introduction

Hadley and Young (1990) provide a useful summary of different critiques of the organization of public services, while the context of some recent approaches to public-sector reform is set out by Hambleton and Hoggett (1988). Deakin (1987) examines the origins of the ideas which have underpinned the attack on the welfare state.

Chapter 2   Central government and welfare

The historical development of central government's social service departments up to the late 1980s can be traced through a reading of the second edition of Chester and Willson (1968), Pollitt (1984) and Hennessy (1990). A good account of the breaking up of the DSS into Next Steps agencies is provided by Greer (1994). For more detail on the role of central government departments in controlling the activities of local authorities and health authorities, see Wilson *et al.* (1994) and Ham (1992).

Chapter 3   The government of welfare outside Whitehall

Stoker (1990) provides a good overview of government beyond Whitehall. Wilson *et al.* (1994) is the most up-to-date survey of local government, while Ham (1992) and Baggott (1994) discuss the changing organization of the NHS. Weir and Hall (1994) provide a critical commentary on the extent and implications of quasi-governmental bodies.

Chapter 4   The coordination of planning and welfare

Challis *et al.* (1988) discuss the practice of policy coordination in the social services, including an account of the CPRS and JASP, together with local case studies. Although now dated in its details, Heclo and Wildavsky (1981) remains the best account of the Whitehall expenditure process, whilst Glennerster (1992a) provides a concise account of the role of the Treasury in public spending control. The problems involved in securing effective collaboration between delivery agencies at the local level are outlined by the National Audit Office (1987).

Chapter 5 Accountability and the public

Day and Klein (1987) consider the theories and practices of accountability, with case studies of the local education service and the NHS. The practices of grievance redress are described by Lewis and Birkinshaw (1993), who also set out an agenda for reform. The claims for, and genesis of, participation in the social services are considered by Richardson (1983), while Gyford (1991) provides an overview of the various initiatives developed by local authorities in recent years.

Chapter 6 The rolling back of the local welfare state

See Hartas and Harrop (1991) for a discussion of the relationship between local author-ities and central government in the post-war local welfare state. Stoker (1991) and Wilson et al. (1994) provide detailed discussions of developments in local government since 1979. Rhodes (1992) examines developments in local government finance. On developments in specific local social services, see Ranson (1992) and Whitty (1990) on education, Cole and Furbey (1994) on housing and Wistow et al. (1992 and 1994) on community care. For the debate on the enabling authority, see Ridley (1988), Clarke and Stewart (1988) and Cochrane (1993).

Chapter 7 The privatization of welfare delivery

For definitions and approaches to privatization, see Young (1986). Forrest and Murie (1991) and Mullins et al. (1993) examine the various aspects of the privatization of council housing. The rise of contracting out is discussed by Ascher (1987). Bartlett and Le Grand (1993) is essential reading on quasi-markets. The developing role of the voluntary sector is covered by Brenton (1985) and Waine (1992).

Chapter 8 The search for efficiency and value for money

Pollitt (1993) provides an analysis of the ideas behind the 'new managerialism' of the 1980s and early 1990s, while Taylor-Gooby and Lawson (1993) examine the emer-gence of the managerialist ideology in the delivery of welfare. Contemporary develop-ments in central government departments are discussed by Drewry and Butcher (1991), and Greer (1994) assesses the important Next Steps initiative, including a case study of the Benefits Agency. For managerial developments in local government, see Kelly (1991) and Elcock (1993). Strong and Robinson (1990) discuss management changes in the NHS, while a new addition to the literature in this particular area is Harrison and Pollitt (1994). Carter et al. (1992) discuss performance indicators.

Chapter 9 The customer orientation

The notion of consumerism in the public services is discussed by Connelly (1992) and Potter (1988), while Deakin and Wright (1990) examine user control in the main social services. On the decentralization of social services to the local level, see Hoggett and Hambleton (1988). Burns *et al.* (1994) is a recently published examination of neighbourhood decentralization in practice. Readers requiring an understanding of recent developments in the customer orientation should read the Citizen's Charter (Prime Minister 1991). Useful commentaries on the Charter are provided by Connolly *et al.* (1994) and Barron and Scott (1992).

References

Adam Smith Institute (1984) *The Omega File: Education Policy*, Adam Smith Institute, London.

Albrow, M. (1970) *Bureaucracy*, Pall Mall Press, London.

Alcock, P. (1987) *Poverty and State Support*, Longman, London.

Alexander, A. (1982a) *Local Government in Britain Since Reorganisation*, Allen & Unwin, London.

Alexander, A. (1982b) *The Politics of Local Government in the United Kingdom*, Longman, London.

Allsop, J. (1984) *Health Policy and the National Health Service*, Longman, London.

Allsop, J. (1992) The voice of the user in health care, in E. Beck, S. Lonsdale, S. Newman and D. Patterson (eds) *In the Best of Health? The Status and Future of Health Care in the UK*, Chapman & Hall, London.

Armstrong, Sir W. (1970) The Civil Service Department and its tasks, *O and M Bulletin*, 25, 63–79.

Arnstein, S. (1971) A ladder of citizen participation in the USA, *Journal of the Royal Town Planning Institute*, 57, 176–82.

Ascher, K. (1987) *The Politics of Privatisation: Contracting Out Public Services*, Macmillan, London.

Ashburner, L. and Cairncross, L. (1993) Membership of the 'new style' health authorities: continuity or change?, *Public Administration*, 71, 357–75.

Association of Metropolitan Authorities (1987) *Press Notice 181/87*, 29 October 1987.

Audit Commission (1983) *Handbook on Economy, Efficiency and Effectiveness*, HMSO, London.

Audit Commission (1985) *Managing Social Services for the Elderly*, HMSO, London.

Audit Commission (1986a) *Performance Review in Local Government: A Handbook for Auditors and Local Authorities*, HMSO, London.

Audit Commission (1986b) *Managing the Crisis in Council Housing*, HMSO, London.

Audit Commission (1986c) *Towards Better Management of Secondary Education*, HMSO, London.

Audit Commission (1988a) *The Competitive Council*, Management Paper No. 1, HMSO, London.

Audit Commission (1988b) *Performance Review in Local Government: A Handbook for Auditors and Local Authorities: Action Guide*, HMSO, London.

Audit Commission (1989) *Losing an Empire. Finding a Role. The ILEA of the Future*, Occasional Paper No. 10, HMSO, London.

Audit Commission (1992a) *Community Care: Managing the Cascade of Change*, HMSO, London.

Audit Commission (1992b) *Citizen's Charter Indicators: Charting a Course*, HMSO, London.

Audit Commission (1993) *Who Wins? Voluntary Housing Transfers*, Occasional Paper No. 20, HMSO, London.

Bacon, W. (1978) *Public Accountability and the Schooling System*, Harper and Row, London.

Baggott, R. (1994) *Health and Health Care in Britain*, Macmillan, London.

Bailey, S.J. (1993) Public choice theory and the reform of local government, *Public Policy and Administration*, 8, 7–24.

Bains Report (1972) *The New Local Authorities: Management and Structure*, HMSO, London.

Barclay, P.M. (1982) *Social Workers: Their Role and Tasks*, Bedford Square Press, London.

Baker, L. (1993) HATs brim with success, *Housing*, 29(5), 4.

Barnett, J. (1982) *Inside the Treasury*, Andre Deutsch, London.

Barron, A. and Scott, C. (1992) The Citizen's Charter Programme, *Modern Law Review*, 55, 526–46.

Bartlett, W. and Le Grand, J. (1993) The theory of quasi-markets, in J. Le Grand and W. Bartlett (eds) *Quasi-Markets and Social Policy*, Macmillan, London.

Bassett, K. (1980) The sale of council houses as a political issue, *Policy and Politics*, 8, 290–307.

Beresford, P. and Croft, S. (1990) Opportunity knocks, *Insight*, 18 July, 18–21.

Best, G. (1987) *The Future of NHS General Management: Where Next?*, King's Fund, London.

Bexley, London Borough of (1984) *Annual Review of Service Performance, 1983–84*.

Birkinshaw, P. (1985) *Grievances, Remedies and the State*, Sweet and Maxwell, London.

Blackstone, T. and Plowden, W. (1988) *Inside the Think Tank: Advising the Cabinet 1971–83*, Heinemann, London.

Boaden, N. (1971) *Urban Policy-Making*, Cambridge University Press, Cambridge.

Boaden, N., Goldsmith, M., Hampton, W. and Stringer, P. (1982) *Public Participation in Local Services*, Longman, London.

Boardman, B. (1991) *Fuel Poverty: From Cold Homes to Affordable Warmth*, Bellhaven Press, London.

Boyne, G. and Law, J. (1993) Bidding for unitary status: an evaluation of the contest in Wales, *Local Government Studies*, 19, 537–57.

Bradshaw, J. (1992) Social security, in D. Marsh and R.A.W. Rhodes (eds) *Implementing Thatcherite Policies: Audit of an Era*, Open University Press, London.

Bramley, G. (1993) Quasi-markets and social housing, in J. Le Grand and W. Bartlett (eds) *Quasi-Markets and Social Policy*, Macmillan, London.

Brenton, M. (1985a) *The Voluntary Sector in British Social Services*, Longman, London.

Brenton, M. (1985b) Privatisation and voluntary social services, in M. Brenton and C. Jones (eds) *The Year Book of Social Policy in Britain 1984–5*, Routledge & Kegan Paul, London.

Brown, R.G.S. (1973) *The Changing National Health Service*, Routledge & Kegan Paul, London.

Brown, R.G.S. (1975) *The Management of Welfare*, Fontana, London.

Brown, R.G.S. (1979) *Reorganising the National Health Service: A Case Study of Administrative Change*, Basil Blackwell/Martin Robertson, Oxford.

Brown, R.G.S. and Steel, D.R. (1979) *The Administrative Process in Britain*, 2nd edn., Methuen, London.

Bulpitt, J. (1983) *Territory and Power in the United Kingdom*, Manchester University Press, Manchester.

Bulpitt, J. (1989) Walking back to happiness? Conservative Party governments and elected local authorities in the 1980s, in C. Crouch and D. Marquand (eds) *The New Centralism: Britain Out of Step in Europe?*, Blackwell, Oxford.

Burningham, D. (1992) An overview of the use of performance indicators in local government, in S. Harrison and C. Pollitt (eds) *Handbook of Public Services Management*, Blackwell, Oxford.

Burns, D., Hambleton, R. and Hoggett, P. (1994) *The Politics of Decentralisation: Revitalising Local Democracy*, Macmillan, London.

Butler, E. (1988) Cure for health service ills, *The Guardian*, 5 May 1988.

Byrne, T. (1990) *Local Government in Britain*, 5th edn., Penguin Books, Harmondsworth.

Cairncross, L., Clapham, D. and Goodlad, R. (1994) Tenant participation and tenant power in British council housing, *Public Administration*, 72, 177–200.

Callaghan, J. (1987) *Time and Chance*, Collins, London.

Carr-Hill, R., McIver, S. and Dixon, P. (1989) *The NHS and its Customers: Executive Summary*, Centre for Health Economics, University of York, York.

Carter, N. (1989) Performance indicators: 'backseat driving' or 'hands-off' control?, *Policy and Politics*, 17, 131–8.

Carter, N. and Greer, P. (1993) Evaluating agencies: Next Steps and performance indicators, *Public Administration*, 71, 407–16.

Carter, N., Klein, R. and Day, P. (1992) *How Organisations Measure Success: The Use of Performance Indicators in Government*, Routledge, London.

Castle, B. (1980) *The Castle Diaries 1974–76*, Weidenfeld & Nicolson, London.

Central Policy Review Staff (1975) *A Joint Framework for Social Policies*, HMSO, London.

Central Policy Review Staff (1977) *Relations Between Central Government and Local Authorities*, HMSO, London.

Challis, L., Day. P. and Klein. R. (1984) Residential care on demand, *New Society*, 5 April, 32.

Challis, L., Fuller, S., Henwood, M., Klein, R., Plowden, W., Webb, A., Whittingham, P. and Wistow, G. (1988) *Joint Approaches to Social Policy: Rationality and Practice*, Cambridge University Press, London.

Chancellor of the Duchy of Lancaster (1994) *Next Steps Agencies in Government Review: 1994*, Cm 2750, HMSO, London.

Chandler, J.A. (1991) *Local Government Today*, Manchester University Press, Manchester.

Chester, D.N. and Willson, F.M.G. (1957) *The Organisation of British Central Government 1914–56*, Allen & Unwin, London.

Chester, D.N. and Willson, F.M.G. (1968) *The Organization of British Central Government 1914–64*, 2nd edn., Allen & Unwin, London.

Clapham, D. (1989) The new housing legislation: what impact will it have? *Local Government Policy Making*, 15(4), 3–10.

Clapham, D. (1990) Housing, in N. Deakin and A. Wright (eds) *Consuming Public Services*, Routledge, London.

Clapham, D., Kemp, P. and Smith, S.J. (1990) *Housing and Social Policy*, Macmillan, London.

Clarke, M. and Stewart, J. (1985) *Local Government and the Public Service Orientation: or does a public service provide for the public?*, Local Government Training Board, Luton.

Clarke, M. and Stewart, J. (1988) *The Enabling Council: Developing and Managing a New Style of Local Government*, Local Government Training Board, Luton.

Clothier, Sir C. (1986) The value of an Ombudsman, *Public Law*, Summer, 204–11.

Cochrane, A. (1993) *Whatever Happened to Local Government?* Open University Press, Buckingham.

Cole, I. (1993) The decentralization of housing services, in P. Malpass and R. Means (eds) *Implementing Housing Policy*, Open University Press, Buckingham.

Cole, I. and Furbey, R. (1994) *The Eclipse of Council Housing*, Routledge, London.

Coleman, V. (1989) *The Health Scandal: Your Health in Crisis*, Mandarin, London.

Commission for Local Administration in England (1994) *Annual Report 1993–1994*, Commission for Local Administration in England, London.

Common, R. and Flynn, N. (1992) *Contracting for Care*, Joseph Rowntree Foundation, York.

Compton, Sir Edmund (1970) The administrative performance of government, *Public Administration*, 48, 3–14.

Connelly, J. (1992) All customers now? Some notes on consumerism in the public services, *Teaching Public Administration*, 12, 29–32.

Connolly, M., McKeown, P. and Milligan-Byrne, G. (1994) Making the public sector more user friendly? A critical examination of the Citizen's Charter, *Parliamentary Affairs*, 47, 21–37.

Conservative Party (1983) *The Challenge of Our Times*, Conservative Party, London.

Corrigan, P., Jones, T., Lloyd, J. and Young, J. (1988) *Socialism, Merit and Efficiency*, Fabian Tract 530, Fabian Society, London.

Council of Europe (1993) *The Role of Competitive Tendering in the Efficient Provision of Local Services*, Council of Europe Press, Strasbourg.

Council on Tribunals (1985) *Annual Report 1984–85*, HC 54, HMSO, London.

Council on Tribunals (1986) *Social Security – Abolition of Independent Appeals Under the Proposed Social Fund*, Cmnd 9722, HMSO, London.

Council on Tribunals (1993) *Annual Report 1992–93*, HC 78, HMSO, London.

Crosland, S. (1982) *Tony Crosland*, Jonathan Cape, London.

Crossman, R.H.S. (1976) The role of the volunteer in the modern social services, Sydney Ball Memorial Lecture 1973, in A.H. Halsey (ed.) *Traditions in Social Policy*, Blackwell, Oxford.

Crossman, R.H.S. (1977) *The Diaries of a Cabinet Minister*, Volume 3, Hamish Hamilton and Jonathan Cape, London.

Davidson, N. (1987) *A Question of Care: The Changing Face of the National Health Service*, Michael Joseph, London.

Davies, B.P. (1968) *Social Needs and Resources in Local Services*, Michael Joseph, London.

Davies, B.P. (1972) *Variations in Children's Services Among British Urban Authorities*, Bell, London.

Day, P. and Klein, R. (1983) The mobilisation of consent versus the management of conflict: decoding the Griffiths Report, *British Medical Journal*, 287, 1813–16.

Day, P. and Klein, R. (1987) *Accountabilities: Five Public Services*, Tavistock, London.

Deakin, N. (1987) *The Politics of Welfare*, Methuen, London.

Deakin, N. and Wright, A. (1990) *Consuming Public Services*, Routledge, London.

Department of the Environment (1971) *Local Government in England: Government Proposals for Reorganisation*, Cmnd 4584, HMSO, London.

Department of the Environment (1977) *Local Government Finance*, Cmnd 6813, HMSO, London.

Department of the Environment (1986) *Paying for Local Government*, Cmnd 9721, HMSO, London.

Department of the Environment (1987) *Housing: the Government's Proposals*, Cm 214, HMSO, London.

Department of the Environment (1989) *Local Authorities Housing Role: 1989 HIP Round*. Appendix to letter from DoE to local authorities inviting annual submission of Housing Strategy and Investment Programme. Department of the Environment, London.

Department of the Environment (1991a) *The Structure of Local Government in England: a Consultation Paper*, HMSO, London.

Department of the Environment (1991b) *The Internal Management of Local Authorities in England: a Consultation Paper*, HMSO, London.

Department of Health (1989a) *Working for Patients*, Cm 555, HMSO, London.

Department of Health (1989b) *Caring for People: Community Care in the Next Decade and Beyond*, Cm 849, HMSO, London.

Department of Health (1990) *Community Care in the Next Decade and Beyond: Policy Guidance*, HMSO, London.

Department of Health (1991a) *Purchase of Service*, HMSO, London.

Department of Health (1991b) *The Patient's Charter*, HMSO, London.

Department of Health (1993) *Managing the New NHS: Background Document*, Department of Health, London.

Department of Health (1994) *Being Heard: The Report of a Review Committee on NHS Complaints Procedures*, Department of Health, London.

Department of Health and Social Security (1972a) *National Health Service Reorganisation*, Cmnd 5055, HMSO, London.

Department of Health and Social Security (1972b) *Management Arrangements for the Reorganised National Health Service*, HMSO, London.

Department of Health and Social Security (1976) *Priorities for Health and Personal Social Services in England*, HMSO, London.

Department of Health and Social Security (1982) *Social Security Operational Strategy: a Framework for the Future*, HMSO, London.

Department of Social Security (1989) *Our Business is Service*, DSS, London.

Department of Social Security (1993) *Social Security Statistics 1993*, HMSO, London.

Doern, B. (1993) The UK Citizen's Charter: origins and implications, *Policy and Politics*, 21, 17–29.

Donnison, D. (1982) *The Politics of Poverty*, Martin Robertson, Oxford.

Donnison, D. (1984) The progressive potential of privatisation, in J. Le Grand and R. Robinson (eds) *Privatisation and the Welfare State*, Allen & Unwin, London.

Drewry, G. (1988) Rubbing noses in the future: social policy and the demise of CPRS, in M. Bury and J. Macnicol (eds) *Aspects of Ageing: Essays on Social Policy and Old Age*, Social Policy Paper No. 3, Department of Social Policy and Social Science, Royal Holloway and Bedford New College, Egham.

Drewry, G. (1993) Mr Major's charter: empowering the consumer?, *Public Law*, Summer, 248–56.

Drewry, G. and Butcher, T. (1991) *The Civil Service Today*, 2nd edn., Blackwell, Oxford.

Dunleavy, P. (1989) The architecture of the British central state, part I: framework for analysis, *Public Administration*, 67, 249–76.

Dunleavy, P. and Rhodes, R.A.W. (1983) Beyond Whitehall, in H. Drucker, P. Dunleavy, A. Gamble and G. Peele (eds) *Developments in British Politics*, Macmillan, London.

Dunleavy, P. and Rhodes, R.A.W. (1986) Government beyond Whitehall, in H. Drucker, P. Dunleavy, A. Gamble and G. Peele (eds) *Developments in British Politics 2*, Macmillan, London.

Dunsire, A. (1981) Central control over local authorities: a cybernetic approach, *Public Administration*, 59, 173–88.

Dunsire, A. (1982) Challenges to public administration in the 1980s, *Public Administration Bulletin*, No. 39, 8–21.

Dunsire, A. and Hood, C. (1989) *Cutback Management in Public Bureaucracies: Popular Theories and Observed Outcomes in Whitehall*. Cambridge University Press, Cambridge.

Eardley, T. and Sainsbury, R. (1993) Managing appeals: the control of housing benefit internal reviews by local authority officers, *Journal of Social Policy*, 22, 461–85.

Efficiency Unit (1988) *Improving Management in Government: The Next Steps*, HMSO, London.

Elcock, H. (1983) Disabling professions: the real threat to local democracy, *Public Money*, 3, 23–7.

Elcock, H. (1986a) *Local Government: Politicians, Professionals and the Public in Local Authorities*, 2nd edn., Methuen, London.

Elcock, H. (1986b) Going local on Humberside: decentralisation as a tool for social services management, *Local Government Studies*, 3, 35–49.

Elcock, H. (1988) Alternatives to representative government in Britain: going local, *Public Policy and Administration*, 3, 38–50.

Elcock, H. (1990) Administrative justice and the citizen, *Teaching Public Administration*, 10, 33–46.

Elcock, H. (1991) *Change and Decay? Public Administration in the 1990s*, Longman, London.

Elcock, H. (1993) Local government, in D. Farnham and S. Horton (eds) *Managing the New Public Services*, Macmillan, London.

Elcock, H., Jordan, A.G. and Midwinter, A.F. (eds) (1989) *Budgeting in Local Government: Managing the Margins*, Longman, London.

Else, P. and Marshall, G.P. (1979) *The Management of Public Expenditure*, Policy Studies Institute, London.

Elston, M.A. (1991) The politics of professional power: medicine in a changing health service, in J. Cabe, M. Calnan and M. Bury (eds) *The Sociology of Health*, Routledge, London.

Enthoven, A. (1985) *Reflections on the Management of the National Health Service*, Nuffield Provincial Hospitals Trust, London.

Enthoven, A. (1991) Internal market reform of the British NHS, *Health Affairs*, 10, 60–70.

Expenditure Committee (1977) 11th Report, Session 1976–77, *The Civil Service*, HC 535, HMSO, London.

Farnham, D. (1992) The Citizen's Charter: improving the quality of the public services or furthering market values?, *Talking Politics*, 4, 75–8.

Fenwick, J. (1989) Consumerism and local government, *Local Government Studies*, 16, 45–52.

Fenwick, J. and Harrop, K. (1990) The customer and local services: a model for practitioners, *Public Money and Management*, 10, 41–5.

Flynn, R. (1992) *Structures of Control in Health Management*, Routledge, London.

Forrest, R. (1993) Contracting housing provision: competition and privatization in the housing sector, in P. Taylor-Gooby and R. Lawson (eds) *Markets and Managers: New Issues in the Delivery of Welfare*, Open University Press, Buckingham.

Forrest, R. and Murie, A. (1991) *Selling the Welfare State: the Privatisation of Public Housing*, revised edition, Routledge, London.

Fowler, N. (1967) The Home Office: ragbag of Whitehall, *New Society*, 24 August, 251–3.

Fowler, N. (1991) *Ministers Decide*, Chapmans, London.

Franks Report (1957) *Report of the Committee on Administrative Tribunals and Inquiries*, Cmnd 218, HMSO, London.

Fudge, C. (1984) Decentralisation: Socialism goes local?, in M. Boddy and C. Fudge (eds) *Local Socialism*, Macmillan, London.

Fulbrook, J., Brooke, R. and Archer, P. (1973) *Tribunals: a Social Court?*, Fabian Tract 427, Fabian Society, London.

Garrett, J. (1980) *Managing the Civil Service*, Heinemann, London.

Giddings, P. (1993) Complaints, remedies and the Health Service Commissioner, *Public Administration*, 71, 377–94.

Gladstone, F.J. (1979) *Voluntary Action in a Changing World*, Bedford Square Press, London.

Glennerster, H. (1992a) *Paying for Welfare: the 1990s*, Harvester Wheatsheaf, Hemel Hempstead.

Glennerster, H. (1992b) *Paying for Welfare: Issues for the Nineties*, Welfare State Programme Paper No. 82, London School of Economics, London.

Glennerster, H., with Korman, N. and Marslen-Wilson, F. (1983) *Planning for Priority Groups*, Martin Robertson, Oxford.

Glennerster, H., Power, A. and Travers, T. (1991) A new era for social policy: a new enlightenment or a new leviathan?, *Journal of Social Policy*, 20, 389–414.

Godber, Sir G. (1975) Regional devolution and the National Health Service, in E. Craven (ed.) *Regional Devolution and Social Policy*, Macmillan, London.

Goldsworthy, D. (1993) Efficiency and effectiveness in public management: A UK perspective, *Administration*, 41, 137–48.

Goodwin, M. and Duncan, S. (1989) The crisis of local government: uneven development and the Thatcher administrations, in J. Mohan (ed.) *The Political Geography of Modern Britain*, Macmillan, London.

Gould, F. and Roweth, B. (1980) Public spending and social policy: the United Kingdom 1950–1977, *Journal of Social Policy*, 9, 337–57.

Gray, A. and Jenkins, W.I. (1982) Efficiency and the self-evaluating organisation – the central government experience, *Local Government Studies*, 8, 47–54.

Gray, A. and Jenkins, W.I. (1985) *Administrative Politics in British Government*, Wheatsheaf Books, Brighton.

Gray, A. and Jenkins, W.I. (1986) Accountable management in British government: some reflections on the financial management initiative, *Financial Accountability and Management*, 2, 171–87.

Greenwood, J. and Wilson, D. (1989) *Public Administration in Britain Today*, 2nd edn., Unwin Hyman, London.

Greenwood, R., Walsh, K., Hinings, C.R. and Ranson, S. (1980) *Patterns of Management in Local Government*, Martin Robertson, Oxford.

Greer, P. (1994) *Transforming Central Government: The Next Steps Initiative*, Open University Press, Buckingham.

Gregory, R. and Pearson, J. (1992) The Parliamentary Ombudsman after twenty-five years, *Public Administration*, 70, 469–98.

Griffith, J.A.G. (1966) *Central Departments and Local Authorities*, Allen & Unwin, London.

Griffiths, R. (1983) *National Health Service Management Enquiry*, DHSS, London.

Griffiths, R. (1988a) *Community Care: Agenda for Action*, HMSO, London.

Griffiths, R. (1988b) Does the public service serve? The consumer dimension, *Public Administration*, 66, 195–204.

Gunn, L.A. (1988) Public management: a third approach?, *Public Money and Management*, 1, 21–6.

Gyford, J. (1985) *The Politics of Local Socialism*, Allen & Unwin, London.

Gyford, J. (1991) *Citizens, Consumers and Councils*, Macmillan, London.

Gyford, J., Leach, S. and Game, C. (1989) *The Changing Politics of Local Government*, Unwin Hyman, London.

Hadley, R. and Hatch, S. (1981) *Social Welfare and the Future of the State*, Allen & Unwin, London.

Hadley, R. and Young, K. (1990) *Creating a Responsive Public Service*, Harvester Wheatsheaf, Brighton.

Hague, D.C. (1971) The Ditchley Conference: a British view, in B.C.R. Smith and D.C. Hague (eds) *The Dilemma of Accountability in Modern British Government: Independence Versus Control*, Macmillan, London.

Haldane Report (1918) *Report of the Machinery of Government Committee*, Cd 9230, HMSO, London.

Ham, C. (1977) Power, patients and pluralism, in K. Barnard and K. Lee (eds) *Conflicts in the National Health Service*, Croom Helm, London.

Ham, C. (1992) *Health Policy in Britain*, 3rd edn., Macmillan, London.

Ham, C. (1994) Where now for the NHS reforms? *British Medical Journal*, 309, 351–2.

Hambleton, R. (1992) Decentralization and democracy in UK local government, *Public Money and Management*, 12, 9–20.

Hambleton, R. and Hoggett, P. (1988) Beyond bureaucratic paternalism, in P. Hoggett and R. Hambleton (eds) *Decentralisation and Democracy: Localising Public Services*, Occasional Paper 28, School of Advanced Urban Studies, University of Bristol, Bristol.

Hambleton, R., Hoggett, P. and Tolan, F. (1989) The decentralisation of public services: a research agenda, *Local Government Studies*, 15, 39–56.

Hamnett, C. (1993) Running housing policy and the British housing system, in R. Maidment and G. Thompson (eds) *Managing the United Kingdom: an Introduction to its Political Economy and Public Policy*, Sage, London.

Hampton, W. (1991) *Local Government and Urban Politics*, 2nd edn., Longman, London.

Hanson, H. and Walles, M. (1984) *Governing Britain*, 4th edn., Fontana, London.

Harden, I. and Lewis, N. (1986) *The Noble Lie: The British Constitution and the Rule of Law*, Hutchinson, London.

Harris, M. (1986) Looking at voluntary agencies, *RIPA Report*, 7(1), 11–12.

Harrison, S. (1988) *Managing the National Health Service: Shifting the Frontier?*, Chapman & Hall, London.

Harrison, S. and Pollitt, C. (1994) *Controlling Health Professionals: The Future of Work and Organization in the National Health Service*, Open University Press, Buckingham.

Harrison, S., Hunter, D.J. and Pollitt, C. (1990) *The Dynamics of British Health Policy*, Unwin Hyman, London.

Harrop, K.J., Mason, C., Vielba, C.A. and Webster, B.A. (1978) *The Implementation and Development of Area Management*. University of Birmingham, Institute of Local Government Studies.

Harrow, J. and Willcocks, L. (1990) Public services management: activities, initiatives and limits to learning, *Journal of Management Studies*, 27, 281–304.

Hartas, W. and Harrop, K. (1991) Patterns of change in local government since 1945, *Teaching Public Administration*, 11 (1), 25–36.

Hatch, S. (1980) *Outside the State*, Croom Helm, London.

Hatch, S. (1986) Review of M. Brenton, 'The Voluntary Sector in British Social Services', *Journal of Social Policy*, 15, 389–90.

Haynes, R.J. (1980) *Organisation Theory and Local Government*, Allen & Unwin, London.

Haywood, S.C. and Elcock, H.J. (1982) Regional Health Authorities: regional government or central agencies?, in B.W. Hogwood and M. Keating (eds) *Regional Government in England*, Clarendon Press, Oxford.

Heclo, H. and Wildavsky, A. (1981) *The Private Government of Public Money*, 2nd edn., Macmillan, London.

Henkel, M. (1992) The Audit Commission, in S. Harrison and C. Pollitt (eds) *Handbook of Public Services Management*, Blackwell, Oxford.

Hennessy, P. (1990) *Whitehall*, Fontana Press, London.

Henney, A. (1984) *Inside Local Government: A Case for Radical Reform*, Sinclair Browne, London.

H.M. Treasury (1991) *Competing for Quality: Buying Public Services*, Cm 1730, HMSO, London.

H.M. Treasury (1993a) *Public Expenditure Analyses to 1995–6: Statistical Supplement to the 1992 Autumn Statement*, Cm 2219, HMSO, London.

H.M. Treasury (1993b) *Economic Briefing*, No. 5, August.

Heseltine, M. (1980) Ministers and management in Whitehall, *Management Services in Government*, 35, 61–8.

Higgins, J. (1988) *The Business of Medicine*, Macmillan, London.

Hill, M. (1993) *The Welfare State in Britain*, Edward Elgar, Aldershot.

Hill, M. (1994) Social security policy under the Conservatives, in S.P. Savage, R. Atkinson and L. Robins (eds) *Public Policy in Britain*, Macmillan, London.

Hillgate Group (1986) *Whose Schools? A Radical Manifesto*, Hillgate Group, London.

Hills, J. (1987) *The Voluntary Sector in Housing: the Role of British Housing Associations*, Welfare State Programme Paper No. 20, London School of Economics, London.

Hills, J. and Mullings, B. (1991) Housing: a decent home for all at a price within their means?, in J. Hills (ed.) *The State of Welfare: The Welfare State in Britain Since 1974*, Clarendon Press, Oxford.

Hirschman, A. (1970) *Exit, Voice and Loyalty*, Harvard University Press, Cambridge, Massachusetts.

Hogg, C. (1990) Health, in N. Deakin and A. Wright (eds) *Consuming Public Services*, Routledge, London.

Hoggett, P. (1991) A new management for the public sector?, *Policy and Politics*, 19, 243–56.

Hoggett, P. and Hambleton, R. (eds) (1988) *Decentralisation and Democracy: Localising Public Services*, Occasional Paper 28, School of Advanced Urban Studies, University of Bristol, Bristol.

Hogwood, B.W. and Gunn, L.A. (1984) *Policy Analysis For the Real World*, Oxford University Press, Oxford.

Hollis, G., Ham, G. and Ambler, M. (eds) (1992) *The Future Role and Structure of Local Government*, Longman, Harlow.

Hood, C. (1982) Governmental bodies and government growth, in A. Barker (ed.) *Quangos in Britain: Government and the Networks of Public Policy-Making*, Macmillan, London.

Hudson, B. (1986) In pursuit of coordination: housing and the personal social services, *Local Government Studies*, 12, 53–66.

Hudson, B. (1992) Quasi-markets in health and social care in Britain: can the public sector respond?, *Policy and Politics*, 20, 131–42.

Hunter, D.J. (1984) Managing health care, *Social Policy and Administration*, 18, 41–67.

Hunter, D.J. and Wistow, G. (1987) *Community Care in Britain: Variations on a Theme*, King's Fund, London.

Jackman, R. (1982) Does central government need to control the total of local government spending?, *Local Government Studies*, 8, 75–90.

Jackman, R. (1985) Local government finance, in M. Loughlin, M.D. Gelfand and K. Young (eds) *Half a Century of Municipal Decline 1935–1985*, Allen & Unwin, London.

Jenkins, P. (1987) *Mrs Thatcher's Revolution: The Ending of the Socialist Era*, Jonathan Cape, London.

Jennings, R.E. (1977) *Education and Politics: Policy-Making in Local Education Authorities*, Batsford, London.

John, P. (1990) *Recent Trends in Central–Local Government Relations*, Joseph Rowntree Foundation/Policy Studies Institute, London.

John, P. (1991) The restructuring of local government in England and Wales, in R. Batley and G. Stoker (eds) *Local Government in Europe: Trends and Developments*, Macmillan, London.

Johnson, N. (1974) Defining accountability, *Public Administration Bulletin*, No. 17, December, 3–13.

Johnson, N. (1987) *The Welfare State in Transition*, Wheatsheaf Books, Brighton.

Johnson, N. (1990) *Reconstructing the Welfare State: A Decade of Change 1980–1990*, Harvester Wheatsheaf, London.

Jones, G. and Stewart, J. (1983) *The Case for Local Government*, Allen & Unwin, London.

Jones, G. and Stewart, J. (1992) Choice in education – but who benefits?, *Local Government Chronicle*, 11 September.

Jordan, A.G. and Richardson, J.J. (1987) *British Politics and the Policy Process*, Allen & Unwin, London.

Judge, K. (1982) The public purchase of social care: British confirmation of the American experience, *Policy and Politics*, 10, 397–416.

Justice–All Souls (1988) *Administrative Justice: Some Necessary Reforms: Report of the Committee of the Justice–All Souls Review of Administrative Law in the United Kingdom*, Clarendon Press, Oxford.

Karn, V. (1985) Housing, in S. Ranson, G. Jones and K. Walsh (eds) *Between Centre and Locality*, Allen & Unwin, London.

Karn, V. (1993) Remodelling a HAT: the implementation of the Housing Action Trust legislation 1987–92, in P. Malpass and R. Means (eds) *Implementing Housing Policy*, Open University Press, Buckingham.

Keith-Lucas, B. and Richards, P.G. (1978) *A History of Local Government in the Twentieth Century*, Allen & Unwin, London.

Kelly, A. (1991) The new managerialism in the social services, in P. Carter, T. Jeffs and M.K. Smith (eds) *Social Work and Social Welfare Yearbook 3*, Open University Press, Buckingham.

Key, T. (1988) Contracting out ancillary services, in R. Maxwell (ed.) *Reshaping the National Health Service*, Policy Journals, Hermitage.

Kingdom, J. (1991) *Local Government and Politics in Britain*, Philip Allan, London.

King's Fund Institute (1989) *Managed Competition: A New Approach to Health Care in Britain*, King's Fund Institute, London.

Klein, R. (1973) *Complaints Against Doctors: A Study in Professional Accountability*, Charles Knight, London.

Klein, R. (1989) *The Politics of the National Health Service*, 2nd edn., Longman, London.

Klein, R. (1990) What future for the Department of Health?, *British Medical Journal*, 301, 481–4.

Kogan, M. (ed.) (1971) *The Politics of Education*, Penguin Books, Harmondsworth.

Kogan, M. (1978) *The Politics of Educational Change*, Fontana/Collins, London.

Kogan, M. (1987) Education, in M. Parkinson (ed.) *Reshaping Local Government*, Policy Journals, Hermitage.

Labour Party (1991) *Citizen's Charter: Labour's Better Deal for Consumers and Citizens*, Labour Party, London.

Labour Party (1992) *It's Time to Get Britain Working Again*, Labour Party, London.

Laffin, M. (1986) *Professionalism and Policy: The Role of the Professions in the Central–Local Government Relationship*, Gower, Aldershot.

Laffin, M. and Young, K. (1990) *Professionalism in Local Government*, Longman, Harlow.

Lansley, S., Goss, S. and Woolmar, C. (1989) *Councils in Conflict: the Rise and Fall of the Municipal Left*, Macmillan, London.

Lapping, A. (1968) A Ministry of Social Welfare? *New Society*, 23 May, 748–9.

Lawson, N. (1980) *The New Conservatism*, Centre for Policy Studies, London.

Layfield Report (1976) *Local Government Finance: Report of the Committee of Enquiry*, Cmnd 6453, HMSO, London.

Leach, S. (1992) The disintegration of an initiative, in S. Leach, J. Stewart, K. Spencer, K. Walsh and J. Gibson, *The Heseltine Review of Local Government: A New Vision or Opportunities Missed?*, Institute of Local Government Studies, University of Birmingham.

Le Grand, J. (1990) The state of welfare, in J. Hills (ed.) *The State of Welfare: the Welfare State in Britain Since 1945*, Clarendon Press, Oxford.

Le Grand, J. (1991) Quasi-markets and social policy, *Economic Journal*, 101, 1256–67.

Levitt, R. and Wall, A. (1992) *The Reorganized National Health Service*, Chapman & Hall, London.

Lewis, N. (1985) Who controls quangos and the nationalized industries?, in J. Jowell and D. Oliver (eds) *The Changing Constitution*, Clarendon Press, Oxford.

Lewis, N. and Birkinshaw, P. (1993) *When Citizens Complain: Reforming Justice and Administration*, Open University Press, Buckingham.

Liberal Democrats (1991) *Citizens' Britain: Liberal Democrat Policies for a People's Charter*, Liberal Democrats, London.

Lipsky, M. (1979) The assault on human services: street-level bureaucrats, accountability and the fiscal crisis, in S. Greer, R.D. Hedlund and J.L. Gibson (eds) *Accountability in Urban Society: Public Agencies Under Fire*, Vol. 15, *Urban Affairs Annual Review*, Sage, Beverley Hills, California.

Local Government Information Unit (1991) *The Citizen's Charter*, Special Briefing No. 36, September.

Long, A.F. (1992) Evaluating health services: from value for money to the valuing of health services, in C. Pollitt and S. Harrison (eds) *Handbook of Public Services Management*, Blackwell, Oxford.

Longley, D. (1993) *Public Law and Health Service Accountability*, Open University Press, Buckingham.

Loughlin, M. (1985) Administrative law, local government and the courts, in M. Loughlin, M.D. Gelfand and K. Young (eds) *Half a Century of Municipal Decline 1935–1985*, Allen & Unwin, London.

Loughlin, M. (1986) *Local Government in the Modern State*, Sweet & Maxwell, London.

Lowe, R. (1993) *The Welfare State in Britain Since 1945*, Macmillan, London.

Lowndes, V. (1992) Decentralisation: the potential and the pitfalls, *Local Government Policy Making*, 18, 53–63.

Lowndes, V. and Stoker, G. (1992) An evaluation of neighbourhood decentralisation – Part 1, *Policy and Politics*, 20, 47–61.

Maclennan, D., Clapham, D., Goodlad, M., Kemp, P., Malcolm, J., Satsangi, M., Stanforth, J. and Whitefield, L. (1989) *The Nature and Effectiveness of Housing Management in England*, HMSO, London.

Macpherson, S. (1987) Department of Health and Social Security, in A. Harrison and A. Gretton (eds) *Reshaping Central Government*, Policy Journals, Hermitage.

Malpass, P. (1992) Housing policy and the disabling of local authorities, in J. Birchall (ed.) *Housing Policy in the 1990s*, Routledge, London.

Malpass, P. and Murie, A. (1990) *Housing Policy and Practice*, 3rd edn., Macmillan, London.

Malpass, P. and Means, R. (1993) The politics of implementation, in P. Malpass and R. Means (eds) *Implementing Housing Policy*, Open University Press, Buckingham.

Margetts, H. (1991) The computerization of social security: the way forward or one step backwards?, *Public Administration*, 69, 325–43.

Marshall, T. (1963) *Sociology at the Crossroads*, Heinemann, London.

Marwick, A. (1982) *British Society Since 1945*, Allen Lane, London.

Mason, P. (1993) Market mayhem, *Nursing Times*, 15 September, 19.

Mather, G. (1989) Thatcherism and local government, in J. Stewart and G. Stoker (eds) *The Future of Local Government*, Macmillan, London.

Maud Report (1967) *Committee on the Management of Local Government*, Vol. I: Report, HMSO, London.

McAuslan, P. (1983) Administrative law, collective consumption and judicial policy, *Modern Law Review*, 46, 1–20.

McCarthy, M. (1989) Personal social services, in M. McCarthy (ed.) *The New Politics of Welfare: An Agenda for the 1990s?*, Macmillan, London.

McGregor, G. (1990) Privatisation on parade, *Health Service Journal*, 3 May, 670–1.

McKnight, J. (1985) Pressure points: the crisis in management, in S. Ward (ed.) *DHSS in Crisis: Social Security Under Pressure and Under Review*, Child Poverty Action Group, London.

McLachlan, G. (1979) Foreword, in W.J.M. Mackenzie, *Power and Responsibility in Health: The National Health Service as a Political Institution*, Oxford University Press, Oxford.

McSweeney, B. (1988) Accounting for the Audit Commission, *Political Quarterly*, 59, 28–43.

McVicar, M. (1993) Education, in D. Farnham and S. Horton (eds) *Managing the New Public Services*, Macmillan, London.

Means, R. (1993) Perspectives on implementation, in P. Malpass and R. Means (eds) *Implementing Housing Policy*, Open University Press, Buckingham.

Merrison Report (1979) *Royal Commission on the National Health Service*, Report, Cmnd 7615, HMSO, London.

Metcalfe, L. and Richards, S. (1990) *Improving Public Management*, 2nd edn., Sage, London.

Midwinter, A. and Monaghan, C. (1993) *From Rates to the Poll Tax*, Edinburgh University Press, Edinburgh.

Minister of Reconstruction (1944) *Social Insurance: Part I*, Cmnd 6550, HMSO, London.

Moodie, M., Mizen, H., Heron, R. and Mackay, B. (1988) *The Business of Service: the Report of the Regional Organization Scrutiny*, DHSS, London.

Moon, G. and Kendall, I. (1993) The National Health Service, in D. Farnham and S. Horton (eds) *Managing the New Public Services*, Macmillan, London.

Mullins, D., Niner, P. and Riseborough, M. (1993) Large-scale voluntary transfers, in P. Malpass and R. Means (eds) *Implementing Housing Policy*, Open University Press, Buckingham.

Nairne, Sir P. (1983) Managing the DHSS elephant: reflections on a giant department, *Political Quarterly*, 54, 243–56.

National Audit Office (1986) *The Rayner Scrutiny Programme: 1979–83*, HC 322, HMSO, London.

National Audit Office (1987) *Community Care Developments*, HC 108, HMSO, London.

National Audit Office (1988) *Department of Health and Social Security: Quality of Service to the Public*, HC 451, HMSO, London.

National Consumer Council (1986) *Measuring Up: Consumer Assessment of Local Authority Services: A Guideline Study*, National Consumer Council, London.

National Health Service Management Executive (1991) *NHS Reforms: the First Six Months*, Department of Health, London.

Newton, K. and Karran, T.J. (1985) *The Politics of Local Expenditure*, Macmillan, London.

Niskanen, W. (1971) *Bureaucracy and Representative Government*, Aldine, Chicago.

Norton, P. (1982) 'Dear Minister' – the importance of MP-to-minister correspondence, *Parliamentary Affairs*, 35, 59–72.

Oliver, D. (1991) *Government in the United Kingdom: The Search for Accountability, Effectiveness and Citizenship*, Open University Press, Buckingham.

Osborne, D. and Gaebler, T. (1992) *Reinventing Government: How the Entrepreneurial Spirit is Transforming the Public Sector*, Addison-Wesley, Reading, Massachusetts.

Packwood, T., Buxton, H. and Keen, J. (1990) Resource management in the National Health Service: a first case history, *Policy and Politics*, 18, 245–55.

Paris, C. and Blackaby, B. (1979) *Not Much Improvement*, Heinemann, London.

Parliamentary Commissioner for Administration (1992) *Second Report 1990–91. Annual Report for 1991*, HC 347, HMSO, London.

Parliamentary Commissioner for Administration (1994) *Annual Report 1993*, HC 290, HMSO, London.

Pater, J.E. (1981) *The Making of the National Health Service*, King's Fund, London.

Perrin, J. (1992) Administrative and financial management of local health services, in E. Beck, S. Lonsdale, S. Newman and D. Patterson (eds) *In the Best of Health? The Status and Future of Health Care in Britain*, Chapman & Hall, London.

Peters, T.J. and Waterman, R.H. (1982) *In Search of Excellence: Lessons From America's Best-Run Companies*, Harper and Rowe, New York.

Pickvance, C. (1991) The difficulty of control and the case of structural reform: British local government in the 1980s, in C. Pickvance and E. Preteceille (eds) *State Restructuring and Local Power*, Gower, London.

Pinker, R.A. (1992) Making sense of the mixed economy of welfare, *Social Policy and Administration*, 26, 273–84.

Pitt, D. and Smith, B. (1981) *Government Departments: An Organizational Perspective*, Routledge & Kegan Paul, London.

Plowden Report (1961) *The Control of Public Expenditure*, Cmnd 1432, HMSO, London.

Plowden Report (1967) *Children and their Primary Schools*, HMSO, London.

Pollitt, C. (1980) Rationalising the machinery of government: the Conservatives 1970–74, *Political Studies*, 28, 84–98.

Pollitt, C. (1984a) *Manipulating the Machine: Changing the Pattern of Ministerial Departments 1960–83*, Allen & Unwin, London.

Pollitt, C. (1984b) Professionals and public policy, *Public Administration Bulletin*, No. 44, April, 29–46.

Pollitt, C. (1985) Measuring performance: a new system for the National Health Service, *Policy and Politics*, 13, 1–15.

Pollitt, C. (1986) Beyond the managerial model: the case for broadening performance assessment in government and the public services, *Financial Accountability and Management*, 2, 155–70.

Pollitt, C. (1987) Performance measurement and the consumer: hijacking a bandwagon?, in National Consumer Council, *Performance Measurement and the Consumer*, NCC, London.

Pollitt, C. (1988) Bringing consumers into performance measurement: concepts, consequences and constraints, *Policy and Politics*, 16, 77–87.

Pollitt, C. (1991) *The Politics of Quality: Managers, Professionals and Consumers in the Public Services*, Royal Holloway and Bedford New College, Egham.

Pollitt, C. (1993) *Managerialism and the Public Services*, 2nd edn., Blackwell, Oxford.

Pollitt, C. and Harrison, S. (eds) (1992) *Handbook of Public Services Management*, Blackwell, Oxford.

Ponting, C. (1986) *Whitehall: Tragedy and Farce*, Hamish Hamilton, London.

Poole, K.P. (1978) *The Local Government Service in England and Wales*, Allen & Unwin, London.

Potter, J. (1988) Consumerism and the public sector: how well does the coat fit?, *Public Administration*, 66, 149–64.

Powell, J.E. (1966) *A New Look at Medicine and Politics*, Pitman, London.

Power, A. (1987) *The Crisis in Council Housing: Is Public Housing Manageable?*, Welfare State Programme Paper No. 21, London School of Economics, London.

Power, A. (1988) *Under New Management: The Experience of Thirteen Islington Cooperatives*, Priority Estates Project, London.

Priestley, C. (1986) Promoting the efficiency of central government, in A. Shenfield *et al. Managing the Bureaucracy*, Adam Smith Institute, London.

Prime Minister (1991) *The Citizen's Charter: Raising the Standard*, Cm 1599, HMSO, London.

Prime Minister (1992) *The Citizen's Charter: First Report 1992*, Cm 2101, HMSO, London.

Public Accounts Committee (1971) *Third Report 1970–71*, HC 537, HMSO, London.

Public Accounts Committee (1976) *Sixth Report 1975–76*, HC 584, HMSO, London.

Public Accounts Committee (1977) *Ninth Report 1976–77*, HC 532, HMSO, London.

Public Accounts Committee (1978) *Ninth Report 1977–78*, HC 622, HMSO, London.

Public Accounts Committee (1981) *Seventeenth Report 1980–81. Financial Control and Accountability in the National Health Service*, HC 255, HMSO, London.

Public Accounts Committee (1988) *Forty-Fourth Report 1987-88. Quality of Service to the Public at DHSS Local Offices*, HC 491, HMSO, London.

Radford, M. (1991) Auditing for change: local government and the Audit Commission, *Modern Law Review*, 54, 912–32.

Ranade, W. (1994) *A Future for the NHS? Health Care in the 1990s*, Longman, London.

Randolph, B. (1993) The re-privatization of housing associations, in P. Malpass and R. Means (eds) *Implementing Housing Policy*, Open University, Buckingham.

Ranson, S. (1985) Education, in S. Ranson, G. Jones and K. Walsh (eds) *Between Centre and Locality*, Allen & Unwin, London.

Ranson, S. (1990) Education, in N. Deakin and A. Wright (eds) *Consuming Public Services*, Routledge, London.

Ranson, S. (1992a) *The Role of Local Government in Education: Assuring Quality and Accountability*, Longman, Harlow.

Ranson, S. (1992b) Education, in F. Terry and P. Jackson (eds) *Public Domain Yearbook 1992*, Public Finance Foundation, London.

Ranson, S. and Thomas, H. (1989) Education reform: consumer democracy or social democracy?, in J. Stewart and G. Stoker (eds) *The Future of Local Government*, Macmillan, London.

Ranson, S. and Travers, T. (1994) Education, in P. Jackson and M. Lavender (eds) *The Public Services Yearbook 1994*, Chapman & Hall, London.

Raynsford, N. (1986) The 1977 Housing (Homeless Persons) Act, in N. Deakin (ed.) *Policy Change in Government: Three Case Studies*, Royal Institute of Public Administration, London.

Redcliffe-Maud, Report (1969) *Royal Commission on Local Government in England: 1966–1969*, Vol. I: Report, Cmnd 4040, HMSO, London.

Redcliffe-Maud, Lord and Wood, B. (1974) *English Local Government Reformed*, Oxford University Press, London.

Regan, D. (1977) *Local Government and Education*, Allen & Unwin, London.

Rhodes, R.A.W. (1979) Research into central–local relations in Britain: a framework for analysis, Appendix I, in *Central–Local Government Relationships*, Social Science Research Council, London.

Rhodes, R.A.W. (1987) Developing the public service orientation, or let's add a soupçon of political theory, *Local Government Studies*, 13, 63–73.

Rhodes, R.A.W. (1988) *Beyond Westminster and Whitehall: the Sub-Central Governments of Britain*, Unwin Hyman, London.

Rhodes, R.A.W. (1992a) Local government finance, in D. Marsh and R.A.W. Rhodes (eds) *Implementing Thatcherite Policies: Audit of an Era*, Open University Press, Buckingham.

Rhodes, R.A.W. (1992b) Local government, in B. Jones and L. Robins (eds) *Two Decades in British Politics*, University of Manchester Press, Manchester.

Richards, P.G. (1972) *The Backbenchers*, Faber, London.

Richards, S. (1992) *Who Defines the Public Good? The Consumer Paradigm in Public Management*, Public Management Foundation, London.

Richardson, A. (1983) *Participation*, Routledge & Kegan Paul, London.

Ridley, N. (1973) Efficiency begins at home, in W.A. Niskanen, *Bureaucracy: Servant or Master?*, Institute of Economic Affairs, London.

Ridley, N. (1988a) *The Local Right: Enabling not Providing*, Centre for Policy Studies, London.

Ridley, N. (1988b) *Speech to Institute of Housing Conference, 17 June 1988*, Department of the Environment News Release.

Robinson, R. (1988) *Efficiency and the NHS: A Case For Internal Markets?*, Institute of Economic Affairs, London.

Robson, W.A. (1935) The public utilities services, in H. Laski, W.I. Jennings and W.A. Robson (eds) *A Century of Municipal Progress*, Allen & Unwin, London.

Robson, W.A. (1966) *Local Government in Crisis*, Allen & Unwin, London.

Rose, R. (1989) *Politics in England*, 5th edn., Macmillan, London.

Sargeant, T. (1979) Joint care planning in the health and personal social services, in T. Booth (ed.) *Planning For Welfare*, Blackwell and Martin Robertson, Oxford.

Scrivens, E. (1988) Consumers, accountability and quality of service, in R. Maxwell (ed.) *Reshaping the National Health Service*, Policy Journals, Hermitage.

Seebohm Report (1968) *Report of the Committee on Local Authority and Personal Allied Social Services*, Cmnd 3703, HMSO, London.

Select Committee on the Parliamentary Commissioner for Administration (1992) *Second Report 1991–92. The Implications of the Citizen's Charter for the Work of the Parliamentary Commissioner for Administration*, HC 158, HMSO, London.

Seneviratne, M. and Cracknell, S. (1988) Consumer complaints in public sector services, *Public Administration*, 66, 2, 181–93.

Sharp, E. (1969) *The Ministry of Housing and Local Government*, Allen & Unwin, London.

Sharpe, L.J. (1970) Theories and values of local government, *Political Studies*, 18, 153–74.

Smith, B.C. (1981) Control in British government: a problem of accountability, *Policy Studies Journal*, 9, 1163–74.

Smith, B.C. and Stanyer, J. (1976) *Administering Britain*, Martin Robertson, London.

Social Services Committee (1980) *Third Report 1979–80. The Government's White Papers on Public Expenditure: The Social Services*, HC 702–1, HMSO, London.

Spencer, K.M. (1989) Local government and the housing reforms, in J. Stewart and G. Stoker (eds) *The Future of Local Government*, Macmillan, London.

Stanyer, J. (1976) *Understanding Local Government*, Fontana, London.

Stewart, J. (1986) *The New Management of Local Government*, Allen & Unwin, London.

Stewart, J. (1987) Has decentralisation failed?, *Local Government Policy Making*, 14, 49–53.

Stewart, J. (1989) The changing organisation and management of local authorities, in J. Stewart and G. Stoker (eds) *The Future of Local Government*, Macmillan, London.

Stewart, J. (1992) The rebuilding of public accountability, in J. Stewart, N. Lewis and D. Longley (eds) *Accountability and the Public*, European Policy Forum, London.

Stewart, J. (1993) The limitations of management by contract, *Public Money and Management*, 13, 1–6.

Stewart, J. and Clarke, M. (1987) The public service orientation: issues and dilemmas, *Public Administration*, 69, 161–77.

Stewart, J. and Stoker, G. (eds) (1989) Introduction, in *The Future of Local Government*, Macmillan, London.

Stewart, J. and Walsh, K. (1992) Change in the management of public services, *Public Administration*, 70, 499–518.

Stoker, G. (1988) *The Politics of Local Government*, Macmillan, London.

Stoker, G. (1990) Government beyond Whitehall, in P. Dunleavy, A. Gamble and G. Peele (eds) *New Developments in British Politics 3*, Macmillan, London.

Stoker, G. (1991) *The Politics of Local Government*, 2nd edn., Macmillan, London.

Stott, T. (1994) Market testing and beyond: privatisation and contracting out in British central government, *Teaching Public Administration*, 14, 36–48.

Strong, P. and Robinson, J. (1990) *The NHS under New Management*, Open University Press, Buckingham.

Sugden, R. (1984) Voluntary organisations and the welfare state, in J. Le Grand and R. Robinson (eds) *Privatisation and the Welfare State*, Allen & Unwin, London.

Taylor, M. (1982) Looking at voluntary agencies, *RIPA Report*, 7(1), 11–12.

Taylor, M. (1992) The changing role of the nonprofit sector in Britain: moving toward the market, in B. Gidron, R.M. Kramer and L.M. Sulaman (eds) *Government and the Third Sector*, Jossey-Bass, San Francisco.

Taylor-Gooby, P. and Dale, J. (1981) *Social Theory and Social Welfare*, Edward Arnold, London.

Taylor-Gooby, P. and Lawson, R. (eds) (1993) *Markets and Managers: New Issues in the Delivery of Welfare*, Open University Press, Buckingham.

Thorpe-Tracey, S.F. (1987) The financial management initiative in practice: Newcastle Central Office, *Public Administration*, 65, 331–8.

Titmuss, R.M. (1974) *Social Policy*, Allen & Unwin, London.

Townsend, P., Davidson, N. and Whitehead, M. (1988) Introduction, in P. Townsend, N. Davidson and M. Whitehead, *Inequalities in Health*, Penguin Books, Harmondsworth.

Travers, T. (1986) *The Politics of Local Government Finance*, Allen & Unwin, London.

Treasury and Civil Service Committee (1989) *Fifth Report 1988–89. Developments in the Next Steps Programme*, HC 348, HMSO, London.

Treasury and Civil Service Committee (1990) *Eighth Report 1989–90. Progress in the Next Steps Initiative*, HC 481, HMSO, London.

Treasury and Civil Service Committee (1993) *Sixth Report 1992–93. The Role of the Civil Service: Interim Report*, HC 370–I, HMSO, London.

Trippier, D. (1989) Speech reported in *Voluntary Housing*, February 1989.

Waine, B. (1992) The voluntary sector – the Thatcher years, in N. Manning and C. Ungerson (eds) *Social Policy Review 5*, Longman, Harlow.

Waldegrave, W. (1987) *Some Reflections on Housing Policy*, Conservative Party News Service, 19 May 1987.

Waldegrave, W. (1993) *Public Services and the Future: Reforming Britain's Bureaucracy*, Conservative Political Centre, London.

Walker, A. (1989) Community care, in M. McCarthy (ed.) *The New Politics of Welfare: An Agenda for the 1990s?*, Macmillan, London.

Walsh, K. (1989) Competition and service in local government, in J. Stewart and G. Stoker (eds) *The Future of Local Government*, Macmillan, London.

Walsh, K. and Davis, H. (1993) *Competition and Service: the Impact of the Local Government Act 1988*, HMSO, London.

Wandsworth, London Borough of (1991) *Wandsworth's Manager's Handbook: A Reference Guide for Managers*.

Warner, N. (1984) Raynerism in practice: anatomy of a Rayner scrutiny, *Public Administration*, 62, 7–22.

Warner, N. (1992) Organizing for strategic management: the personal social services, in C. Pollitt and S. Harrison (eds) *Handbook of Public Services Management*, Blackwell, Oxford.

Webb, A. (1991) Coordination: a problem in public sector management, *Policy and Politics*, 19, 229–40.

Webb, A. and Wistow, G. (1982) *Whither State Welfare? Policy and Implementation in the Personal Social Services: 1979–80*, Royal Institute of Public Administration, London.

Webb, A. and Wistow, G. (1987) *Social Work, Social Care and Social Planning: The Personal Social Services since Seebohm*, Longman, London.

Webb, A., Day, L. and Weller, D. (1976) *Voluntary Social Service Manpower Resources*, Personal Social Services Council, London.

Weber, M. (1964) *The Theory of Social and Economic Organization*, translated by A.M. Henderson and T. Parsons, Free Press, New York.

Webster, B. (1991) *Customer Service in the Counties*, Association of County Councils, London.

Weir, S. and Hall, S. (1994) *Extra-Governmental Organisations in the United Kingdom and Their Accountability*, Charter 88 Trust, London.

Welsh Office (1993) *Local Government in Wales: A Charter for the Future*, HMSO, London.

Wheatley Report (1969) *Royal Commission on Local Government in Scotland*, Report, Cmnd 4150, HMSO, London.

Whitehead, P. (1985) *The Writing on the Wall: Britain in the Seventies*, Michael Joseph, London.

Whitty, G. (1990) The politics of the 1988 Education Reform Act, in P. Dunleavy, A. Gamble and G. Peele (eds) *Developments in British Politics 3*, Macmillan, London.

Wicks, M. (1987) *A Future For All? Do We Need a Welfare State?*, Penguin Books, Harmondsworth.

Widdicombe Report (1986) *The Conduct of Local Authority Business: Report of the Committee of Inquiry into the Conduct of Local Authority Business*, Cmnd 9797, HMSO, London.

Wikeley, N. and Young, R. (1992) The administration of benefits in Britain: adjudication officers and the influence of social security appeal tribunals, *Public Law*, Summer, 238–62.

Wilcox, B. (1989) The Education Reform Act (1988): implications for schools and local education authorities, in M. Brenton and C. Ungerson (eds) *Social Policy Review 1988–9*, Longman, Harlow.

Wilding, P. (1982) *Professional Power and Social Welfare*, Routledge & Kegan Paul, London.

Willcocks, A.J. (1967) *The Creation of the National Health Service*, Routledge & Kegan Paul, London.

Willmore, N. (1992) The Citizen's Charter brings out the cynics, 20 October.

Wilson, D. (1993) Turning drama into crisis: perspectives on contemporary local government, *Public Policy and Administration*, 8(1), 30–45.

Wilson, D. and Game, C., with Leach, S. and Stoker, G. (1994) *Local Government in the United Kingdom*, Macmillan, London.

Winkler, F. (1987) Consumerism in health care: beyond the supermarket model, *Policy and Politics*, 15, 1–8.

Wistow, G. (1992a) The National Health Service, in D. Marsh and R.A.W. Rhodes (eds) *Implementing Thatcherite Policies: Audit of an Era*, Open University Press, Buckingham.

Wistow, G. (1992b) The health service policy community: professionals pre-eminent or under challenge?, in D. Marsh and R.A.W. Rhodes (eds) *Policy Networks in British Government*, Clarendon Press, Oxford.

Wistow, G., Knapp, M., Hardy, B. and Allen, C. (1992) From providing to enabling: local authorities and the mixed economy of care, *Public Administration*, 70, 25–45.

Wistow, G., Knapp, M., Hardy, B. and Allen, C. (1994) *Social Care in a Mixed Economy*, Open University Press, Buckingham.

Wolfenden Committee (1978) *The Future of Voluntary Organisations*, Croom Helm, London.

Wood, B. (1988) Privatisation: local government and the health service, in C. Graham and T. Prosser (eds) *Waiving the Rules: The Constitution Under Thatcherism*, Open University Press, Milton Keynes.

Wright, M.W. (1977) Public expenditure in Britain: the crisis of control, *Public Administration*, 55, 143–59.

Young, S. (1986) The nature of privatisation in Britain 1979–85, *West European Politics*, 9, 235–52.

Younghusband, E. (1978) *Social Work in Britain, 1950–1975*, Vol. 1, Allen & Unwin, London.

Index

THE DEVELOPMENT OF SOCIAL WELFARE IN BRITAIN

Eric Midwinter

This textbook is aimed at undergraduate and diploma students across a wide range of the social sciences, with particular reference to those preparing for or involved in careers in social and public administration. It provides, in compact and accessible form, the story of social provision from medieval times to the present day, systematically examining major themes of:

- the relief of poverty and social care,
- healthcare and housing,
- crime and policing,
- education.

With the rise of the welfare state, and its current questioning as a chief focus, the book sets out to analyse how the state has responded to the social problems that have beset it. Consideration is given to comparative elements in Europe, North America and elsewhere, together with specific reference to issues of race, ethnicity and gender. A specially prepared glossary completes what is a well-packaged review and description of the growth and present disposition of the full range of social and public services in Britain.

Contents

Preface: How best to use this book — Introduction: Social casualty and political response — Medieval life and welfare — The nation-state and the money-economy — Industrialism's impact and the initial response — Piecemeal collectivism: Precursors of the welfare state — The silent revolution of the 1940s — The Butskellite consensus (c. 1951–1973/9) — The questioning of the welfare state — General advice on further reading — Glossary of terms — Index.

208pp   0 335 19104 5 (Paperback)   0 335 19105 3 (Hardback)

SOCIAL CARE IN A MIXED ECONOMY

Gerald Wistow, Martin Knapp, Brian Hardy and Caroline Allen

This book describes the mixed economy of community care in England and analyses the efforts and activities of local authorities to promote and develop it. It is based on national documentary and statistical evidence and on more detailed research with twenty-four local authorities; and includes a case study on the transfer of residential homes to the independent sector.

The roles of Social Services Departments have been progressively redefined to emphasize responsibility for creating and managing a mixed economy. This entails a major cultural shift for departments which may be summarized as involving moves from providing to enabling, and from administration to management. It also implies the need for new skills and structures. *Social Care in a Mixed Economy* traces the historical changes; the local interpretations of central government policy; how authorities actually have been developing mixed economies; the main opportunities or incentives for promoting a mixed economy; and the main obstacles to its development.

Contents
Introduction: historical and policy context – Community care: markets and enabling – The mixed economy in 1991 – Local responses to the legislation and guidance – Building a mixed economy – Social care is different – Residential care home transfers – Conclusions – References – Index.

176pp   0 335 19043 X (Paperback)   0 335 19044 8 (Hardback)

MARKETS AND MANAGERS
NEW ISSUES IN THE DELIVERY OF WELFARE

Peter Taylor-Gooby and Robyn Lawson (eds)

Over the past decade, the British welfare state has undergone the most fundamental reforms since the Second World War. Much discussion of current policy focuses on the global issues of cuts, privatization and the scope of the state sector. This book argues that the organizational reforms of the 1990s are also of far-reaching significance and will play a major role in setting the agenda for welfare policy into the next century. The new welfare settlement emphasizes decentralization, the use of markets, an autonomous managerialism, a stronger voice for consumers and a greater role for the private sector. Reformers claim that the changes allow a more efficient, flexible and responsive welfare system, while critics argue that they will lead to greater inequality and to discrimination against the most vulnerable groups of service users.

This book differs from other recent publications in its emphasis on the changes in the organization and delivery of services. It examines the emergence of the new managerial ideology in central and local government, considers the similarities and differences between the UK and other European countries and reviews policy change across the range of public services. The concluding chapter evaluates competing explanations of why the transformation has occurred and discusses future developments. The book provides a practical discussion of the issues, and will be of value to a wide range of students and welfare practitioners.

Contents
Markets, managers and the public service: the changing of a culture – Patterns of change in the delivery of welfare in Europe – Contracting housing provision: competition and privatization in the housing sector – A case study in the National Health Service: Working for Patients – *The new technology of management in the personal social services – Social security: the income maintenance business – The new educational settlement: National Curriculum and local management – The legacy of the Manpower Services Commission: training in the 1980s – Where we go from here: the new order in welfare – References – Index.*

Contributors
Pat Ainley, John Baldock, John Butler, Hartley Dean, Ray Forrest, Andrew Gray, Bill Jenkins, Robyn Lawson, Peter Taylor-Gooby.

192pp   0 335 15789 0 (Paperback)   0 335 15790 4 (Hardback)